NOLS Wilderness Medicine
Seventh Edition

Tod Schimelpfenig
Illustrated by Joan Safford

A publication of the National Outdoor Leadership School and

STACKPOLE
BOOKS
Guilford, Connecticut

Published by Stackpole Books
An imprint of The Rowman & Littlefield Publishing Group, Inc.
4501 Forbes Blvd., Ste. 200
Lanham, MD 20706
www.rowman.com

Distributed by NATIONAL BOOK NETWORK

British Library Cataloguing in Publication Information Available

Library of Congress Cataloging-in-Publication Data Available
ISBN 978-0-8117-3996-2 (paper: alk. paper)
ISBN 978-0-8117-6981-5 (electronic)

♾️ The paper used in this publication meets the minimum requirements of American National Standard for Information Sciences—Permanence of Paper for Printed Library Materials, ANSI/NISO Z39.48-1992.

FSC
www.fsc.org
MIX
Paper from
responsible sources
FSC® C005010

NOLS books are printed by FSC® certified printers. The Forest Stewardship Council® encourages responsible management of the world's forests.

NOLS Wilderness Medicine
Seventh Edition

To the students at NOLS.
I hope this text helps you to be better outdoor leaders.

To all NOLS field and wilderness medicine instructors,
who on a daily basis teach and practice first aid and safety
in the wilderness and are the source of the practical experience
that is the foundation of this text.

To Betsy, Sam, Dave, Mara, and Emily
for their support and patience during
the time I devoted to this project.

To the St. Michael's College Rescue Squad,
where I first learned quality patient care.

QUICK-REFERENCE INDEX

CONTENTS

PREFACE TO THE 7TH EDITION

In most first aid programs, instruction focuses on simple interventions that can be done while waiting for emergency medical services to arrive on scene. In the context of wilderness medicine, though, access to emergency services and definitive care is delayed, resources are limited, communication is difficult, and conditions may be austere.

True, improved satellite communications have made it easier for modern backcountry travellers to ask for help than it was in 1991 when the first edition of *NOLS Wilderness Medicine* was published. Treks out to a trailhead to find a payphone and multi-day improvised litter carries are rarer than they used to be because it's often easier to make a satellite phone call or text and ask for proper equipment and providers to come to you.

Yet those resources cannot be taken for granted. Satellite phones break. Cell phones and radio reception may be blocked. Weather and terrain can still hamper rescue. Even in areas where we can usually rely on help, we can find ourselves without it. Wilderness medicine providers have utilized their skills by the sides of lonely highways, and in cities ravaged by natural disasters. And as this book goes to press, much of the world is experiencing healthcare systems overwhelmed by COVID-19. All these things mean that, while making a phone call for help might be your first plan, managing an illness or injury for extended periods without outside help is always a possibility, whether you're in the "wilderness" or in "civilization."

This 7th edition of *NOLS Wilderness Medicine* is an extension of over half a century of practical experience of managing illnesses and injuries away from the medications, equipment, and interventions of modern medicine. It relies on the lessons learned by generations of NOLS field and wilderness medicine instructors, managing injuries and illnesses in the backcountry, on expeditions, in ambulances and emergency rooms, and on scene at disasters around the world. It is also informed by the development of professional medical expertise in the practice of wilderness medicine.

The author, Tod Schimelpfenig, has been on the forefront of wilderness medicine since he began teaching medical courses for NOLS staff in the 1970s. Tod developed the NOLS field incident database in 1984. That database—the largest of its kind—tells us what injuries and illnesses actually occur and what decisions wilderness leaders make, and thus informs what curriculum they teach. Tod also helped found the Wilderness Risk Management Conference in 1992 with the goal of sharing best practices in the industry. After NOLS purchased the Wilderness Medicine Institute in 1999, Tod became the school's Wilderness Medicine Curriculum Director, a position he has held for nearly 20 years.

Over the decades, NOLS has developed a more broad set of educational offerings to train truly skilled outdoor leaders. In addition to expeditionary travel, we've increased our focus on the ability to anticipate and prevent injury and illness—and minimizing negative outcomes when they do occur—as critical to successful remote area ventures. Formal training in wilderness medicine and risk management disciplines has become equally important for the wilderness leaders that NOLS trains and employs.

Leadership remains fundamental in all those skill areas. The concept of expedition behavior, initially described by NOLS founder Paul Petzoldt "an awareness and attention to all relationships that influence an outdoor experience," also comes into play within leadership and decision making dynamics. Any time a group of people are working together toward a goal, awareness of, and attention to, these dynamics play significant roles in producing successful outcomes. This 7th edition has significant revisions in the chapters on leadership, teamwork, communication and decision-making. We continue to see how emphasis on these skills influences patient outcomes in the field, as well as assists caregiving teams in delivering the best care possible.

Tod has also given attention in this edition to ensuring that the language and reference to patients and assessments are more inclusive in their approach, and more attentive to implicit biases in caregivers. From discussing differences in illness presentation across sexes, to using language that centers on the patient vs. their condition ("a person with diabetes" vs. "a diabetic"), to introducing language that instructs accurate assessment of signs and symptoms regardless of skin pigmentation or gender presentation, Tod's matter-of-fact manner of ensuring each patient receives great care with dignity and respect is a hallmark of his style.

Stress injury and psychological first aid, topics that first appeared several editions ago, are updated to reflect their developing importance in both emergency response and our lives.

Overall, Tod works to highlight what is accurate, realistic, and practical in a field setting, instead of attempting to comprehensively cover all that could be written on a given topic.

Wilderness medicine is still very much an evolving discipline. Overall, this new edition updates, improves, and expands upon a body of knowledge informed by ongoing experience, research, and understanding. But, as has always been the case, wilderness medicine cannot be learned solely from books. It requires expert instruction, practice, and refreshing of skills. By reading this text, you're taking the first, critical step in learning to care for others in remote, austere environments. To round out your toolbox, follow up this read by taking a wilderness medicine or expedition skills course. We'd love to have you join with NOLS to continue the lifelong learning that is the practice of wilderness medicine.

I want to close with praise of the author, Tod Schimelpfenig. He has devoted nearly 50 years of his life to the staff and students of NOLS. I've been privileged to know Tod for 30 of those years, and what I have seen in him is a profound consistency, a common sense that is uncommon, a passion for the logical and practical that truly serves "real life" in remote situations, and a deep kindness toward those he works with. The content of this book is solid, based in real-life experience and deep exploration of wilderness medicine across many sources. Its presentation by someone as trusted and experienced as Tod lends it an additional credibility, and I will continue to keep the latest copy in my personal library.

I'm proud to present this 7th edition of *NOLS Wilderness Medicine* to our community of practice, and I look forward to seeing you "out there."

Terri Watson
President, NOLS
January 2021

ACKNOWLEDGMENTS

This book and its six previous editions owe much to the assistance of:

Linda Lindsey, Human Resources Director for NOLS, who coauthored the first three editions of this text.

Shana Tarter, Gates Richards, and Ben Lester of NOLS Wilderness Medicine for their editorial suggestions.

Jo Rolls PA-C for her work on the chapter on genitourinary medicine.

Herb Ogden, M.D., NOLS Medical Advisor, for his advice and support of NOLS instructors and students.

Laura McGladrey PMHNP for her work on stress injury management.

Cynthia B. Stevens, M.D. for her assistance to NOLS on matters of mental health and work on the mental health chapter.

Charles "Reb" Gregg for his assistance with the medical legal chapter.

NOLS Wilderness Medicine Instructors Javier Cea, Felipe Jácome, and Gabriel Puma for their review and help with the translation of this text.

And the generations of NOLS field and wilderness medicine instructors whose suggestions and experience are vital in helping this text be as relevant and practical as possible.

INTRODUCTION

Linda Lindsey and I wrote the first edition of this book in 1991. It seems appropriate for this, the 7th edition, to reflect on the evolution of the manuscript over 30 years, and indeed the evolution of the practice of wilderness medicine.

For decades, people who recreated and worked outdoors learned their first aid from isolated, small-scale "mountain medicine" educational programs, often hosted by outdoor organizations such as the Seattle Mountaineers or the Adirondack Mountain Club. The instructors for these early courses were people who were passionate about wilderness, medicine, and education. They took what they had learned in urban-oriented Advanced First Aid or Emergency Medical Technician (EMT) courses and adapted this curriculum—based on experience and opinion—to fit their needs. Published research was sparse. Many of the wilderness medicine textbooks of the time contain techniques, such as incision and suction for snakebite, suturing wounds, and administration of a plethora of medications, that are now considered either ineffective or beyond the scope of practice of a lay medical provider. At the time it was the best advice available.

I became interested in wilderness medicine when I began working summers as a field instructor for NOLS in 1973 and realized that among the most difficult decisions I would face—and where I was lacking in experience—was in wilderness medicine. It was much easier to hone my rock climbing skills than to learn how to help the ill or injured in the wilderness. This was the dawn of modern emergency medical services, and I was able to join a volunteer ambulance service during winters in college. After several years of training and experience, I found myself teaching what was an early version of the Wilderness First Responder (WFR) course for NOLS field instructors, now at the dawn of modern wilderness medicine curriculum.

As I write this, the bookshelf in my office sags with tomes on wilderness medicine. But when we were laying out the curriculum for NOLS wilderness medicine courses in the late 1970s, none of those existed. We crafted the curriculum focusing on three themes: what is practical, what is accurate, and what is relevant. We worked to make sure that the skills we were teaching would actually work in the field, not just in the classroom. We asked ourselves, have we ever done this—build this type of splint, for example—and could we actually do it in the field? Is it a realistic skill?

We worked to make sure that what we were teaching was accurate. In the era before the modern concept of evidence-based medicine, and before the ease of access the Internet provides, we tried to determine whether what we were teaching was based on science, was an educated opinion, or was myth or lore. The former would be part of the curriculum, the latter we would try to purge.

We sought relevance; of everything we could teach, what should we teach? What was the wilderness medicine provider likely to *need* to know? In this we had the benefit of the experience of NOLS field instructors and of the NOLS Incident database.

When NOLS began gathering information on injuries and illnesses in the field it became clear that small wounds, sprains and strains, diarrhea, and flu-like illness were the day-to-day experience of the outdoor leader, and serious injury and illness were rare. These observations were confirmed as the pace of wilderness medicine research and textbook publication increased. There is now a substantial body of work that can inform our practice and help us focus our training and decision-making tools. We can study incident data collected on youth groups, outdoor programs, park visitors, search and rescue teams, climbing programs, trekking organizations, and boating groups.

There is also a growing literature on specific issues in wilderness medicine, and first aid in general. In some ways, wilderness medicine feels like a mature discipline. In others, we're still very much peeling the onion, asking critically if traditional techniques work and if hallowed information is accurate. We study the arguments on the need for, and efficacy of, traction splints, on which dislocation techniques are relevant and realistic for an outdoor leader to perform, and whether pre-hospital providers can make accurate decisions on the need for spine immobilization. We're seeing rational discussion on wilderness water quality, hygiene, and water disinfection.

Wilderness medicine courses remain "evidence-informed"— perhaps a more honest phrase than "evidence-based" in that it reflects the limits and biases of the science, and the ever-present influence of human experience and opinion. Our wilderness medicine courses continue to reflect the direct experience of outdoor leaders whose expertise is in the outdoors, not medicine. Often there is little that can be done for a patient in the wilderness besides providing comfort while evacuating, and the crux is the decision whether or not to evacuate, and if so, how quickly. This decision impacts the expedition, the rescuers, and the patient. We listen to outdoor leaders explain how they made their decisions on the need for, and urgency of, evacuation. These observations inform our decisions on what to include in our programs.

Guidance on evacuation decisions is not found in urban first aid courses, which assume ready access to the physician. It is a crucial difference in wilderness medicine and weaves judgment and decision making into first aid training. To ignore this in a leader's training is to ignore a reality of the field. Decision tools such as protocols have been tightened over the years. In the future, accurate case reports may allow validation or abandonment of these decision tools. The curriculum is dynamic and changes to stay current and relevant. WFR instructors of the

2020s do not teach a 1970s curriculum; they teach a course that continues to evolve to meet the needs of the outdoor leader.

This new edition has many changes woven into the text, reflecting our evolving practice. You will read a new approach to spine injury; about the concept of stress injury and psychological first aid; and about the latest understanding of hyponatremia, drowning, and marine animal envenomation, among others. The chapters on leadership, teamwork, and decision making in particular saw significant revisions to reflect our current curriculum on these topics. Throughout the text we worked hard to make our language more inclusive, use gender-neutral descriptors, and avoid labels (e.g., "diabetic" versus "person with diabetes") that are unfortunately common.

NOLS Wilderness Medicine may be used as a text for any wilderness medicine course. This text covers the material commonly taught by reputable wilderness first responder (WFR) programs and published in the Wilderness First Responder Scope of Practice document curated by the Wilderness Medicine Education Collaborative. People using this as a WFR textbook should seek supplementary background information and training on cardiopulmonary resuscitation (CPR).

Simply reading the text or successfully completing a NOLS course does not qualify a person to perform any procedure. The text is not a substitute for thorough, practical training, experience in emergency medicine and the outdoors, critical analysis of the needs of specific situations, or the continued education and training necessary to keep skills sharp.

In the first edition of this text, the late Jim Ratz, NOLS Instructor and Executive Director from 1983 to 1994, commented that on his student course NOLS founder Paul Petzoldt began the first aid class with the observation that we would be better off spending our time learning how to avoid accidents.

> *Paul's class was short on detail—wilderness medicine had hardly begun—and long on common sense. Paul had his priorities in order; good judgement, prior planning, and an appreciation for accident prevention will dramatically decrease your odds of an accident. Petzoldt's first aid class was an eye-opener for me; his was the first*

class that I had ever heard that placed good judgment before the rote learning of technical skills. Having recently finished school, I wasn't accustomed to such down-to-earth statements. I realize now that Paul wasn't simply teaching a class, he was setting the direction that has made NOLS a leader in the field of wilderness education and safety. This book is one more step in a great tradition.

Many things have changed in the 30 years of this textbook, and in my 47 years in wilderness and emergency medicine, but Paul Petzoldt's advocacy for good judgment still rings true.

Tod Schimelpfenig
Lander, Wyoming
September 2020

PATIENT ASSESSMENT

Many outdoor leaders, skilled in wilderness living and travel yet inexperienced in first aid, have wondered if they will be able to care for an ill or injured companion. They can and do provide this care using the patient assessment system as their foundation—their tool for checking for life-threatening problems, surveying the patient for injury and illness, and gathering the information needed to prioritize treatment and evacuation decisions. Generations of wilderness first responders and NOLS Field Instructors have proven this true. The foundation of their first aid and medical judgment has been common sense, good training, and the thoroughness and care by which they gather information in the patient assessment.

CHAPTER 1 | PATIENT ASSESSMENT SYSTEM

INTRODUCTION

Imagine yourself kneeling beside a fallen hiker, deep in the wilderness. The 911 call, the ambulance, and expectations of prompt advanced medical care don't apply to this situation. As you examine the person, thoughts of your remoteness, the safety of your companions, the incoming weather, evacuation, communication, and shelter possibilities swirl through your brain. You are about to make decisions and initiate a series of events that will affect the safety and well-being of the patient, your group, and outside rescuers.

In the city, the patient could be transported quickly to a hospital. In the wilderness, patient care may be your responsibility for hours or days. The rescue or evacuation may be strenuous and could jeopardize the safety of the group and the rescuers. You need information to help determine how best to manage risk, care for, and transport the patient. You gather that information during the patient assessment, the foundation of your care.

SCENE SIZE-UP

Assessing the scene is the first step in assessing the patient. Your observations of weather, terrain, any bystanders, and the position of the patient are your first clues as to how an injury occurred, the patient's condition, and possible scene hazards. Sizing up the scene begins a process of making sense of the situation, a process that continues as more information is gathered in the patient assessment.

Scene Safety
Before focusing on the patient, evaluate and manage hazards, and make decisions on acceptable risk. As a WFR you will manage many risks: moving water, falling rock, the possibility of a fall, dangerous animals, and other hazards. Your outdoor skills and experience, beyond the scope of this text, will help you make wise and competent risk assessments.

Look for danger to yourself, other rescuers or companions, and to the patient. Cold, driving rain may make constructing shelter a priority to avoid hypothermia. Falling rock or an avalanche may dictate a rapid carry of the patient out of the path of danger. A cliff edge may mean you can't approach the scene or the patient without additional protection.

We also make risk assessments for blood-borne, respiratory, and other pathogens—the COVID-19 pandemic is a striking example—and based on our assessment, don personal protective gear (PPE). Before you approach the patient, make an intentional decision about what PPE to put on—mask, gloves, eyewear, and a gown or protective clothing. Similarly, early in your patient assessment make a decision about whether to ask the patient to wear a mask.

In addition to protection from exposure to blood and other body fluids, responders need to consider appropriate vaccinations and a larger concept of personal protective equipment to include items such as a helmet, a harness, rope, heavy gloves, insulated clothing, or a personal flotation device.

Mechanism of Injury
Assess the mechanism or cause of injury (MOI). Look around. Your observations of the scene and questions of the patient and others involved in the event can elicit clues about what happened. You are trying to make sense of the scene, to understand what is going on. Is the patient ill or injured? If ill, gather a short

history of the illness. If injured, what is the mechanism? If the patient fell, find out how far and if they were wearing a helmet. Did the person land on soft ground, snow, or rocks? Did they fall free or tumble? Mechanism can give us critical information about the location and severity of injuries.

Do you have more than one patient? If so, an initial assessment may tell you who needs your immediate attention, and how best to use your companions or teammates to organize the scene and care for the patients.

Is the patient quiet (possibly a bad sign), or are they talking and moving (often a good sign)? Are they holding an ankle and wincing in pain, or having trouble breathing? Does the person look seriously ill or injured, or do you perceive a mild illness or injury? These observations form your first impression of the patient's condition.

Body Substance Isolation
As a healthcare worker, you must practice body substance isolation (BSI) to protect yourself against infectious disease that may be present in the patient or the environment, and to protect the patient from any infectious agents you may harbor. What we tend to loosely refer to as "bloodborne pathogens," viruses such as hepatitis B (HBV) and human immunodeficiency virus (HIV), which cause hepatitis and AIDS, respectively, can be carried in body fluids such as saliva, tears, sputum and, of course, blood. We protect ourselves by wearing primarily gloves, but also gowns and goggles, to minimize contact, especially exposure through breaks in the skin, and by hand washing.

We can also pick up pathogens from fecal matter and surfaces, and with our hands, and transport them to our face, where we may inhale or swallow them, thus becoming infected. We use gloves, clean surfaces, wash our hands, and try not to touch our face.

Respiratory pathogens such as influenza and coronavirus, which can cause the flu and COVID-19, respectively, can float in the air. We use primarily masks, but also eyewear, to protect ourselves.

We consider all body fluids and tissues presumptively infectious, and after the emergence of the COVID-19 pandemic, appropriate respiratory precautions are taken as standard practice. Protect yourself by washing your hands; using personal protective equipment (PPE) such as face masks, gloves, eyewear, and protective clothing; properly disposing of soiled bandages, dressing, and clothing; and avoiding needlestick injury.

Hand Hygiene

Hand hygiene is fundamental to infection control. Ideally, hands are cleaned before and after contact with each individual patient, and when you change gloves. Perform hand hygiene using either soap and water for at least 20 seconds or an alcohol-based hand sanitizer that contains at least 60 percent alcohol. Soap and water remove pathogens through mechanical action. Alcohol-based sanitizers kill or inactivate pathogens through chemical action. Common errors with handwashing are to not wash for 20 seconds, or to not scrub the entire hand surface. Common errors with alcohol-based sanitizers are not using sufficient sanitizer to cover the entire surface of the hands (web spaces especially), not scrubbing sufficiently, and not waiting until the sanitizer has dried. If hand sanitizer is used on dirty or greasy hands the alcohol may not penetrate deep enough to disinfect; if your hands are visibly dirty, wash with soap and water.

Masks

The rescuer dons a mask and asks the patient to wear a mask, primarily to protect against respiratory pathogens. In order of preference, choose: N95 (or similar standards such as FFP2), surgical, or cloth.

In potentially infectious environments, medical professionals use the N95 respirator, which is designed to filter 95 percent of particulate matter out of inhaled air. Proper function depends on a proper fit and tight face seal so air can't leak around the edges. Facial hair must be properly trimmed for a good mask fit.

Surgical and cloth masks, on the other hand, contain exhaled airborne droplets emitted by the mask-wearer; they primarily protect other people from our exhalations. It is more likely that a lay responder will use a surgical or medical mask, a cloth mask or an improvised mask. A bandana, neck gaiter, or scarf is not considered PPE for a healthcare provider in a clinical setting, but it might be the best option available in the outdoors.

Donning a surgical or cloth mask

- If your mask has pleats, pull at the bottom to expand.
- If your mask has a nose piece, pre-bend it.
- Place the mask on your face making sure to cover your nose.
- Pull the bottom of the mask under your chin.
- If your mask secures behind the ears, secure it now.
- If your mask ties around your head, secure the top ties around the crown of your head, and then tie bottom ties securely at the nape of your neck.

Doffing a mask

- Handle only the ties to remove the mask.
- Remove the bottom tie first, then the top tie.
- Remove the mask from your face.
- Properly dispose of the mask, touching only the ties.

Gloves

In the field, in order of protection, we use medical, food service or work/recreational gloves. Disposable nitrile, vinyl, or other synthetic or natural rubber gloves should be in your first aid kit (people allergic to latex will need nonlatex gloves). SAR teams may wear work gloves, especially when they handle ropes. These should be sanitized after patient contact. Hand hygiene is performed, ideally before, and certainly after removing gloves. To remove gloves:

- Grasp the outside of one glove at the wrist. Do not touch your bare skin.
- Peel the glove away from your body, pulling it inside out.
- Hold the glove you just removed in your gloved hand.
- Peel off the second glove by putting your fingers inside the glove at the top of your wrist.
- Turn the second glove inside out while pulling it away from your body, leaving the first glove inside the second.

Eyewear

Wear eye protection (in order of preference: a face shield, glasses or goggles with full side protection, standard eyeglasses or sunglasses).

Gowns

Organized responders may carry medical gowns as part of their equipment. In lieu of purpose-made gowns, water- or wind-proof outerwear can serve the same function. When removing potentially contaminated outerwear, turn the garment inside out and touch only the inside. Outerwear can be stored and washed later with soap and water. Gowns can be disposed of.

Surface Cleaning

Clean and disinfect frequently touched objects and surfaces, such as litters, splinting materials, stethoscopes etc., with a commercial or household disinfectant spray or wipe.

Place contaminated items such as gloves and bandages in sealed plastic bags labeled as a biohazard, or incinerate such items in a hot fire.

INITIAL ASSESSMENT

The initial assessment, also called the primary survey or primary assessment, is performed on every patient. Designed to find and treat life-threatening medical problems, it provides order during the first frantic minutes of an emergency. Problems in the critical respiratory and circulatory systems are identified and managed. If a mechanism for spine injury is present, disability is presumed and the spine protected. Obvious injuries are exposed and those that threaten life are treated.

Scene Size-up
- Identify hazards to self, other rescuers, and patient.
- Determine mechanism of injury.
- Form a general impression of seriousness.
- Determine the number of patients.
- Don personal protective equipment.

Establishing Responsiveness

As you approach the patient, introduce yourself and ask if you may help. You're obtaining consent to treat, being polite, and finding out if the patient is responsive. Ideally you have a brief conversation with the patient who, if they agree to allow you to help, will have given informed consent. If there is no response, say a greeting such as "hello!" loudly. If this fails to arouse the patient, try a painful stimulus, such as pinching the shoulder or knuckle-rubbing the breastbone. Permission to treat an unresponsive patient, or a patient with altered mental status, is assumed through the legal concept of implied consent. See Chapter 30 ("Medical Legal Concepts in Wilderness Medicine"). This is the point in the assessment where you may ask a responsive patient to don a mask, or drape a mask over the mouth and nose of an unresponsive patient.

This is also the point where, if there is a mechanism for spine injury or uncertainty of the mechanism, protect the spine. Use soft supportive head blocks or a rescuer's hands on the side of the head to protect against neck movement.

ABCDE

The initial assessment checks the airway, breathing, and circulation; looks for serious bleeding; includes a decision on possible spine injury; and exposes obvious injuries. We use ABCDE (airway, breathing, circulation, disability, expose) as a memory aid for this initial assessment sequence.

Airway. The airways, consisting of the mouth, nose, throat, trachea, and bronchi, are the path air travels from the atmosphere into the lungs. An obstructed airway is a medical emergency because oxygen cannot reach the lungs, a condition we can tolerate only for a few minutes. Ask the patient to remove anything in their mouth that could become an airway obstruction, such as gum or broken teeth. If the patient is unresponsive, open the airway with the head-tilt–chin-lift method or the jaw thrust, and look inside the mouth. If you see an obvious obstruction—a piece of food, perhaps—take it out.

If you can see, hear, or feel air moving from the lungs to the outside, the airway is open. A patient making sounds is able to move air from the lungs and past the vocal cords, indicating that the airway is at least partially open.

The Initial Assessment

- Assess for responsiveness.
- Obtain consent to treat.
- Protect the spine.

A—Assess the airway.
- Open the airway.
- Clear obvious obstructions.

B—Assess for breathing.
- Look, listen, feel.

C—Assess for circulation.
- Check pulse.
- Look and sweep for severe bleeding.

D—Decision on disability.
- Decide if further spine protection is needed.

E—Expose and examine major injuries.

Signs of an obstructed airway are lack of air movement, labored or noisy breathing, use of neck and upper chest muscles to breathe, and pale gray or bluish skin or mucous membranes such as the gums. If you discover an airway obstruction, attempt to clear the airway before proceeding to assess breathing. The appropriate techniques for treating a foreign body airway obstruction are those taught in Basic Life Support (BLS) or cardiopulmonary resuscitation (CPR) courses.

Breathing. If the patient is awake, ask them to take a deep breath. If the patient's breathing is labored or painful, expose the chest and look for life-threatening injuries. If the patient is unresponsive, look for the rise and fall of the chest as air enters and leaves the lungs. The abdomen also moves as we breathe, as the diaphragm rises and falls. Listen for the sound of air passing through the upper airway. If the patient is not breathing, give two slow, even breaths using a barrier device, then check for a pulse.

Circulation. Check for the presence or absence of a pulse. If the patient is unresponsive, place the tips of your middle and index fingers over the carotid artery for at least 10 seconds. The carotid is a large artery accessible at the neck. If the patient is responsive, this assessment is often done at the radial artery in the wrist.

Finding a pulse is not always easy, especially in a patient suffering from cold or shock. If you are unsure about the presence of the carotid pulse, try the femoral or the radial pulse.

The INITIAL ASSESSMENT

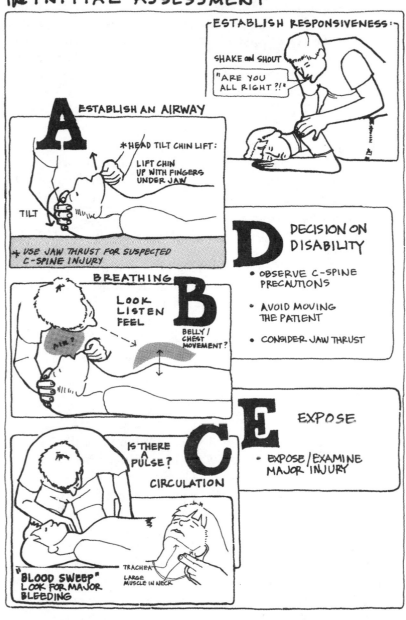

If there is no pulse and no signs of life (moving, moaning, coughing, or breathing), start CPR. If there is a pulse but no breathing, start rescue breathing with a barrier device.

Blood Sweep. Severe bleeding can be fatal within minutes. Look for obvious bleeding or wet places on the patient's clothing. Run your gloved hands over and under the patient's clothing, especially bulky sweaters or parkas, to find moist areas that may be caused by serious bleeding. Look for blood that may be seeping into snow or the ground. Most external bleeding can be controlled with direct pressure. Chapter 7 ("Soft Tissue Injuries") addresses bleeding control in detail.

Decision on Disability. Make a decision on whether you need to continue to protect the spine. If there is no mechanism for spine injury, you can release spine protection. If there is a mechanism or you are unsure, your decision should be to continue to protect the spine. An airway-opening technique for someone who is unresponsive and has a known or possible spine-injury mechanism is the jaw thrust. It does not require shifting the neck or spine. See Chapter 4 ("Brain and Spinal Cord Injuries").

Expose. Without moving the patient, search for major injuries that may be hidden under bulky outdoor clothing. Quickly unzip zippers, open cuffs, and look under parkas. Re-zip to keep the patient warm.

ABC or CAB?

The first five letters of the alphabet remind us of the parts of the initial assessment. The *flow* of the initial assessment, the sequence of steps, is determined by the context in which we are assessing the patient. The ABC flow—checking the airway, then breathing, then circulation—is appropriate for most patients. It's appropriate for a patient who may be suffering from hypoxia, perhaps an avalanche or submersion victim, and for pediatric patients. CPR courses teach a CAB initial assessment sequence, where checking for circulation takes precedence over airway and breathing. This is appropriate for the person who may have suffered a cardiac arrest due to heart disease. In this case, early chest compressions are key to survival. In a tactical context, massive bleeding may immediately threaten life, which is why the combat medic focuses on bleeding control before airway and breathing. They may use the memory aid MARCH for major hemorrhage, airway, respirations, circulation, head injury, hypothermia/shock. Whether you focus your initial assessment on bleeding, on the airway and breathing, or on circulation depends on the context of the event. Your understanding of the scene size-up guides your decision on the sequence. This is a stressful part of the patient assessment; take time at the outset to decide what order you will use, and then see that system through. This phase of the patient assessment system is not complete until all parts of it, represented by all five letters of the alphabet, have been done and any identified threats to life have been treated.

ABC, CAB, or MARCH?

Scene size-up

Context?

Urban Cardiac?	Patient without apparent life-threats?	Tactical?
	Avalanche?	Obvious massive injury?
CAB	ABC	Blood Sweep first

SECONDARY ASSESSMENT

Now pause a moment. The initial assessment is complete. Immediate threats to life have been addressed. Take a deep breath and consider the needs of the patient and the rescuers. If the location of the incident is unstable—such as on or near loose boulders or a potential avalanche slope—move to a safer position. Provide insulation, adjust clothing, rig a shelter. Assign tasks: boil water for hot drinks, set up camp, write down vital signs. Delegate tasks; ensuring everyone has something to do helps rescuers by creating a sense of self-efficacy and helps the patient by creating an atmosphere of order and leadership. This weaves psychological first aid into the patient assessment. See Chapter 29 ("Stress and the Responder") for more on rescue stress and psychological first aid.

Focused Exam and History

PATIENT EXAM	VITAL SIGNS	MEDICAL HISTORY
• Look	• Responsiveness	• Chief Complaint (OPQRST)
• Listen	• Heart Rate	• SAMPLE
• Feel	• Respiration	
• Smell	• Skin	
• Ask	• Temperature	
	• Blood Pressure	
	• Pupils	

The secondary assessment, also known as the focused exam and history, is done after life-threatening conditions have been treated. It consists of a head-to-toe physical exam, measurement of vital signs, and a medical history.

Much of the secondary assessment can feel personal, so take time at the outset to help the patient feel comfortable. Introduce yourself more fully. Ask the patient how they would like to be addressed, and use their preferred name and honorific. The patient may be more comfortable if the person doing the patient assessment matches their biological sex or gender-identity. The patient may want a friend or companion present for their comfort, which can reduce stress and is good psychological first

FOCUSED ASSESSMENT and HISTORY

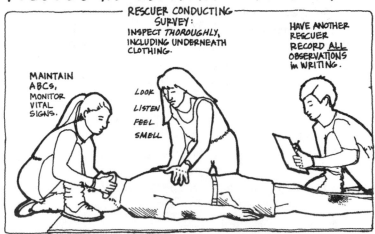

aid. Some programs and agencies require that two responders are present during patient assessment and care, especially if the patient is a minor. As you perform the assessment, avoid assumptions about injuries, medical history and vital signs. Ask and assess. Explain what you are doing and why. Besides demonstrating simple courtesy, this involves the patient in their care, another principle of psychological first aid. Ongoing consent is also a medical-legal principle.

Head-to-Toe Examination
The head-to-toe exam is a physical examination starting with the head and systematically checking the body down to the toes. Ideally, one person should perform the survey, in order to avoid confusion, provide consistent results, and minimize discomfort to the patient. If possible, designate a notetaker to record the results of the focused exam and history.

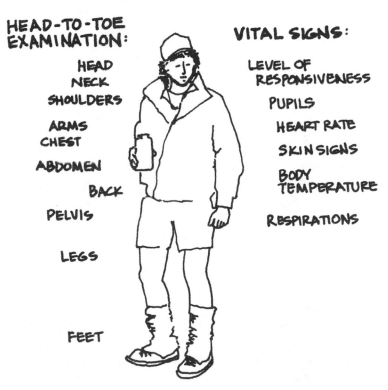

HEAD-TO-TOE EXAMINATION:

HEAD
NECK
SHOULDERS
ARMS
CHEST
ABDOMEN
BACK
PELVIS
LEGS
FEET

VITAL SIGNS:

LEVEL OF RESPONSIVENESS
PUPILS
HEART RATE
SKIN SIGNS
BODY TEMPERATURE
RESPIRATIONS

The Focused Exam and History: Head-to-Toe Patient Examination
- **Look** for wounds, bleeding, unusual movements or shapes, deformities, penetrations, excretions, vomit.
- **Listen** for abnormal sounds, such as crepitus and airway noises or moaning in response to pain.
- **Feel** for wounds, rigidity, hardness, softness, tenderness, deformity.
- **Smell** for unusual odors.
- **Ask** if anything hurts or feels odd or numb.

The examination technique consists of looking, listening, feeling, smelling, and asking. Your hands should be clean, warm, and gloved. Whenever you touch the patient, do so with enough firmness to elicit any response that might indicate tenderness in the area, without causing undue pain. If you are uncertain of what is abnormal, ask the patient, or compare the injured extremity with the other side of the body or with that of a healthy or uninjured person.

Head. Check the ears and nose for fluid, and the mouth for injuries that may affect the airway. Observe the face for symmetry; all features are typically symmetrical down the midline from the forehead to the chin. The cheekbones are usually accurate references for facial symmetry. Feel the entire skull for depressions, tenderness, and irregularity. Run your fingers through the hair to detect hidden bleeding or cuts. Check the eyes for injuries and pupil abnormalities, and ask about vision disturbances.

Neck. The trachea or windpipe should be in the middle of the neck. Feel the entire cervical spine from the base of the skull to the top of the shoulders to identify pain, tenderness, muscle rigidity, and deformity.

Shoulders. Examine the shoulders and the collarbones for signs of deformity, tenderness, and pain. If possible, collarbones should be touched along their entire length.

Arms. Feel the arms from the armpit to the wrist, and check circulation, sensation, and motion (CSM) in each hand, one hand at a time. CSM assessment tests whether there is injury to nerves in the extremity or at the spine, or injury to blood vessels in an extremity. Assess for radial pulse in the wrist to check circulation. Ask the patient if they have any abnormal sensations such as tingling, numbness, hot, or cold, and assess for sensitivity to light touch on a pinky and thumb. Having the patient squeeze your hands and extend their wrist will enable you to identify issues with motion.

Chest. Feel the chest for deformity or tenderness. Push in from the sides. Ask the patient to breathe deeply as you compress the chest. Look for open chest wounds. Observe the rise and fall of the chest for symmetry.

Abdomen. Feel the abdomen for tenderness or muscle rigidity with light pressure. Look for distension, discoloration, and bruising (abdominal injuries are discussed further in Chapter 18).

Back. Feel each vertebra from the neck to the pelvis. If the patient is on their back, logroll to press on the spine and look at the back. This is a good time to place the patient on a pad or in a sleeping bag.

Pelvis. Press in from the sides of the pelvis. Avoid aggressive or rocking motions on an injured pelvis.

Genitals or breasts are assessed only if a patient complains of injury and in the presence of whomever the patient is most comfortable with. The patient may be able to self-assess.

Legs. Check the legs from the groin to the ankle. Check CSM in the feet, one foot at a time. Assess for pedal pulse in the foot or posterior tibia pulse in the ankle. The pulses in the foot and ankle can be hard to find, and in such cases, warmth and color can instead be used as indicators of good circulation. Warm feet with pink skin or nail beds have good circulation. Ask the patient if they have any abnormal sensations: tingling, numbness, hot, or cold, and assess for sensitivity to light touch on a small toe and the big toe. Assess the ability to move by asking the patient to push and pull the feet against your hand pressure.

Vital Signs

Vital signs are objective indicators of airway, breathing, circulation, brain function, and body temperature. Check airway and breathing by noting the color of the skin or mucous membranes and the breathing effort. Good color and easy, regular breathing indicate that the airway and lungs are working well. Evaluate circulation by pulse, skin or mucous membrane color, skin

---

Focused Exam and History: Vital Signs
- **Level of Responsiveness**—Assess with AVPU.
- **Heart rate**—Assess pulse rate, rhythm, strength.
- **Skin signs**—Assess skin or mucous membrane color, temperature, and moisture.
- **Respiration**—Assess rate, rhythm, effort.
- **Temperature**—Assess temperature with a thermometer.
- **Blood Pressure**—Assess with a stethoscope and a sphygmomanometer, or radial pulse.
- **Pupils**—Assess size, shape, and reactivity to light.

---

temperature, and level of responsiveness. Effective circulation gives us warm, perfused skin and enough oxygen to keep the brain alert.

As a general rule, measure and record vital signs every 15 to 20 minutes—more frequently if the patient is seriously ill or injured. The initial set of vitals—responsiveness, pulse, respiration, skin, blood pressure, pupils, and temperature—provides baseline data on the patient's condition. The changes that occur thereafter provide information on the progress of the patient.

Level of Responsiveness (LOR). Brain function—also known as mental status and reflected in how responsive we are to our environment—may be affected by toxic chemicals such as drugs or alcohol, low blood sugar, shock, abnormally high or low temperature, low blood oxygen from airway or breathing problems, diseases of the brain such as stroke, or pressure from bleeding or swelling caused by a head injury.

You begin assessing responsiveness when you approach the patient, introduce yourself, say hello, and ask if you can help. You're being polite as well as finding out if the patient is awake, asleep, or possibly unresponsive. A simple classification system for level of responsiveness is AVPU (awake, not awake but responsive to a verbal stimulus, not awake but responsive to only a painful stimulus, unresponsive). AVPU gives us structure to evaluate responsiveness and vocabulary to communicate our findings to other healthcare providers.

Awake. Normally we are awake (or we wake quickly from sleep) and know who we are, where we are, the date or time, and recent events. Depending on whether the patient knows who they are, where they are, what date or time it is, and recent events they are described as "A (awake) and O (oriented) times 0, 1, 2, 3, or 4." The order in which a patient loses this information may vary, but in general the trend is:

- A+Ox4   The person knows person, place, time, and event.
- A+Ox3   The person knows person, place, and time, but not event.
- A+Ox2   The person knows person and place, but not time and event.
- A+Ox1   The person knows person, but not place, time, and event.

A patient who is awake but not oriented to person, place, time, or event can be described as "disoriented" or "A+Ox0." The spoken response may be incoherent, confused, inappropriate, or incomprehensible.

Not awake but responsive to Verbal Stimulus. The patient is not awake but responds to a verbal stimulus, such as the rescuer saying, "Hello, how are you?" If the patient does not respond, repeat louder: "Hey! Wake up!" The patient's response may be opening the eyes, grunting, or moving. Higher levels of brain function respond to verbal input, lower levels to pain. Test first for responsiveness to verbal stimuli, and if no response, painful stimuli.

Not awake and responsive only to Pain. The patient is not awake, does not respond to verbal stimuli, but does respond to painful stimuli by moving, opening the eyes, or groaning. To stimulate for pain, pinch the muscle at the back of the shoulder or neck, rub the sternum with knuckles, or squeeze a fingernail.

AVPU: Assessing Level of Responsiveness
- **A**wake
- Not awake but responsive to **V**erbal Stimulus
- Not awake and responsive only to **P**ain
- **U**nresponsive

Unresponsive. The patient is not awake and does not respond to verbal or painful stimuli.

Report the patient's initial state, the stimulus you gave, and the response. For example: "This patient is awake and oriented times four." Or, "This patient is not awake, but is responsive to a verbal stimulus. When awake, the patient knows their name but is otherwise disoriented."

Heart Rate, Rhythm, Strength. Every time the heart beats, a pressure wave is transmitted through the arteries. We feel this pressure wave as the pulse. The pulse rate indicates the number of heartbeats over a period of time. For an adult, the normal range is 50 to 100 beats per minute. A well-conditioned athlete may have a normal pulse rate below 50. Shock, exercise, altitude, illness, emotional stress, or fever can increase the heart rate. Hypothermia, some forms of heart disease and some medications can decrease the heart rate.

The heart rate can be measured most easily at the radial artery on the thumb side of the wrist or at the carotid artery in the neck. Place the tips of the middle and index fingers over the artery. If it is not practical to count the pulse for an entire minute, count the number of beats for 15 seconds and multiply by four or 30 seconds and multiply by 2.

In addition to rate, note the rhythm and the quality or strength of the pulse. Normally, the pulse has a steady beat. Irregular rhythms can be associated with heart disease and are frequently rapid. The strength of the pulse is the amount of pressure you feel against your fingertips. It may be weak or strong.

A standard pulse reading includes the rate, rhythm, and quality/strength. For example: "The pulse is 110, irregular, and weak." Or, "The pulse is 60, regular, and strong."

Skin. Skin color, temperature, and moisture—often abbreviated as SCTM—indicates the condition of the respiratory and cardiovascular systems.

Pinkness. Skin that is well perfused with blood is often described with the adjective pink, which refers not necessarily to skin color, which can vary with the degree of pigmentation, but rather to the color of our mucous membranes (and non-pigmented areas such as nail beds).

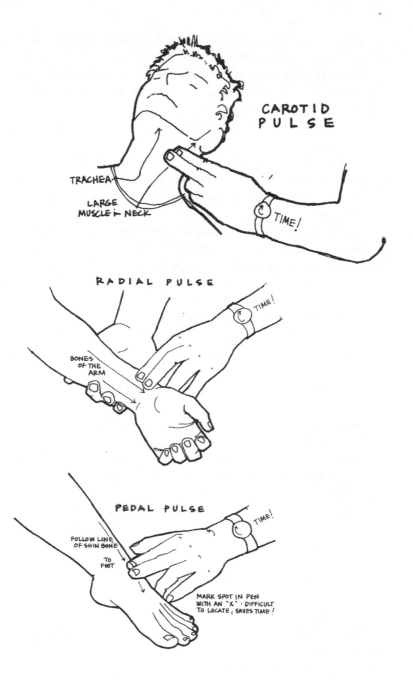

CAROTID PULSE

TRACHEA

LARGE MUSCLE in NECK

TIME!

RADIAL PULSE

BONES OF THE ARM

TIME!

PEDAL PULSE

FOLLOW LINE OF SHIN BONE

TO FOOT

TIME!

MARK SPOT IN PEN WITH AN "X" : DIFFICULT TO LOCATE, SAVES TIME!

Redness. Red skin or mucous membranes may indicate heat-stroke, carbon monoxide poisoning, fever, or allergic reaction.

Paleness. Pale skin or mucous membranes indicates that blood has withdrawn from the skin, due to fright, shock, fainting, or cooling of the skin.

Cyanosis. Blue skin or mucous membranes, also called cyanosis, appears when circulation to the skin is reduced or the level of oxygen in the blood falls. Well-oxygenated blood is brighter red than poorly oxygenated blood. Cyanosis indicates that oxygen levels have fallen significantly, or that the patient may be cold.

Jaundice. Yellow skin or mucous membranes combined with yellow eyes—jaundice—is a sign of liver or gallbladder disease. The condition results from excess bile pigment in the blood.

Temperature and Moisture. Quickly assess the temperature and moisture of the skin. In cold environments the face and hands may be unreliable places to assess skin temperature. Instead, slip your warm hand under clothing to check the trunk. In a healthy person, the skin is warm and relatively dry. Skin temperature rises when the body attempts to rid itself of excess heat, as in fever or environmental heat problems. Hot, dry skin can be a sign of fever or heatstroke. Hot, sweaty skin occurs when the body attempts to eliminate excess heat, and can also be a sign of fever or heat illness.

Skin temperature falls when the body attempts to conserve heat by constricting blood flow to the skin—for example, during exposure to cold. Cool, moist (clammy) skin is an indicator of extreme stress and a sign of shock.

A report on skin condition should include color, temperature, and moisture. For example: "The patient's mucous membranes are pink, and their skin is cool and clammy."

Respiratory Rate, Rhythm, Effort. Respiratory (breathing) rate is counted in the same manner as the pulse: each rise of the chest is counted over 15 seconds and multiplied by four, or 30 seconds and multiplied by two. Watch the chest rise and fall, or observe the belly move with each breath. Normal adult breathing rate is 12 to 20 breaths per minute.

The patient's depth and effort of breathing enable you to gauge their need for air and the presence or absence of chest injury. A healthy individual's breathing is relatively effortless.

A patient experiencing breathing difficulty may exhibit air hunger with deep, labored inhaling efforts. A patient with a chest injury may have shallow, rapid breathing accompanied by pain. Irregular breathing is a sign of a brain disorder. Noisy breathing indicates some type of airway obstruction. Assess and, if necessary, clear the airway.

Smell the breath. Fruity, acetone breath can be a sign of diabetic coma. Foul, fecal-smelling breath may indicate a bowel obstruction.

Report respirations by their rate, rhythm, effort, depth, noises, and odors. For example, a patient in diabetic ketoacidosis may have respirations described as "20 per minute, regular, labored, deep. There is a fruity breath odor."

Temperature. Temperature measurement is an important component of a thorough patient assessment, but it is probably the vital sign that is measured least often in the field. Although a normal temperature is around 98.6°F (37°C), daily variation in body temperature is also normal, usually rising a degree during the day and decreasing through the night. A report on temperature should include the method, such as "100°F oral" or "37°C rectal."

Temperature can be measured by first aid providers orally or rectally, in the ear, or on the forehead. Ear and forehead temperatures are considered unreliable in a cold person. Axillary (taken under the armpit) readings are also unreliable. Rectal temperatures are the most accurate indication of the core temperature available to first responders. However, rectal temperature, sometimes considered necessary for suspected hypothermia, is rarely measured due to exposure issues in cold environments, and because it lags behind core temperature when warming or cooling. Diagnosis of hypothermia in the outdoors, discussed in Chapter 9 ("Cold Injuries"), is often based on other factors such as behavior, history, appearance, and mental status.

Pupils. Pupils are clues to brain function. They can indicate head or eye injury, stroke, drug abuse, or lack of oxygen to

PUPIL SIZE:

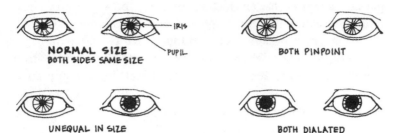

NORMAL SIZE — IRIS
BOTH SIDES SAME SIZE — PUPIL

BOTH PINPOINT

UNEQUAL IN SIZE

BOTH DIALATED

the brain. Both pupils should be round and equal in size. They should contract symmetrically when exposed to light and dilate when the light dims. Evaluate pupils by noting size, equality, and reaction to light.

In the absence of a portable light source, such as a flashlight or headlamp, ask the patient to close their eyes or shield the patient's eyes for 5 seconds, then expose them to ambient light. Both pupils should contract equally. When in doubt, compare the patient's reactions with those of a healthy individual in the same light conditions.

A patient deficient in oxygen may have equal but slow-to-react pupils. A wide, nonreactive pupil on one side and a small, reactive pupil on the other side may indicate brain damage or disease on the side with the larger pupil. Very small, equal pupils may indicate drug intoxication. Pupils are reported for size, equality, whether they are round and reactive to light, e.g., "Pupils are normal size, equal, round and react to light" or "Pupils are constricted, equal, round and slow to respond to light."

Blood Pressure. The concept of blood pressure is discussed in Chapter 2 ("Shock"). Accurate blood pressure measurement requires a stethoscope and a sphygmomanometer—equipment rarely carried on wilderness trips. However, a strong radial or pedal pulse provides useful information, in that they suggest that the patient has a cardiovascular system healthy enough to pump blood to the hands and feet. A weak or absent radial or pedal pulse, unless explainable by limb injury, suggests that blood pressure may be low. If this is the case, other signs of shock are likely present as well.

Medical History

The patient's medical history provides background that may be relevant to the present problem. An accurate history depends greatly on the quality of communication between you and the patient. Building this rapport begins as soon as you approach the scene. Communicating clearly, acting in an orderly fashion and with respect, using plain language, and listening carefully make it easier to obtain an accurate history.

> **Focused Exam and History: Medical History**
> - Chief Complaint (OPQRST)
> - SAMPLE

Chief Complaint. Obtain the patient's chief complaint—the problem that caused them to solicit help. Pain is a common complaint—for example, abdominal pain or pain in an arm or leg after a fall. In lieu of pain, a chief complaint may be nausea or dizziness. A memory aid for investigating the chief complaint is OPQRST.

Onset. Did the chief complaint appear suddenly or gradually?

Provokes/Palliates. What provoked the injury? If the problem is an illness, under what circumstances did it occur? What makes the problem worse, and what makes it better?

Quality. What qualities describe the pain? Adjectives may include stabbing, cramping, burning, sharp, dull, or aching.

Radiate/Region/Referred. Where is the pain? Does it move or radiate? What causes it to move? Chest pain from a heart attack can

> **OPQRST: Assessing the Chief Complaint**
> - **O**nset
> - **P**rovokes/Palliates
> - **Q**uality
> - **R**adiates/Region/ Referred
> - **S**everity
> - **T**ime/Trend

radiate from the chest into the neck and jaw. Pain from a spleen injury may be felt in the left shoulder.

Severity. On a scale of 1 to 10 (with 1 being no pain or discomfort and 10 being the worst pain or discomfort the patient has ever experienced), how does the patient rate this pain? This question can reveal the level of discomfort the patient is experiencing and help us evaluate changes over time. Or you can describe the effect of pain on the patient's affect, e.g., "The patient is obviously uncomfortable from pain or the patient is distracted and moaning from pain."

Time/Trend. When did the pain start? How frequently does it occur? How long does it last? Is it getting better or worse?

SAMPLE. This is a memory aid for a series of questions that complete the medical history.

Symptoms. In addition to the chief complaint, what symptoms does the patient have? Nausea? Dizziness? Headache? Ask the patient how they are feeling or if anything is causing discomfort. A symptom is something the patient perceives and must tell you about (e.g., pain). A sign, on the other hand, is something you can see, or find when you touch or expose an injury during a patient exam.

Allergies, Medications. Ask whether the patient is allergic to medications or has other environmental allergies, such as food, insects, or pollen. If so, find out if they have been exposed to the allergen and what is their usual response. Ask if the patient is currently taking any medications. Ask about non-prescription, prescription, and herbal medications, as well as possible alcohol or drug use. Ask whether the patient is supposed to be taking medication and is not, or has missed a dose.

**SAMPLE:
Assessing the
History**
- **S**ymptoms
- **A**llergies
- **M**edications
- **P**ast Pertinent
  medical history
- **L**ast intake/output
- **E**vents

Pertinent Medical History. The history consists of a series of questions you ask the patient to discover any previous and relevant medical problems. How—and how deeply—you probe the medical history is based on your sense of what is relevant, and on your level of medical training. If the patient has a broken leg, for example, it's unlikely you need to know about childhood illness. Begin with general questions: Has the patient ever been in a hospital? Is the patient currently seeing a physician? Next, ask about specific body systems. Avoid medical jargon. For instance, asking the patient about any previous heart problems may be less confusing than asking, "Do you have a cardiac history?"

Additional sources of information may include a medical-alert tag or a medical-information questionnaire. A medical-alert tag is a necklace, bracelet, or wallet card that identifies the patient's medical concerns. It may report a history of diabetes, hemophilia, epilepsy, or other disorder; allergies to medication; and other pertinent information. Medical forms are common to many outdoor schools, camps, and guide services.

Last Intake and Output. Ask the patient when they last ate and drank. This information may tell you whether the patient is hydrated, dehydrated or overhydrated, or give you important history if, for example, the patient is diabetic. Also find out when the patient last urinated and defecated. Clear, copious urine indicates good hydration; dark, smelly urine suggests dehydration. A patient with diarrhea or vomiting may be dehydrated.

Recent Events. Recent events are unusual circumstances that have occurred within the past few days that may be relevant to the patient's present situation. Recent events might include symptoms of mountain sickness preceding pulmonary edema or changes in diet preceding stomach upset.

Helpful Hints for the Patient Interview
- Establish a relationship:
  —Introduce yourself. Explain your training. Ask permission to help.
  —Allow the patient to dictate the distance between you.
  —Ask the patient what they would like to be called, and use their preferred name.
  —Do not use the patient's first name or a nickname without permission.
  —In some cultures, it is important to always address the person by the appropriate honorific (Mrs., Mr., Dr., etc.)
  —Speak to the person with respect: use words like "please" and "thank you."
  —Ask permission to touch the patient.
  —Do not make assumptions. Ask.
- Communicate calmly: Make eye contact. Relax. Be aware of your tone of voice and body language.
  —Tell the patient what you are doing and why.
  —Ask open-ended questions. Closed questions can be answered "yes" or "no." Open questions solicit a longer answer, e.g., "How do you feel?" "How would you describe your pain?"
  —If necessary, explain why you are asking the question.
  —Listen carefully to the patient's responses. If necessary, clarify answers.
  —Take notes.

THE ASSESSMENT

The assessment is a review of the information gathered and the development of a "problem list." It might include "the patient has a possible dislocated shoulder" or "the patient has anxiety, hyperventilation, and an unusable ankle injury."

Create a problem list by first thinking of all possible explanations. Then try to rule out those that don't fit the findings of the patient assessment. Physicians make many diagnoses on the basis of what a condition isn't, rather than what it could be. Is chest pain a muscle pull or a heart attack? Does the patient have the flu, mountain sickness, or early cerebral edema? If you can't rule out a possible problem, then it needs to stay on your list.

The Assessment
- Review available information.
- Rule out other possibilities.

The Plan
- Prioritize and treat.
- Review and repeat exam.
- Make an evacuation decision.

THE PLAN

Next, prioritize the problem list and develop a "treatment plan" for each. If "possible spine injury" is on your list, your plan may include "protect the spine and request evacuation support." If mild hypothermia is on your list, your plan may include "remove wet clothing, dry the patient, and insulate in a hypothermia wrap."

ANTICIPATED PROBLEMS

A list of concerns that you will monitor may include weather delaying evacuation or a condition worsening.

The initial patient assessment provides a baseline. Periodically repeat the exam to judge the patient's response to treatment and any changes for better or worse. Any change or deterioration in the patient calls for repeating your assessment.

SOAP Notes

Write down the results of your assessment. Not only will it help your own memory, but you also may need to communicate with

VERBAL SOAP REPORT

Subjective/Summary/Story (*Who, What, Where*)

_____

"This is (name/s) with a patient report/evacuation request."

"We are currently located at"

"I have a (age)-year-old (sex) whose chief complaint is"

"The MOI is"

"The patient is currently (LOR)"

Objective/Observations/Findings (*Head to Toe, Vitals, History*)

_____

"Patient has" (List relevant injuries/key signs of illness.)

"The patient's vital signs are (LOR, HR, RR, Skin, BP, Pupils, Temperature)"

"Pertinent SAMPLE history includes" (Include only relevant findings.)

Assessment (*Problem List*)
"We suspect the following problems"

Plan
Treatment
"Our treatment has included"

Evacuation
"Our evacuation/bivouac plan is to"

"We request the following supplies/support"

an evacuation or rescue party or the emergency room physician. Healthcare professionals commonly organize and communicate their medical information in the SOAP format: subjective, story or summary; objective or observations; the assessment; and the plan.

The patient or bystanders tell you subjective or summary information, the "story" of this event. It includes the patient's age, sex, mechanism of injury, chief complaint, and OPQRST findings.

Objective information is measurable or observable: "vital" signs and results called "findings" from the SAMPLE history and the patient exam.

The assessment section categorizes the patient's medical concerns in a problem list. For example, a problem list might be "sprained ankle, mild hypothermia," or "chest pain, possible heart attack."

The plan, the "P" of SOAP, is the list of interventions or treatment for each problem. It is also where you sketch how you plan to evacuate the patient, if necessary.

EXTENDED PATIENT CARE

Emergency medical care in the wilderness may be prolonged over hours or days in isolated locations. Splints, shelter, and litters may need to be improvised. In addition to first aid, basic nursing care is necessary to manage the physical and emotional needs of the patient.

Daily Needs
Keep the patient warm, clean, and comfortable. Remove soiled and wet clothing, and wash the patient. An individual immobilized on a litter may need extra insulation to keep warm and occasional position changes to avoid pressure sores. Hot water bottles, heat packs, or fires may be needed as sources of warmth.

If the patient can drink, give water or clear soups and juices. Avoid lots of coffee, tea, or other beverages with high concentrations of sugar or caffeine. Excess sugar can delay fluid absorption; excess caffeine increases fluid loss. Drinking and eating are not appropriate for patients who cannot protect their airway while they swallow.

Over a period of a few days, fluid intake is more important than solid food, as dehydration can complicate any existing medical condition. Dehydration is discussed in Chapter 23 ("Hydration").

Arrange for the patient to urinate and defecate as comfortably as possible. These basic body functions are essential to overall well-being, despite embarrassment or temporary discomfort. The first responder's sensitivity to and support for the patient are essential.

A patient with a penis who is immobile may be able to use a water bottle as a urine receptacle. For other patients, a bedpan can be fashioned from a frying pan or a large-mouth water bottle, or an article of clothing can be used as a diaper. Bowel movements can be managed by assisting the patient with an improvised bedpan.

Emotional Support: Psychological First Aid
An ill or injured patient experiences a variety of emotions, including fear about the quality of care and the outcome of the injury or illness, the length of evacuation, loss of control and independence, loss of self-esteem, and embarrassment. Reassurance, concern, and sympathy are appropriate, but avoid making promises of which you are unsure, such as, "You're going to be just fine." It's healthy to allow the patient to discuss the incident. Talking about an incident begins the process of emotional healing. Do not critique the incident or lay blame on any party involved.

Use the simple concepts of Psychological First Aid to help ameliorate the patient's stress. Creating a sense of safety, fostering calm, supporting patient self-efficacy, connecting them with loved ones and support groups, and overall creating a sense of hope can go a long way to reduce emotional stress. See Chapter 29 ("Stress and the Responder") for more on rescue stress and psychological first aid.

FINAL THOUGHTS—THE EVACUATION DECISION

An incomplete patient assessment system that fails to measure vital signs or review history and physical findings may lead to unnecessary and needlessly rushed evacuations. Helicopters have flown into wilderness areas for simple knee sprains and for hyperventilation misdiagnosed as a head injury. Rescue teams have hiked through the night expecting to treat serious injuries, only to find a walking patient with minor injuries. The patient, rescuers, and expedition members are needlessly put at risk.

Likewise, the same mistake has delayed evacuations. Life-threatening fevers have been overlooked because a temperature was not measured. Diabetic complications have been missed because no one asked about the patient's medical history.

A significant difference between urban and wilderness medicine lies in the decision-making process. In the emergency medical services system, ambulance personnel rarely make a decision to transport a patient or not. If they are called to help, an ambulance crew either transports the patient or obtains a patient signature on a refusal of treatment form. In the wilderness, the leader must decide if a patient needs to see a physician, and if so, with what urgency. The patient assessment system is an invaluable tool for making these decisions.

This text will suggest evacuation decision points, noting the thresholds for when patients should be evacuated, and when they need to be evacuated rapidly. These are guidelines that you can use, in conjunction with your physician advisor, to develop a protocol for your expedition or program.

There are many stories of outdoor leaders who lacked medical experience, but following their training performed a simple and methodical assessment, checked the ABCs for life-threatening problems, and then followed the focused history and exam protocols. They used a checklist, took their time, and made a written record of their findings. The information gathered was the foundation for quality first aid. Good medical decisions and judgment make for a sound evacuation plan.

NATIONAL OUTDOOR LEADERSHIP SCHOOL
FIELD EVACUATION REPORT

Name of Evacuee _____ Course/Section _____

Course Leader _____ Date & Time of Incident _____

SUBJECTIVE: Age___ Sex___ Location of Patient: Common name _____

Mechanism of Injury/Illness _____

_____

_____

_____

Chief Complaint (OPQRST*) _____

_____

_____

_____

OBJECTIVE: Vital Signs**

Date/Time	LOR	Pulse	RR	Skin	Pupils	T

Signs/Symptoms (patient exam) _____

_____

_____

_____

_____

Allergies _____ Medications _____

Past Medical History _____

Last Oral Intake _____

Events (recent, relevant) _____

ASSESSMENT: Problem list (prioritize) _____

_____

_____

PLAN: Emergency Care Rendered/Changes in Patient's Condition _____

_____

_____

_____

_____

_____

Evacuation Plan (timetable, backup, pickup point) _____

_____

_____

_____

_____

Instructor Signature _____ Date _____ Time _____

*OPQRST = onset, provocation, quality, region/radiation, severity, time sequence.
**LOR = alert x 4 (person, place, time, event), verbal, pain, unresponsive; pulse = rate, strength, and rhythm; RR = respiratory rate, depth, and rhythm; skin = color, temperature, moisture; pupils = equality, roundness, reactivity to light; T = temperature.

TRAUMATIC INJURIES

The incident data collected over three decades by the National Outdoor Leadership School shows that sprains, strains, and small wounds are the common injuries experienced on wilderness expeditions. Serious injury is uncommon. Regardless, in the wilderness we need to be prepared to manage fractures and dislocations as well as head, spine, or chest injuries until we can deliver the patient to the physician. This section covers field first aid treatment principles for this spectrum of injuries, from bleeding control and wound care to splinting, moving, and immobilizing a possible spine injury, stabilizing a chest injury, taping an ankle, and aiding a person in shock.

CHAPTER 2 | SHOCK

INTRODUCTION

Shock is a simple name for a complex disorder in which the circulatory system is unable to provide oxygen to the body's tissues. Mid-nineteenth century descriptions of shock as "a deadly downward spiral" and "a rude unhinging of the machinery of life" accurately portray a condition in which the circulatory system can collapse in apparent disproportion to the initial injury. When burns, serious illnesses, fractures, injuries to the chest and abdomen, severe bleeding, and catastrophic injuries become fatal, shock is often the reason. A first responder must anticipate, recognize, and treat shock.

THE CIRCULATORY SYSTEM

The circulatory system is composed of the heart, the blood vessels, and the blood. Its primary function is to deliver a constant supply of oxygen to the tissues. An interruption in that oxygen supply causes cells and tissues to malfunction and eventually die. The circulatory system also transports carbon dioxide from the cells to the lungs, keeps the body's electrolyte environment stable, delivers hormones from their source to their place of action, and mobilizes body defenses.

The HEART

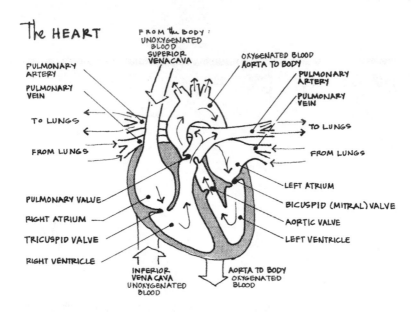

FROM the BODY:
UNOXYGENATED BLOOD
SUPERIOR VENACAVA

OXYGENATED BLOOD
AORTA TO BODY

PULMONARY ARTERY

PULMONARY VEIN

TO LUNGS

FROM LUNGS

PULMONARY ARTERY

PULMONARY VEIN

TO LUNGS

FROM LUNGS

LEFT ATRIUM

BICUSPID (MITRAL) VALVE

AORTIC VALVE

LEFT VENTRICLE

PULMONARY VALUE

RIGHT ATRIUM

TRICUSPID VALVE

RIGHT VENTRICLE

INFERIOR VENA CAVA
UNOXYGENATED BLOOD

AORTA TO BODY
OXYGENATED BLOOD

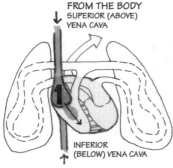

FROM THE BODY
SUPERIOR (ABOVE) VENA CAVA

INFERIOR (BELOW) VENA CAVA

1
• BLOOD FROM BODY DELIVERED THROUGH VENA CAVA
• ENTERS RIGHT ATRIUM
• PASSES THROUGH TRICUSPID VALVE

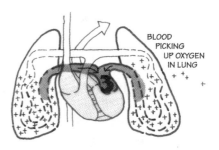

BLOOD PICKING UP OXYGEN IN LUNG

3
• FROM LUNGS, PICKS UP OXYGEN
• PASSES THROUGH PULMONARY VEINS
• ENTERS LEFT ATRIUM

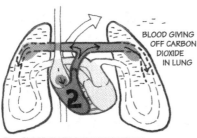

BLOOD GIVING OFF CARBON DIOXIDE IN LUNG

2
• BLOOD ENTERS RIGHT VENTRICLE
• PASSES THROUGH PULMONARY VALVE
• THROUGH PULMONARY ARTERIES
• TO LUNGS (GIVES UP CO_2)

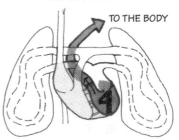

TO THE BODY

4
• PASSES THROUGH BICUSPID VALVE
• ENTERS LEFT VENTRICLE
• PASSES THROUGH AORTIC VALVE
• PASSES THROUGH AORTA TO BODY

The heart is a two-sided pump that propels blood through a system of pipes (arteries, veins, and capillaries). The right side receives blood from the veins and pumps it through the lungs for oxygen replenishment. The left side pumps the oxygen-rich blood from the lungs to the rest of the body. Blood leaves the heart through arteries, which narrow into smaller vessels called arterioles and eventually become a vast network of microscopic vessels called capillaries.

Capillaries are woven throughout the tissues. The exchange of nutrients and waste products between the blood to the cells takes place across capillary walls only one cell thick. Blood vessels leaving the capillary beds widen into veins, conduits for blood returning to the heart. The venous blood returns to the right side of the heart and then to the lungs to be replenished with oxygen. The circuit is complete.

Roughly half of our blood is a water-based plasma in which are dissolved electrolytes, proteins, oxygen, carbon dioxide, glucose, and other vital compounds. The other half consists of formed elements: oxygen-carrying hemoglobin in red blood cells, infection-fighting white blood cells, and clot-forming platelets.

The circulatory system adjusts automatically to our energy demands, activity level, position, and temperature. The rate and force of pumping, the diameter of the vessels, and the amount of fluid in the system vary to meet the requirements of exercise, stress, sleep, and relaxation.

SHOCK

The late cardiologist and wilderness medicine specialist Dr. Bruce Paton suggested the following analogy for shock: Imagine the body as a healthy wetland with a river running through lush vegetation. The vegetation depends on the river's flow of pure, unpolluted water and the nutrients it carries. If the river dries up or the water becomes poisoned, the plants shrivel and die.

The maintenance of a healthy, well-oxygenated flow of blood through the tissues is called good perfusion. Shock is the inadequate perfusion of tissue with oxygenated blood, due to a

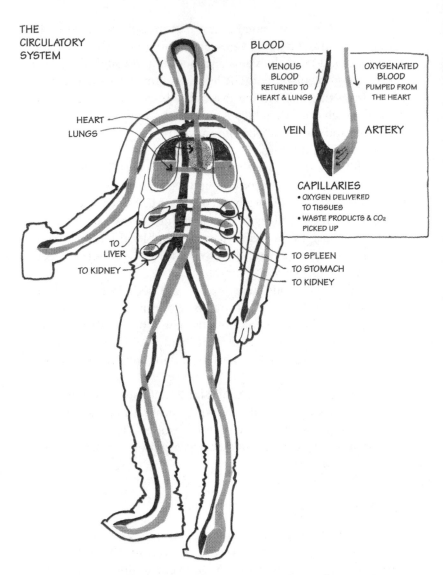

THE CIRCULATORY SYSTEM

BLOOD

VENOUS BLOOD RETURNED TO HEART & LUNGS

OXYGENATED BLOOD PUMPED FROM THE HEART

VEIN   ARTERY

CAPILLARIES
• OXYGEN DELIVERED TO TISSUES
• WASTE PRODUCTS & CO_2 PICKED UP

HEART
LUNGS

TO LIVER
TO KIDNEY

TO SPLEEN
TO STOMACH
TO KIDNEY

failure of any or all of three basic components of the circulatory system—heart, blood vessels, and blood—to deliver oxygenated blood to the tissues. Insufficient blood flow to the tissues causes inadequate oxygen and nutrient delivery and waste product removal. Shock is a state in which poor perfusion leads first to reversible, then to irreversible tissue damage.

Causes of Shock

Adequate blood pressure, like a healthy river flowing at a proper level into the wetland, is essential to maintaining perfusion of vital organs. Three factors influence blood pressure: blood volume, cardiac output (the volume of blood pumped per minute by the heart), and the state of constriction or dilation of the blood vessels (peripheral resistance). Changes in any of them can have serious consequences.

Fluid Loss. Fluid loss is a major cause of shock. The primary causes of fluid loss are bleeding, infections, extensive burns, and metabolic disorders. Massive bleeding results in reduced blood volume. Shock can also develop from fluid loss during watery diarrhea, dehydration, illness such as diabetes, or hidden bleeding into fractures of the femur and pelvis. Any of these mechanisms can result in reduced blood pressure.

The average adult has 6 liters of blood. A 10 percent loss (0.5 liter) is enough to affect blood pressure. A 25 percent blood volume loss (1.5 liters) can cause moderate shock. A 30 percent loss (2 liters) is considered serious shock. Shock secondary to fluid or blood loss is referred to as hypovolemic shock.

Decreased Cardiac Output. The heart muscle may become so damaged by a heart attack that it cannot maintain adequate output (pump failure). Shock secondary to a heart attack is referred to as cardiogenic shock.

Blood Vessel Dilation. Dilated blood vessels cause blood pressure and perfusion to decrease. If a spinal cord injury damages nerves controlling vessel diameter, they may widen and cause shock. However, changes in blood vessel diameter are generally not an important cause of shock, except in overwhelming infection or anaphylaxis where there is widespread dilation of small vessels. Shock secondary to blood vessel dilation is referred to as distributive or vasogenic shock.

Assessment of Shock

A patient in shock has pale, cool, clammy skin, pale mucous membranes, and a rapid pulse rate that may feel weak and irregular. These signs and symptoms are due to our "fight or flight" response—our body's response to danger—wherein release of adrenaline increases heart rate and causes the skin to sweat and skin and mucous membranes to pale, as well as causing nausea and restlessness. Blood is routed away from the digestive tract and concentrates around the muscles and essential organs. These changes pump the blood faster, reduce the size of the blood vessels, and route the blood to essential organs, attempting to enable the body to compensate for the shock.

Signs and Symptoms of Shock

EARLY CHANGES
- Rapid and/or weak pulse
- Rapid and/or shallow respirations
- Pale, cool, clammy skin, pale mucous membranes
- Anxiety or restlessness
- Nausea, thirst

LATER CHANGES
- Altered mental status
- Slow-to-respond pupils
- Falling blood pressure

When frightened, injured, or ill, most people have a "fight or flight" or acute-stress response. Your heart beats strong and fast; you sweat, skin and mucous membranes pale, and you feel nervous. If you're not seriously ill or injured and your circulatory system is healthy, this response should abate in a short time. The heart rate slows, you relax, and the skin returns to its normal color. When you measure a series of vital signs over time, you may see this initial acute stress diminish as you recover from the initial fright. If the circulatory system cannot adjust due to one of the shock mechanisms listed above, a downward spiral of deterioration may begin, in which tissues, then organs, and finally entire systems fail from lack of oxygen.

A progressively increasing pulse rate is a bad sign, indicating continuing blood loss or increasing shock. The skin becomes sweaty and pale, the mucous membranes pale, and the patient looks very ill. The patient may exhibit shallow, rapid breathing and be restless, anxious, irritable, and thirsty. If shock prevents the brain from being perfused with oxygen-rich blood, the level of responsiveness will deteriorate.

A test of the ability to accommodate positional changes (orthostatic vitals) can be a useful tool to evaluate shock. With the patient lying flat, measure vital signs. Then, if your patient does not have injuries that prevent movement, have the patient sit, and then stand. A healthy cardiovascular system compensates for these changes. A cardiovascular system in shock cannot compensate. The decompensating patient may become pale, and as the heart rate increases, the patient may become dizzy or faint. If, after one minute, the heart rate increases less than 30 beats a minute and the patient can tolerate standing, it is unlikely they are in shock.

Treatment Principles for Shock

Assume that shock may occur and begin treatment before signs and symptoms manifest. Treatment begins with the triad of basic life support—airway, breathing, and circulation (ABC)—as well as control of bleeding, and stabilization of fractures and other injuries. Thereafter, shock treatment moves to a second triad: temperature maintenance, position, and fluids.

Maintain Temperature. Protect the patient from excess heat and cold. Your goal is to maintain body temperature within normal limits. Insulate the patient from the cold ground, provide protection from wind and weather, and remove wet clothes and replace them with dry. This is especially important in patients with serious injuries, where hypothermia aggravates shock by causing acidosis and blood coagulation problems.

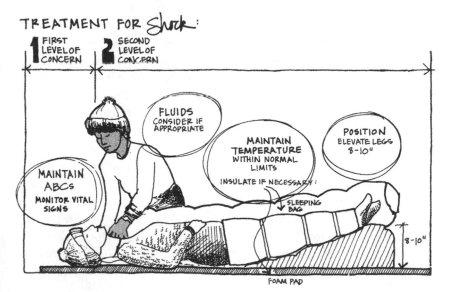

TREATMENT FOR Shock:

1 FIRST LEVEL OF CONCERN 2 SECOND LEVEL OF CONCERN

FLUIDS CONSIDER IF APPROPRIATE

MAINTAIN TEMPERATURE WITHIN NORMAL LIMITS

INSULATE IF NECESSARY:
SLEEPING BAG

POSITION ELEVATE LEGS 8-10"

MAINTAIN ABCs MONITOR VITAL SIGNS

8-10"

FOAM PAD

Elevate Legs. Unless the patient has a head injury, or unless injury to the legs or pelvis prevents it, position the patient with the legs elevated 8 to 10 inches (20-25 cm). Whether this helps return blood to the heart is debatable, but it doesn't harm the patient. Elevating the legs may help shock; it may also relax the lower back and provide comfort to the patient who is supine for a long time. Even with apparently minor injuries, this position can be used until you have assessed the problem and ruled out shock.

Treatment Principles for Shock

- ABCs: open and maintain airway.
- Control bleeding, stabilize fractures.
- Maintain temperature.
- Elevate legs.
- Consider fluids.

Consider Fluids. In the urban setting we rarely give the patient oral fluids because definitive care and efficient hydration methods are usually close by. In the wilderness, fluids may be given if the patient does not have an altered mental status, and they can tolerate the fluids. Oral fluids are unlikely to reverse shock, but they may prevent deterioration and provide comfort to the patient. When giving fluids by mouth, plain water is adequate. Using one teaspoon of salt per liter is acceptable, as are diluted bouillon drinks.

FINAL THOUGHTS

Shock is difficult to treat in the backcountry. Paramedics, nurses, and physicians in urban medical systems are trained to use specialized medical procedures to fight shock and have access to rapid transport, an asset not always available in the wilderness.

The definitive treatment of shock in the backcountry is evacuation. However, the basic treatments of bandages, splints, and physical and emotional support, reinforced by temperature maintenance, position, and fluids, are all assets in the wilderness management of shock.

If the initial patient presentation is not obviously serious, a key to making a decision on the need for evacuation is assessment of trends in vital signs and being watchful for slowly deteriorating signs; an increasing and weakening pulse, persistent or worsening skin pallor and clamminess, increasing breathing rate, and alterations in mental status.

Evacuation Guidelines
- Evacuate any patient whose vital signs do not stabilize or improve over time.
- Evacuate rapidly any patient with decreased mental status or deteriorating vital signs.

| CHEST INJURIES

INTRODUCTION

Chest injuries range from simple (but painful) rib fractures to life-threatening lung injuries. NOLS's incident data show that rib fractures are the most common chest injuries in a wilderness context, but *Accidents in North American Climbing* has documented more than a few instances of mountaineers who have suffered serious chest and lung injuries from falls. Paddlers can experience chest injuries from impact with rocks or the bows of kayaks. Horsepacking and backcountry skiing are other wilderness activities in which there are mechanisms—falls and collisions—for chest trauma. Chest injuries concern us particularly because they can compromise respiratory or cardiovascular functions. Treatment options are limited in the backcountry context, and our primary role is to recognize the injury, assess whether those functions are or may become compromised, and make sound evacuation decisions.

CHEST AND LUNG ANATOMY

The respiratory system provides oxygen to, and removes carbon dioxide from, the body. The cardiovascular system transports these gases, as well as nutrients and waste products, to and from the cells. The chest cavity contains some of the structures

PARTS OF THE RESPIRATORY SYSTEM :

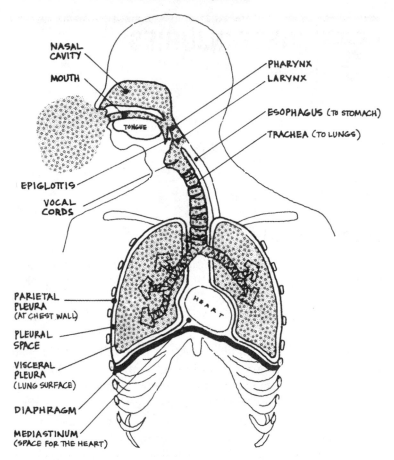

responsible for these processes: airway passages, lungs, heart, and major vessels, the vena cava and the aorta.

The clavicles, rib cage, and diaphragm form the boundaries of the chest cavity. The rib cage consists of twelve pairs of ribs, all attached to the spine in the back. The upper seven pairs are attached to the sternum by cartilage; the next three pairs are attached to cartilage only; and the lowest two pairs ("floating ribs") are attached only to the spine.

The components of the respiratory system are the nose, mouth, pharynx, larynx, epiglottis, trachea, bronchi, bronchioles, and alveoli. The diaphragm and muscles of the chest wall move air in and out of the lungs.

The average healthy adult breathes twelve to twenty times per minute, moving half a liter of air with each breath. Respiratory rate varies with exercise, altitude, emotional state, illness, or injury.

Nose, Mouth, Pharynx, Larynx. As air enters the nose or mouth, it is warmed and humidified by mucous membranes that line the respiratory tract. At the same time, the mucus produced by the membranes and the cilia (microscopic hairlike structures that line the entire tract) help filter foreign material out of the air, preventing it from reaching the alveoli. Air passes from the nose or mouth into the pharynx, past the larynx, and into the trachea. The larynx consists of tiny bones, muscles, cartilage, and two vocal cords. Air forced past the vocal cords causes them to vibrate, producing sound.

Epiglottis. The epiglottis sits above the larynx and prevents food from entering the trachea by closing over the larynx during swallowing. If solids or liquids inadvertently enter the larynx, the vocal cords spasm, causing us to cough.

Trachea. The trachea is approximately 5 inches (12 cm) long and composed of cartilage that prevents the trachea from collapsing under the air pressure changes created by breathing. At the bottom of the trachea, the tube divides into the right and left bronchi. After air enters the lungs via the bronchi, it follows smaller passageways called bronchioles until it enters the alveoli.

Alveoli. The alveoli are small air sacs, surrounded by capillaries, where red blood cells release carbon dioxide and pick up oxygen. Oxygen-rich blood then flows into the pulmonary veins, which carry it to the heart to be pumped to the body.

Lungs. The lungs occupy most of the chest cavity. Each lung is enclosed by a double-layered membrane called the pleura. Between the two layers is the pleural space, which contains a thin film of fluid that lubricates the membranes and allows them to move freely. If air enters the pleural space, as in a pneumothorax, the lung can collapse.

Inspiration is the active motion of breathing. The diaphragm (a muscle dividing the chest from the abdomen) contracts and moves downward, while the intercostal muscles (muscles between the ribs) move the chest wall outward. This increases the volume in the chest, and as the pressure in the lungs decreases relative to the atmospheric pressure, air flows into the lungs. When the pressure within the lungs equals the atmospheric pressure, air stops entering the lungs. At this point, the diaphragm and chest muscles relax, elastic recoil reduces lung size, and air is exhaled (expiration).

Control of Breathing. The level of carbon dioxide in the blood is one of the factors that determines how fast and deeply we breathe. If the level of carbon dioxide in the blood increases, the respiratory center in the brain increases the respiratory rate. If the level of carbon dioxide is too low, the brain slows the breathing rate. We can directly control our breathing by breathing faster, taking deep breaths or by holding our breath, but only for short periods of time, after which the involuntary control centers of the brain take over.

RIB FRACTURES

The most commonly fractured ribs are ribs five through ten. Ribs one through four are protected by the shoulder girdle and are rarely fractured. The floating ribs—eleven and twelve—are more flexible and will give before breaking.

Signs and Symptoms. Rib fractures can cause deformity and/or discoloration over the injured area. The patient complains of tenderness over the fracture (point tenderness) when touched. Breathing or coughing can cause sharp, stabbing pain at the site of the fracture. Breaths become shallow as the patient tries to decrease the pain. The patient may clutch the chest on the fractured side, in an attempt to splint the chest.

Treatment Principles. A single fractured rib often does not require splinting. Pain medication such as acetaminophen or ibuprofen may be all the treatment necessary.

Tape the Fracture Site on One Side of Chest. If the patient is uncomfortable from pain, broadly tape the fractured side from sternum to spine. This may decrease movement at the fracture site and so diminish pain. Avoid wrapping tape completely around the chest, as this can restrict breathing. You may also find that a simple sling and swathe of the arm on the injured side limits movement and provides comfort. A simple rib fracture without shortness of breath does not necessarily need to be evacuated. However, these patients usually leave the field due to pain. If the patient is not in respiratory distress, they may be able to walk out of the wilderness.

Signs and Symptoms of Rib Fractures

- Point tenderness over the fracture
- Pain on inspiration, shallow breathing, coughing
- Shortness of breath during exertion

Treatment Principles for Rib Fractures

- Tape the fracture site.
- Sling and swathe the arm on the injured side.

UNSTABLE CHEST WALL

An unstable chest wall (flail chest) occurs when three or more adjacent ribs are broken in two or more places, loosening a

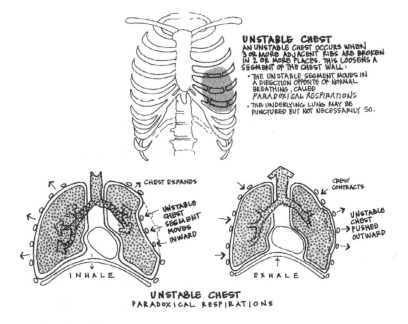

UNSTABLE CHEST
PARADOXICAL RESPIRATIONS

segment of the chest wall. When the patient breathes in, the increased negative pressure pulls the unstable segment inward, and the lung does not fill with air as it should. When the patient breathes out, the unstable segment may move in a direction opposite of normal breathing, giving rise to the term "paradoxical respirations."

Signs and Symptoms of Unstable Chest

- Paradoxical chest movement
- Respiratory distress

Signs and Symptoms. A flail chest develops only with a significant mechanism of injury, such as a heavy fall against a rock. The patient may be in respiratory distress. Put your hands under the patient's shirt, and you may feel a part of the chest moving in while the opposite part of the chest is moving out. This may also be visible upon inspection.

Treatment Principles. Stabilize the chest:
- Position the patient in whatever position is most comfortable to breathe. This may be on the injured side with a rolled-up piece of clothing underneath the unstable segment.
- Tape a large pad firmly over the unstable segment (without circling the chest).

TREATMENT
UNSTABLE CHEST

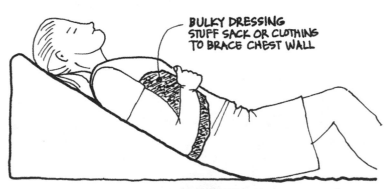

BULKY DRESSING STUFF SACK OR CLOTHING TO BRACE CHEST WALL

PLACE PATIENT IN A POSITION OF COMFORT TO BREATHE!

Treat the patient for shock and evacuate.

INJURIES TO LUNGS

Injuries to the ribs may also damage the lungs. Ruptured and torn blood vessels can cause bleeding into the chest, and punctured lungs may cause air to leak into the chest.

Pneumothorax. When air leaks into the pleural space, it can collapse the lung. A fractured rib that lacerates the lung (traumatic pneumothorax), a weak spot on the lung wall that gives way (spontaneous pneumothorax), or an open chest wound (open pneumothorax) are all potential causes.

Spontaneous Pneumothorax. A weak area of the lung may rupture, creating a spontaneous pneumothorax. The highest incidence occurs in tall, thin men between the ages of twenty and thirty. Eighty percent of spontaneous pneumothoraces occur while the person is at rest. The patient complains of a sudden, sharp pain in the chest and increasing shortness of breath.

Tension Pneumothorax. If a hole opening into the pleural space serves as a one-way valve, allowing air to enter but not to escape, a tension pneumothorax can develop. With each breath, air enters the pleural space, but it cannot escape with expiration. As pressure in the pleural space increases, the lung collapses. Pressure in the pleural space eventually pushes the heart and

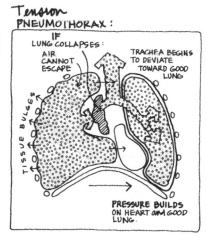

PNEUMOTHORAX

AIR ENTERS
THE PLEURAL
SPACE:

LUNG MAY OR
MAY NOT COLLAPSE
FULLY.

Tension
PNEUMOTHORAX:

IF
LUNG COLLAPSES:
AIR
CANNOT
ESCAPE

TRACHEA BEGINS
TO DEVIATE
TOWARD GOOD
LUNG

TISSUE BULGES

PRESSURE BUILDS
ON HEART and GOOD
LUNG.

large blood vessels to the uninjured side of the chest cavity, impairing blood flow.

As pressure builds, you may see the trachea deviate toward the uninjured side, tissue between the ribs bulge, and the neck veins distend. These are often late and serious signs. Respiration becomes increasingly rapid. The pulse is weak and rapid; cyanosis occurs.

Hemothorax. This occurs when lacerated blood vessels cause blood to collect in the pleural space. The source can be a fractured rib or lacerated lung. If more than 1 liter of blood leaks into the pleural space, a hemothorax may compress the lung and compromise breathing. The loss of blood may also cause shock.

Injury to Lungs

SIGNS AND SYMPTOMS
- Obvious chest trauma
- Shortness of breath
- Rapid, shallow respirations
- Cyanosis
- Shock

Pneumothorax
- Sudden, sharp chest pain

Tension pneumothorax
- Tracheal deviation

Open chest wound
- Sucking noise

TREATMENT PRINCIPLES
- Seal open chest wounds.
- Stabilize rib fractures.
- Stabilize unstable chest walls.
- Position patient for comfort.
- Monitor for shortness of breath.
- Evacuate.

Open Chest Wounds

If a wound through the chest wall breaks into the pleural space, air can enter, creating a pneumothorax. If the wound remains open, air can move through it, in and out of the lung, possibly with a sucking noise.

The goal of treatment is to limit the size of the pneumothorax. Seal the hole, preferably with a commercial vented chest seal. If this is not available, use an occlusive dressing made from any nonporous material, such as a plastic bag or petroleum jelly–impregnated gauze.

Traditionally, the advice was to use a three-sided dressing over the open chest wound to create a flap valve to allow excess air pressure in the chest to release. In practice this doesn't work well. Tape the dressing down on all four sides to seal the hole. If signs of a tension pneumothorax develop, release and then reseal the hole. This might allow trapped air to escape and relieve the tension in the chest.

RESPIRATORY DISTRESS

Respiratory distress is a term that describes any situation in which a patient experiences life-threatening difficulty breathing. It can occur after an injury, with an illness such as pneumonia, during a heart attack or an asthma attack, due to an allergic reaction, or after inhalation of a poisonous gas.

Signs and symptoms of respiratory distress are anxiety and restlessness; shortness of breath; rapid respirations and pulse; signs of shock, including pale, cool, clammy skin and cyanosis of the skin, lips, and fingernail beds; and labored breathing using accessory muscles of the neck, shoulder, and abdomen to achieve maximum effort. The patient is usually more comfortable sitting than lying.

Respiratory distress can be a frightening experience for both the patient and the rescuer. If the underlying cause is emotional, as in hyperventilation syndrome (see Chapter 17), reassurance may be all that's needed to alleviate the problem. If a chest injury with underlying lung damage or an illness such as pneumonia or pulmonary embolism creates the distress, treatment may be far more difficult. The airway must be maintained, the patient

OPEN CHEST WOUND :
A WOUND THROUGH THE CHEST WALL THAT ALLOWS AIR
TO ENTER THE PLEURAL SPACE.

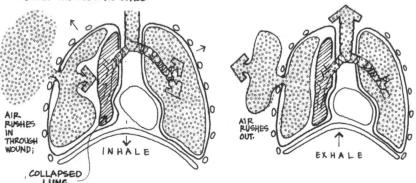

AIR RUSHES IN THROUGH WOUND;

INHALE

COLLAPSED LUNG

AIR RUSHES OUT.

EXHALE

placed in the most comfortable position for breathing, the injury splinted or taped, wounds dressed, and the patient treated for shock until they can be evacuated.

FINAL THOUGHTS

Thankfully, the most common chest injury in the wilderness is the simple rib fracture, painful but not life threatening. Serious injuries of the chest wall, lungs, and heart are far more rare.

Evacuation Guidelines
- The simple rib fracture does not necessarily need to be evacuated unless the patient is uncomfortable with pain, unable to travel, or short of breath. If evacuated, they may be able to walk out of the wilderness.
- Patients with shortness of breath following a blow to the chest, open chest wounds, or other obvious signs of serious chest injury will need to be rapidly evacuated.

BRAIN AND SPINAL CORD INJURIES

INTRODUCTION

Head injuries range from simple scalp lacerations to life-threatening swelling of the brain. Spine injuries range from fractured vertebrae to actual spinal cord injuries that can result in paralysis. According to the data kept by NOLS, serious brain and spine injuries are rare in the wilderness; yet the urgency and care with which we must assess and handle these patients make them some of the more challenging problems to manage in remote areas.

CENTRAL NERVOUS SYSTEM

Together, the brain, spinal cord, and peripheral nerves monitor and control all body functions. The brain governs thoughts, emotions, senses, memory, and movement, as well as basic physiological functions. It processes information from our senses, initiates motor responses, remembers, solves problems, and makes judgments.

The three main divisions of the brain are the cerebrum, the cerebellum, and the brain stem. The cerebrum is the largest part of the brain, the center for our "higher" cognitive functions, including problem solving, memory, speech, hearing, and sight. The cerebellum, in the lower rear of the skull, regulates posture,

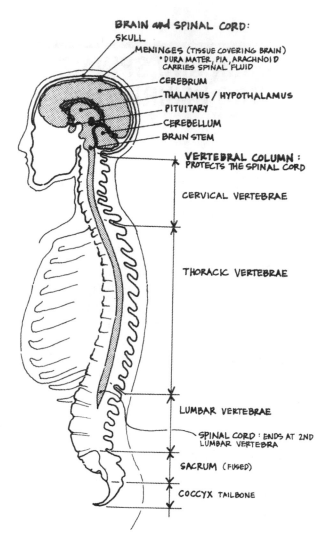

BRAIN and SPINAL CORD:

SKULL

MENINGES (TISSUE COVERING BRAIN)
• DURA MATER, PIA, ARACHNOID
CARRIES SPINAL FLUID

CEREBRUM

THALAMUS / HYPOTHALAMUS

PITUITARY

CEREBELLUM

BRAIN STEM

VERTEBRAL COLUMN:
PROTECTS THE SPINAL CORD

CERVICAL VERTEBRAE

THORACIC VERTEBRAE

LUMBAR VERTEBRAE

SPINAL CORD: ENDS AT 2ND
LUMBAR VERTEBRA

SACRUM (FUSED)

COCCYX TAILBONE

coordination, and motor responses. The brain stem at the base of the brain maintains responsiveness, heart rate, blood pressure, and breathing.

The skull houses and protects the brain. The brain is covered by three layers of tissue known collectively as the meninges: the dura mater, the pia mater, and the arachnoid. Cerebrospinal fluid (CSF) flows within these layers, nourishing and cushioning the brain. Blood vessels are located within the brain and the meninges.

Central nervous system tissue is extremely sensitive to oxygen. Depriving the brain of oxygen for only a few minutes can result in permanent damage.

BRAIN, SCALP, AND SKULL INJURIES

Injuries to the scalp and skull can be serious by themselves, but possible underlying injury to the brain is of greater concern. A large blood supply feeds the scalp, causing it to bleed profusely when cut. A bruised or lacerated scalp can mask injury to the skull or brain. Examine scalp injuries carefully for exposed bone or brain, or an indentation that might be a depressed fracture. Bleeding from the scalp can be controlled by applying gentle pressure on the edges of the wound, being careful to avoid direct pressure on possibly unstable central areas.

The skull consists of 22 fused bones. The strongest are the bones that form the top and sides of the protective box encasing the brain. Fractures of the skull are not life threatening in and of themselves, except when associated with underlying brain or spinal cord injury, if they are open fractures that expose the brain to the outside environment, or when the fracture causes bleeding by tearing the blood vessels that lie between the brain and the skull.

Serious brain injuries can occur with or without skull fractures. The brain can be injured by a direct blow to the head, or by twisting forces that cause deformation and shearing against the inside of the skull. A blow to the head can make the brain move within the skull, tearing blood vessels in the meninges or within the brain itself, stretching and shearing brain cells and the connections between cells.

A mild brain injury, also called a concussion, is temporary brain dysfunction or loss of responsiveness following a blow to the head. Inflammation and disturbances of brain metabolism cause a variety of symptoms, including headache, disorientation, nausea, lethargy, dizziness, amnesia, and photophobia, which can persist for weeks.

Contusions (bruising of brain tissue) and hemorrhages or hematomas (bleeding within the brain) are serious injuries that can lead to increased pressure in the skull. Encased in this rigid box, a swelling or bleeding brain presses against the skull. The body has no mechanism to release such an increase in pressure. As pressure rises, blood supply is shut off by compression of swollen vessels, and brain tissue is deprived of oxygen. The pressure can squash the brain stem, affecting heart and lung function.

Brain injury can be fatal when it disrupts heartbeat and breathing. In the long term, a severe brain injury may leave the patient physically immobile or mentally incompetent, with severely impaired judgment and problem-solving ability, or an inability to process or communicate information properly.

Signs and Symptoms of Brain Injury

Signs and symptoms of brain injury depend on the degree and progression of injury. Some indications of brain injury appear immediately after an accident; others develop slowly.

Changes in Level of Responsiveness. Loss of responsiveness may be transient or may persist for hours or days. The patient may alternate between periods of responsiveness and unresponsiveness, or be responsive but disoriented, confused, and incoherent, exhibiting changes in behavior and personality, or verbal or physical combativeness.

Physical Findings. Headache, vision problems, loss of balance, nausea, vomiting, and paralysis may accompany brain injury. The patient may assume abnormal positions, with the legs and arms stiff and extended, or the arms clutched across the chest. A brain-injured patient may have seizures.

Blood or clear cerebrospinal fluid (CSF) leaking from the ears, mouth, or nose is a sign of a skull fracture. Similarly, pain, tenderness, and swelling at the injury site or obvious penetrating wounds or depressed fractures may indicate a skull fracture. Two other signs of skull fracture—bruising around the eyes (the raccoon sign) and bruising behind the ear (Battle's sign)—usually appear hours after the injury.

Signs and Symptoms of Brain Injury

MILD BRAIN INJURY

- Brief change in mental status or brief loss of responsiveness
- Temporarily blurred vision or "seeing stars"
- Nausea and/or isolated vomiting
- Headache, dizziness, and/or lethargy
- Short-term amnesia

SERIOUS BRAIN INJURY

- Worsening headache, vision disturbances, protracted vomiting, lethargy, excessive sleepiness, ataxia, and seizures
- Disoriented, irritable, combative, unconscious
- Heart rate decreases and bounds
- Hyperventilation, erratic respiration
- Pupils become slow or unequal

Combativeness. A brain-injured patient may become combative, striking out randomly at those trying to help. If the brain is oxygen-deprived, supplemental oxygen and airway maintenance may help alleviate such behavior. Restraint may be necessary to protect the patient and the rescuers.

Slow Pulse, Rising Blood Pressure, Irregular Respirations. All these changes in vital signs indicate a serious and late-stage brain injury. These contrast with the rising pulse, falling blood pressure, and rapid regular respirations seen with shock.

JAW THRUST AIRWAY OPENING FOR SUSPECTED C-SPINE PATIENTS :
- DO NOT MOVE NECK OR SPINE.
- DO NOT TILT HEAD BACK.

PLACE FINGERS IN FRONT OF EARLDBE.
PUSH JAW FORWARD AND UP.

ONE HAND ON EACH SIDE OF HEAD :

JAW

EAR

Assessment for Brain Injury

Initial assessment of brain injury can be difficult because the symptoms of a mild brain injury can be similar to those seen in more serious injuries. The assessment may also be complicated when drugs, alcohol, or other traumatic injuries affect the patient's mental status.

A patient with a brain injury is at risk for cervical spine (neck) injury. If you suspect brain or neck injury, protect the spine. After a thorough physical assessment, evaluate the nervous system. Note the level of responsiveness (LOR) and the patient's ability to feel and move extremities. Use the AVPU (awake and alert; not awake but responsive to a verbal stimulus; not awake but responsive to pain; or not awake and unresponsive) structure, discussed in Chapter 1, to assess mental status. Question the patient or bystanders as to a loss of responsiveness. Was it immediate, or was there a delay before the patient became unresponsive? Has the patient been awake but drowsy, sleepy, confused, or disoriented? Has the patient been going in and out of responsiveness? Are there associated symptoms such as headache, nausea, fatigue, or irritability?

Watch any potentially brain-injured patient carefully, even if at first the injury does not appear serious. Sleep is important for patients with brain injury. If you think the patient has a mild brain injury, allow the patient to sleep. Waking is unnecessary. If you observe any altered mental status or other signs of a worsening brain injury, periodically, every couple of hours, wake the patient and assess LOR and vital signs. Patients with concussion often need physical and cognitive rest, so activities such as reading or camp chores should be avoided.

Treatment Principles for Brain Injury

ABCs. An injured brain needs oxygen. Ensuring an open airway is the first step in treatment.

If Patient IS Vomiting, Position Them on Side. Brain-injured patients have a tendency to vomit. Logrolling the patient onto their side while maintaining cervical spine stabilization helps drain vomit while maintaining the airway.

Control Scalp Bleeding. Cover open wounds with bulky sterile dressings as a barrier against infection. Although it is acceptable to clean scalp wounds, cleaning open-skull injuries may introduce infection into the brain, so leave them as you find them.

Do Not Control Internal Bleeding or Drainage. Do not attempt to prevent drainage of blood or clear CSF from the ears or nose. Blocking the flow could increase pressure within the skull.

Elevate Head. Keep the patient in a horizontal or slightly head-elevated position. Do not elevate the legs, as this may increase pressure within the skull.

Record Neurological Assessment. Watch the patient closely for any changes in mental status. These observations will be valuable to the receiving physician.

Treatment Principles for Brain Injury

- ABCs.
- Protect the spine.
- If patient is vomiting, position on side.
- Control scalp bleeding.
- Do not control internal bleeding or drainage.
- Record neurological assessment.

Brain injuries can be difficult to assess; some that appear initially benign may become serious over time. Thus, we have a low threshold for evacuation. Evacuation is recommended for any patient who was unresponsive, even for a minute or two, or who exhibits vision or balance disturbances, irritability, lethargy, or nausea and vomiting after a blow to the head, regardless of whether the person lost responsiveness. A patient

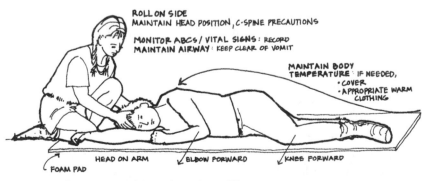

ROLL ON SIDE
MAINTAIN HEAD POSITION, C-SPINE PRECAUTIONS

MONITOR ABCS / VITAL SIGNS: RECORD
MAINTAIN AIRWAY: KEEP CLEAR OF VOMIT

MAINTAIN BODY TEMPERATURE: IF NEEDED,
• COVER
• APPROPRIATE WARM CLOTHING

HEAD ON ARM   ELBOW FORWARD   KNEE FORWARD

FOAM PAD

CARING FOR A BRAIN-INJURED PATIENT

who experiences loss of responsiveness but awakens without any other symptoms, or who may have a concussion, may be walked out of the wilderness with a support party capable of quickly evacuating the patient if their condition worsens.

SPINAL CORD INJURIES

As with head injuries, spinal cord injuries primarily involve young people, with most cases occurring in men between the ages of 15 and 35. An estimated 10,000 spinal cord injuries occur each year in the United States. Because central nervous tissue does not regenerate, victims can be permanently disabled. Motor-vehicle accidents account for the majority of spinal-injury cases, followed by falls.

The spinal cord is the extension of the brain outside the skull, the component of the central nervous system that connects the brain and the rest of the body. The spinal cord is protected by the vertebrae, thirty-three of which form the backbone, or spine. A force driving the spine out of its normal alignment can fracture or dislocate the vertebrae, and pinch, bruise, or cut the spinal cord, damaging the nervous connections. However, vertebral fractures or ligament and muscle damage to the back can occur without damage to the spinal cord.

The smallest vertebrae with the greatest range of motion are in the neck, the most vulnerable part of the spine. From there, the vertebrae become progressively larger as they support more weight. The location of damage to the spinal cord determines whether the patient may die or be left paralyzed from the neck down (quadriplegia) or the waist down (paraplegia).

Signs and Symptoms of Spinal Cord Injury
- Pain or tenderness on the spine
- Weakness in extremities
- Loss of strength or ability to move extremities
- Loss of sensation in extremities
- Numbness and tingling in hands and feet
- Incontinence
- Signs and symptoms of shock
- Shortness of breath

Signs and Symptoms of Spinal Cord Injury

Signs and symptoms of spinal cord injury include weakness, loss of sensation or ability to move, numbness and tingling in the hands and feet, incontinence, soft-tissue injury over or near the spine, and tenderness in the spine.

Assessment for Spinal Cord Injury

Palpate the spine from the top of the neck to the pelvis, touching each vertebra.

Check CSM in the feet and hands, one extremity at a time. Assess for the pedal pulse in the foot or the posterior tibia pulse in the ankle. Ask the patient if they have any abnormal sensations: tingling, numbness, hot, or cold, and assess for sensitivity to light touch on a small toe and the big toe. Assess the ability to move by asking the patient to push and pull the feet against your hand pressure.

IMPROVISED CERVICAL COLLAR

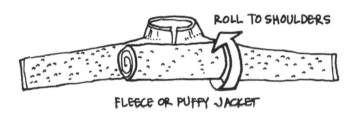

ROLL TO SHOULDERS

FLEECE OR PUFFY JACKET

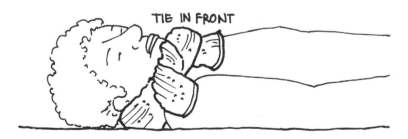

TIE IN FRONT

Treatment Principles for Spinal Cord Injury

Modern spine-injury management is evolving rapidly. Historical practices of strapping patients to backboards with rigid cervical collars are giving way to the concept of protecting the spine, using backboards only as extrication tools, and placing patients comfortably on cots and other firm padded surfaces. The vacuum mattress is becoming a standard tool in mountain rescue.

> **Treatment Principles for Spinal Cord Injury**
> - Stabilize the spine.
> - Check circulation, sensation, and motion (CSM) in the extremities.
> - Establish and maintain neutral alignment of the spine.
> - Carefully move the patient onto a pad.
> - Maintain head stabilization with hands or with head blocks and cervical collar.
> - Evacuate. Ideally utilize a commercial spinal protection device.

Protect the Spine. Place one hand on either side of the head to prevent neck motion. Manual head stabilization is important, but it does not preclude common-sense practices necessary to complete the patient assessment or treat urgent injuries. After assessment, gently return the head to a neutral position, stopping if there is resistance to movement or pain. Clothing or a blanket roll may be used as an improvised cervical or neck collar to aid in stabilization, freeing rescuers for other tasks. The soft collar is

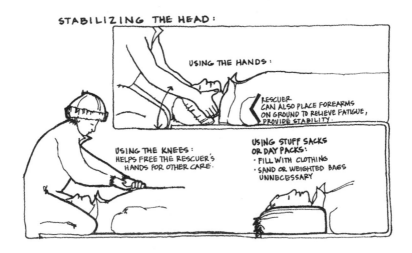

STABILIZING THE HEAD:

USING THE HANDS:

RESCUER CAN ALSO PLACE FOREARMS ON GROUND TO RELIEVE FATIGUE, PROVIDE STABILITY.

USING THE KNEES: HELPS FREE THE RESCUER'S HANDS FOR OTHER CARE.

USING STUFF SACKS OR DAY PACKS:
- FILL WITH CLOTHING
- SAND OR WEIGHTED BAGS UNNECESSARY

replacing the rigid collar as a neck stabilization tool. Soft head blocks—sacks stuffed with clothing or a daypack—can serve to protect the neck from movement.

The patient is commonly placed on their back on a firm surface. In the wilderness this often is a pad on the ground. If necessary to protect the airway, a patient with a possible spine injury can be stabilized on their side. Strapping is only necessary during carries. Wilderness treatment may require prolonged immobilization while a litter is brought to the scene. Padding under the lower back and behind the knees goes a long way toward making the patient who must lie still on a hard surface for hours more comfortable.

Move with Logroll, Lift, or Slide. Assume that the patient may have to be moved at least twice during the rescue—once to place insulation underneath the body to prevent hypothermia, and a second time to place the patient on a litter or backboard. Two common techniques for moving the patient are the logroll and the lift. You may also need to slide the patient.

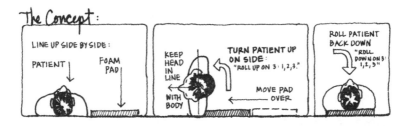

How to Perform a Four-Person Logroll:
1. The rescuers take positions:
   - Rescuer One maintains stabilization of the head throughout the procedure and gives the commands.
   - Rescuer Two kneels beside the patient's chest and reaches across to the patient's shoulder and upper arm.
   - Rescuer Three kneels beside the patient's waist and reaches across to the lower back and pelvis. Rescuers Two and Three can cross their arms, which may help to control the roll.

- Rescuer Four kneels beside the patient's thighs and reaches across to support the legs with one hand on the patient's upper thigh, the other behind the knee.
2. The rescuers roll the patient onto their side:
   - Rescuer One, at the head, gives the command, "Roll on 3; 1, 2, 3," and the rescuers slowly roll the patient toward them, keeping the patient's body in alignment. Rescuer One supports the head and maintains alignment with the spine. Once the patient is on their side, a backboard or foamlite pad can be placed where the patient will be lying when the logroll is complete.
3. The rescuers roll the patient onto their back:
   - When Rescuer One gives the command, "Lower on 3; 1, 2, 3," the procedure is reversed, and the patient is slowly lowered onto the backboard or foamlite pad while the rescuers keep the spine in alignment.

Lifting Technique. A minimum of four people can lift the patient (depending on how large the patient is), enabling a fifth person to slide a backboard, foamlite pad, or litter underneath. The rescuer at the head again maintains stabilization during the entire procedure and gives commands. The other three rescuers

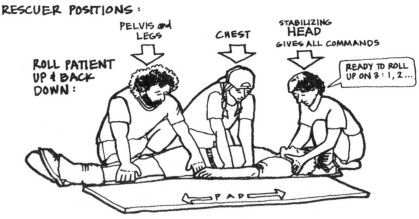

Techniques :

RESCUER POSITIONS :

PELVIS and LEGS

CHEST

STABILIZING **HEAD**
GIVES ALL COMMANDS

ROLL PATIENT UP & BACK DOWN :

READY TO ROLL UP ON 3 : 1, 2 ...

PAD

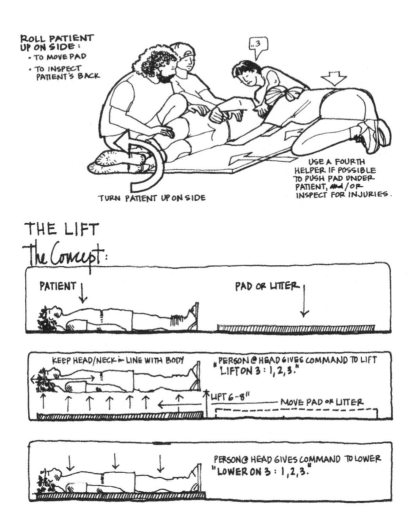

ROLL PATIENT
UP ON SIDE :
• TO MOVE PAD
• TO INSPECT
  PATIENT'S BACK

..3

USE A FOURTH
HELPER IF POSSIBLE
TO PUSH PAD UNDER
PATIENT, and/OR
INSPECT FOR INJURIES.

TURN PATIENT UP ON SIDE

THE LIFT

The Concept :

PATIENT

PAD OR LITTER

KEEP HEAD/NECK in LINE WITH BODY

PERSON @ HEAD GIVES COMMAND TO LIFT
"LIFT ON 3 : 1, 2, 3."

LIFT 6-8"   MOVE PAD OR LITTER

PERSON @ HEAD GIVES COMMAND TO LOWER
"LOWER ON 3 : 1, 2, 3."

position themselves at the patient's sides, one kneeling at chest
level and another at pelvis level on the same side, while the
third rescuer kneels at waist level on the opposite side. Before
lifting, the rescuers place their hands over the patient to visualize their hands in position under the chest, lower back, pelvis,
and thighs. They then slide their hands under the patient as far
as they can without jostling the patient. On the command, "Lift
on 3; 1, 2, 3," rescuers lift the patient then lower him or her onto
the pad or litter.

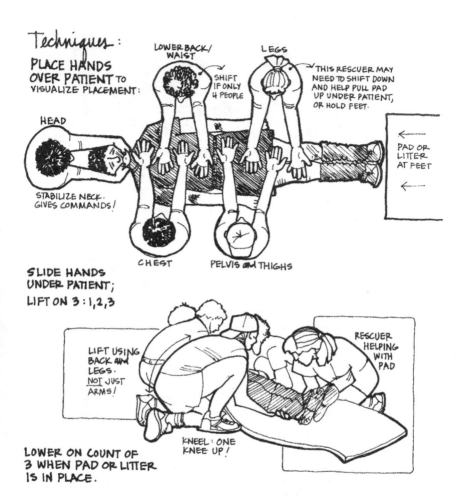

Techniques:

PLACE HANDS
OVER PATIENT TO
VISUALIZE PLACEMENT:

LOWER BACK/
WAIST

LEGS

SHIFT
IF ONLY
4 PEOPLE

THIS RESCUER MAY
NEED TO SHIFT DOWN
AND HELP PULL PAD
UP UNDER PATIENT,
OR HOLD FEET.

HEAD

PAD OR
LITTER
AT FEET

STABILIZE NECK.
GIVES COMMANDS!

CHEST

PELVIS AND THIGHS

SLIDE HANDS
UNDER PATIENT;
LIFT ON 3: 1,2,3

LIFT USING
BACK AND
LEGS.
NOT JUST
ARMS!

RESCUER
HELPING
WITH
PAD

LOWER ON COUNT OF
3 WHEN PAD OR LITTER
IS IN PLACE.

KNEEL: ONE
KNEE UP!

Lift and Slide. One or two people can lift and slide the patient in a head-first direction. This is a difficult technique on most surfaces. The rescuer's hands hold the trapezius muscle at the base of the neck and gently squeeze the head. The patient's upper back is gently lifted, only enough to allow sliding. A second rescuer can place their hands under the upper body to assist in the slide.

LIFT and SLIDE

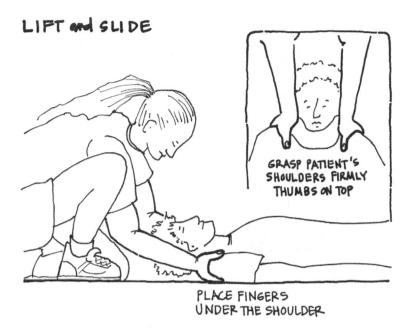

GRASP PATIENT'S
SHOULDERS FIRMLY
THUMBS ON TOP

PLACE FINGERS
UNDER THE SHOULDER

The Focused Spine Assessment. If the patient has a mechanism for a spinal cord injury (e.g., a fall from a height, high-velocity skiing fall, diving accident, or blow to the head with loss of responsiveness or altered mental status), initially assume the worst and control the head. If the mechanism is severe or the patient has signs or symptoms of a spinal cord injury, immobilize the spine. If the mechanism is questionable or no signs of spine injury are found during the patient assessment, you may consider performing a focused spine assessment.

The focused spine assessment is an evidence-based protocol used both in the wilderness context and by urban emergency medical services, and supported by a wide range of prehospital groups including the Wilderness Medical Society. It is a reliable tool to make a decision on the need for spine protection. Without this protocol, we might unnecessarily immobilize patients with low risk of spinal cord injury.

PATIENT PACKAGING POINTS

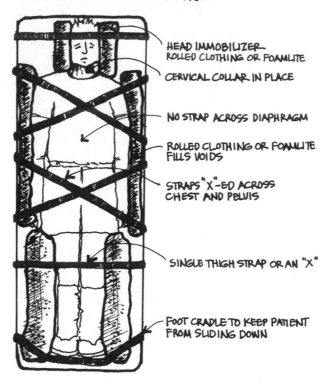

HEAD IMMOBILIZER — ROLLED CLOTHING OR FOAMLITE

CERVICAL COLLAR IN PLACE

NO STRAP ACROSS DIAPHRAGM

ROLLED CLOTHING OR FOAMLITE FILLS VOIDS

STRAPS "X"-ED ACROSS CHEST AND PELVIS

SINGLE THIGH STRAP OR AN "X"

FOOT CRADLE TO KEEP PATIENT FROM SLIDING DOWN

FILL VOIDS NEXT TO HEAD WITH ROLLED CLOTHING OR FOAMLITE

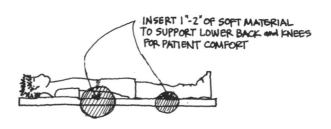

INSERT 1"-2" OF SOFT MATERIAL TO SUPPORT LOWER BACK and KNEES FOR PATIENT COMFORT

The focused spine assessment is an intentional check of parameters that provide the basis for a sound decision on the need for spine protection. It checks the reliability of the patient, CSMs, and the presence of pain or tenderness on the spine. Proceed sequentially through this series of steps:

1. The patient must be reliable. They should be sober, not distracted, able to focus on the assessment, and A+Ox3 or 4.
2. The patient should have normal CSMs in all four extremities.
   • Circulation (warm, pink digits, pedal/radial pulse)
   • Sensation (no numbness, tingling, or other unusual sensations)
   • Motion in all four extremities
3. The patient should be free of spine pain or tenderness when the spine is palpated.

If the patient is reliable, with intact CSMs in all four extremities and no spine pain or tenderness, you can make a decision to end spine immobilization. If the patient fails any step in this process or you're uncertain about the results of your exam, continue to protect the spine. Any time you're uncomfortable with this process, you can choose a conservative plan and continue to immobilize the patient.

FINAL THOUGHTS

Airway maintenance, cervical spine precautions, and patient assessment are important treatments for patients with brain and spine injuries, but they are only stopgap measures. A quarter of all brain and spine injuries result in death or permanent disability. The cost of treating a serious brain injury is staggering. In urban settings, first aid for brain or spine injuries includes rapid transport to neurological care—impossible in a wilderness setting.

Prevention is more effective than treatment: Wear a helmet! Be careful out there.

Evacuation Guidelines
- Evacuate if the patient has:
  —A loss of responsiveness, even if they recover to A+Ox3 or 4
  —Headache, nausea/vomiting, irritability, or other signs and symptoms of mild head injury without loss of responsiveness and is not improving after 24 hours
- Rapidly evacuate if the patient has:
  —Distinct changes in mental status (disoriented, irritable, combative)
  —Persistent vomiting, lethargy, excessive sleepiness, seizures, worsening headache, vision disturbances
  —Signs of skull fracture
- Evacuate any patient with possible spinal cord injury.

CHAPTER 5 | ATHLETIC INJURIES

INTRODUCTION

Living and traveling in the wilderness, carrying a pack, paddling whitewater, mountain biking, and rock climbing can all cause injury to muscle, tendon, or ligament—often as sprains, strains, and tendinitis. These "athletic" injuries account for 50 percent of injuries on NOLS courses and frequently cause evacuations.

Sprains affect ligaments, whereas strains are injuries to muscles and tendons. Both range in severity from stretched tissues to complete tears. A tendon irritated from overuse can develop tendinitis.

In a wilderness context, we don't try to diagnose or "grade" the injury. We make a common-sense decision on whether the injured area is usable or unusable. If usable, we manage pain and may use tape or a brace for support. If unusable, we immobilize and evacuate.

The most common athletic injuries on NOLS courses are ankle and knee sprains, Achilles tendinitis, and forearm tendinitis.

ASSESSMENT FOR ATHLETIC INJURIES

The assessment of an athletic injury includes an evaluation of the mechanism of injury, as well as the signs and symptoms. The mechanism will help you determine whether the occurrence was sudden and traumatic, or whether it was progressive, suggesting an overuse injury.

Signs and symptoms of an injury to muscle, tendon or ligament include swelling, pain, and discoloration. In an acute injury, point tenderness and obvious deformity suggest a fracture. Ask the patient to try to move the joint through its full range of motion. Painless movement is a good sign. If the patient is able to use or bear weight on the injured limb, and pain and swelling are not severe, they may be treated in the field.

Severe pain, the sound of a pop at the time of injury, immediate swelling, and inability to use the joint are signs of a serious muscle, tendon, or ligament injury, possibly a fracture. This injury should be immobilized and the patient evacuated from the field.

General Treatment for Athletic Injuries

- Ice: 20 to 40 minutes every 2 to 4 hours, for 24 to 48 hours
- Compression: elastic bandage may reduce swelling
- Elevation: may reduce swelling
- Support: with tape, brace, or wrap

Signs and Symptoms of a Muscle, Tendon, or Ligament Injury

- Swelling and discoloration
- Pain or tenderness
- Instability and/or loss of range of motion
- Inability to bear weight

GENERAL TREATMENT FOR ATHLETIC INJURIES

Usable athletic injuries are generally treated with pain management and support with tape, wraps or braces.

While there is little evidence supporting the practice of elevating an injured limb or joint above the level of the heart to reduce swelling and pain, it may be helpful and should not cause harm.

Ice, used judiciously in the short term to manage pain—rather than for long periods to suppress inflammation—can be helpful. In warm environments where hypothermia and frostbite are not concerns, ice can be applied with cold packs or ice or snow encased in a plastic bag and wrapped with a sock, or even a shirt soaked in cold water. Cool for 20-40 minutes every 2-4 hours. There is also only equivocal evidence that compression wraps are helpful, but they may reduce swelling and pain and, as long as they do not compromise CSM, are unlikely to cause harm.

Pain Management Principles for the Lay Provider in the Wilderness

Comfort Care

Comfort—both physical and psychological—helps improve a patient's perception of pain. Decrease the patient's anxiety by using their name and keeping the patient informed and involved in their care. Increase their physical comfort by attending to basic needs such as hygiene, warmth, food and hydration, and allowing the patient to place themselves in a position of comfort.

Injury Management

Protection from further injury is an essential pain management tool. Provide stability in the form of taping, bracing, or splinting. Covering open wounds and reducing deformities helps the patient psychologically.

Ice and Elevation

Icing decreases pain by reducing skin temperature to the point where nerve conduction is inhibited and can be an effective non-pharmacological pain intervention. Cooling the area with ice for 20-40 minutes, repeated every 2-4 hours, may help manage pain. Raising the injury above the patient's heart may reduce throbbing pain and allow rest.

Medications (Oral, Non-Opioid, Non-prescription)

OTC dosing of non-steroidal anti-inflammatories (NSAIDs) or acetaminophen can be effective for mild to moderate pain. Before taking any medication:
- Read your protocols/medication information.
- Confirm the dosage.
- Read the label and confirm the medication.
- Ask the patient if they are currently on any medication.
- Ask the patient about previous history with this medication.
- Ask the patient about any known allergies.
- Ask for the patient's consent before administering any medication.

Ankle Sprains

Whether the environment is boulder fields in the backcountry or broken pavement in the city, uneven ground contributes to the likelihood of ankle sprains. Of all ankle sprains, 85 percent are inversion injuries—those in which the bottom of the foot turns in toward the midline of the body and the ankle turns outward. Inversion injuries usually sprain one or more of the ligaments on the outside of the ankle.

Ankle Anatomy. The bones, ligaments, and tendons of the ankle and foot absorb stress and pressure generated by both body weight and activity. They also allow for flexibility and accommodate surface irregularities so that we don't lose our balance.

Bones. The lower leg bones are the tibia and the fibula. The large bumps on either side of the ankle are the lower ends of these bones—the fibula on the outside, and the tibia on the inside. Immediately under the tibia and fibula lies the talus bone, which sits atop the calcaneus (heel bone). The talus and calcaneus act as a rocker for front-to-back flexibility of the ankle. Without them, we would walk stiff-legged.

Ligaments. Due to the number of bones in the foot, ligaments are many and complex. For simplicity, think of there being a ligament on every exterior surface of every bone, attaching to the adjacent articulating bone.

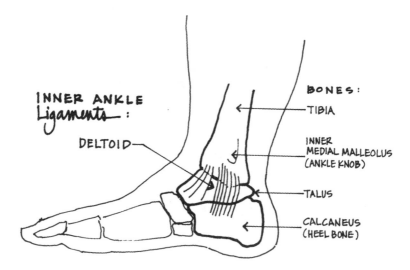

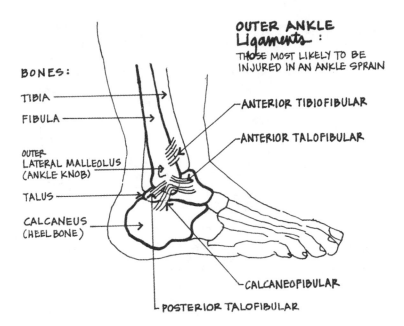

OUTER ANKLE
Ligaments :
THOSE MOST LIKELY TO BE
INJURED IN AN ANKLE SPRAIN

BONES:

TIBIA

FIBULA

OUTER
LATERAL MALLEOLUS
(ANKLE KNOB)

TALUS

CALCANEUS
(HEEL BONE)

ANTERIOR TIBIOFIBULAR

ANTERIOR TALOFIBULAR

CALCANEOFIBULAR

POSTERIOR TALOFIBULAR

Four ligaments are most commonly associated with ankle sprains. On the outside, usually the weaker aspect, three ligaments attach from the fibula to the talus and the calcaneus. Together these three ligaments protect the ankle from turning to the outside.

On the inside of the ankle is the large, fan-shaped deltoid ligament joining the talus, calcaneus, and several of the smaller foot bones to the tibia. Rolling the ankle inward (an eversion sprain) stresses the deltoid ligament. Spraining the deltoid requires considerable force, and due to its size and strength, it is seldom injured. In fact, this ligament is so strong that if a bad twist occurs, it frequently pulls fragments of bone off at its attachment points, causing an avulsion fracture.

Muscles and Tendons. Muscles in the lower leg act on the ankle and foot via long tendons. The calf muscles—the gastrocnemius and soleus—taper into the largest tendon, the Achilles, which attaches to the back of the calcaneus.

Treatment of Ankle Sprains. If a severe sprain or a fracture is suspected, the injury is unusable. Immobilize the ankle with a splint. If the injury is usable, treating with ice, compression,

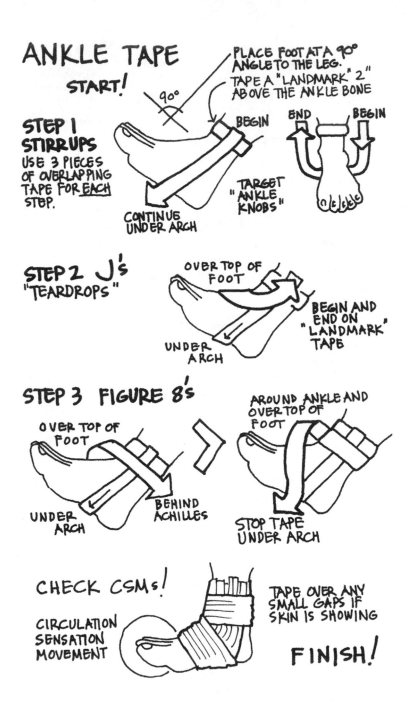

and elevation for the first 24 to 48 hours and resting the injury for a few days may allow a patient to stay in the mountains rather than cut the trip short. Once swelling has abated, taping or wrapping the ankle can provide bracing and allow a patient to walk.

Treatment of Ankle Sprains
- Ice, elevation, and compression
- Taping for support

Knee Pain

Pain in the knee from overuse can be treated by ceasing the activity causing the discomfort, and controlling pain and swelling using ice, compression, and elevation. In the event of a traumatic injury resulting in an unstable knee, splint and evacuate. If the injury is stable and the patient can bear weight, wrap the knee with tape or use a knee brace for support. Ability to walk, your location, distance to the roadhead, and other factors will all influence a decision whether this person stays in the field, or can self-evacuate. If the knee is well braced, risk of further injury during a walking evacuation is low.

TENDINITIS

A tendon is the fibrous cord by which a muscle is attached to a bone. Its structure is similar to that of kernmantle rope, with an outer sheath of tissue enclosing a core of load-bearing fibers. Some tendons, such as those to the fingers, are long. The activating muscles are in the forearm, and the tendons stretch from the forearm across the wrist to each finger.

Tendinitis is inflammation of a tendon, caused by torn fibers or, more commonly, irritation from overuse or infection that inflames the sheath. When the sheath and the tendon become inflamed, movement is restricted and painful, and the patient may feel a grating of the tendon inside the sheath. There may be little pain when the tendon is at rest.

Tendons are poorly supplied with blood, so they heal slowly. However they are well supplied with nerves, which means that an injury may be painful. Tendons can be injured by sudden overloading but are more frequently injured through overuse.

Factors contributing to tendinitis include poor technique, poor equipment, unhealed prior injury, and cool, tight muscles.

Assessment for Tendinitis

Tendinitis causes swelling, redness, warmth, pain to the touch or pinch, painful movement, and sounds of friction or grinding (crepitus). In contrast to ankle sprains, tendinitis is a progressive overuse injury, not an acute injury. Common sites for tendinitis are the Achilles tendon and the tendons of the forearm. The Achilles, the largest tendon in the body, may fatigue and become inflamed during or following lengthy hikes, especially with significant elevation gain. Boots that break down and place pressure on the tendon can provide enough irritation in one day to initiate inflammation.

Signs and Symptoms of Tendinitis

- Swelling
- Redness
- Warmth
- Localized pain

Canoeists and kayakers are prone to forearm tendinitis. Poor technique and inadequate strength and flexibility contribute to the injury. Similar tendinitis comes with repetitive use of ski poles, ice axes, and ice-climbing tools.

Tendinitis may also occur on the front of the foot, usually caused by tight lacing or stiff mountaineering boots. The tendons extending the toes become irritated and inflamed.

Treatment of Tendinitis

Treat tendinitis with ice, compression, and elevation. It may be necessary to cease the aggravating activity until the inflammation subsides. Prevent or ease tendinitis of anterior foot muscles by varying boot lacing. Lace boots more loosely when hiking and more tightly when climbing.

Achilles Tendinitis. To relieve stretch on the Achilles tendon, provide a heel lift. To relieve direct pressure from the boot, place a 6-inch by 1-inch strip of foamlite padding on either side of the Achilles tendon. The placement should take the pressure off without touching the Achilles.

Forearm Tendinitis. Forearm tendinitis is primarily associated with the repetitive motion of paddling. Pay close attention to proper paddling technique. Keep a relaxed open grip on the

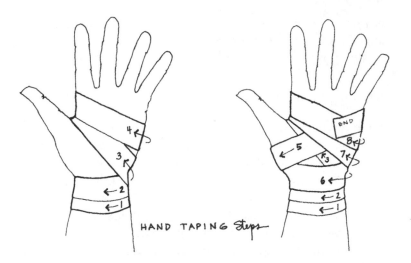

HAND TAPING Steps

paddle. Keep the wrist in line with the forearm during the pull and push, and avoid crossing the upper arm over the midline of the body.

Other paddling techniques that may help prevent forearm tendinitis include keeping the thumb on the same side of the paddle as the fingers, and switching a feathered paddle for an unfeathered one. Feathered paddles require a wrist movement that can sometimes aggravate tendinitis.

Tendinitis of the forearm is treated with ice, compression, and elevation. Also, the wrist can be taped to limit movement that aggravates the condition.

Treatment of Achilles Tendinitis
- Ice, compression, and elevation
- Pads on ankle to protect the tendon
- Padding under the heel to elevate the ankle

Treatment of Forearm Tendinitis
- Ice, compression, and elevation
- Taping wrist to limit range of motion

MUSCLE STRAINS

Muscles can be stretched and torn from overuse or overexertion. Initial treatment is ice, compression, and elevation followed—once the initial inflammation has subsided—by heat, massage, and gentle stretching. Reasons to evacuate the patient for evaluation by a physician include radiating muscle pain, unmanageable pain, pain secondary to an illness, or pain from a severe trauma mechanism.

FINAL THOUGHTS

While it's not clear whether ice, compression, and elevation speed healing any faster than rest and patience, it can make the patient more comfortable by reducing pain and swelling. There is possible benefit, and low risk of harm. Most athletic injuries—sprains, strains, and tendinitis—will take weeks to heal, and this time of reduced activity can impact ability to travel on a wilderness expedition. Prevention is the key.

Errors in technique and inadequate muscular conditioning or warm-up produce injury. Overuse of muscles and joints (when there is no single traumatic event as the cause of injury) generates many of the sprains and strains on NOLS courses.

Jerky movements, excessive force, or an unnecessarily tight grip on the paddle while kayaking contribute to forearm tendinitis. Performing the athletic movements required for difficult rock climbs, without warming up or paying attention to balance and form, can cause injury. Even the seemingly simple actions of lifting a backpack or boat, stepping over logs, and wading in cold mountain streams can be dangerous.

Steep terrain and wet conditions contribute to injuries. Slippery conditions make it harder to balance and can cause falls. Surprisingly, injuries are just as likely to occur when backcountry travelers are not wearing packs as when they are, possibly because people are more attentive to technique when hiking or skiing with a pack.

Injury is more likely when you are tired, cold, dehydrated, rushed, or ill. You're not thinking as clearly, and your muscles are less flexible and responsive. Injuries happen more frequently in late morning and late afternoon, when dehydration and fatigue reduce awareness and increase clumsiness. Shifting from a three-meal-a-day schedule to breakfast and dinner plus three or four light snacks during the day helps keep your food supply constant and energy up.

Haste, often the result of unrealistic timetables, is frequently implicated in accidents. Plan routes so that you negotiate more difficult terrain in the morning when you are fresh. Take rest breaks before difficult sections of a hike or paddle. Stop at the base of the pass, the near side of the river, or the beginning of the boulder field. Drink, eat, and stretch tight muscles. Check equipment for loose gaiters and poorly balanced backpacks.

The sustained activity of life in the wilderness and the need for sudden bursts of power when paddling, skiing, or climbing necessitate physical conditioning prior to a wilderness expedition. A regimen of endurance, flexibility, and strength training will help prevent injuries and promote safety and enjoyment of wilderness activity.

Evacuation Guidelines
- Evacuation decisions about athletic injuries are usually based on practical considerations—continued pain, an injury that does not heal, or inability to travel.

6 | FRACTURES AND DISLOCATIONS

INTRODUCTION

Fractures and dislocations make up less than 7 percent of NOLS's field injury incidents, compared with as much as 20 percent of reported wilderness injuries among the general public. Despite their relative rarity at NOLS, each fracture or dislocation has the potential to be a serious incident requiring skillful management. NOLS instructors have cared for femur fractures in winter in the remote backcountry of Yellowstone National Park and at 16,000 feet on Denali. They've expertly splinted uncomplicated wrist fractures and walked patients 20 miles out of the wilderness. They've accurately diagnosed a complicated elbow fracture requiring an urgent helicopter evacuation. A theme linking all these incidents is sound patient assessment and skillful injury management.

At one time, a fractured femur was a deadly injury. Broken bone ends often did not heal properly. Open fractures frequently became infected, and amputation was a common unpleasant consequence. Modern emergency medicine, especially assessment and splinting in the field, has reduced these complications.

THE SKELETAL SYSTEM

A bony skeleton shapes the body. From this scaffolding the soft tissues hang: the vital organs, blood vessels, muscles, fat, and skin. The skeleton is strong to support and protect internal organs, flexible to withstand stress, and jointed to allow for movement.

Bone is living tissue combined with the mineral calcium and the protein collagen, which make bone rigid. Ligaments and connective tissue join bones. An adult has 206 bones, ranging in size from the femur, or thighbone—the largest—to the tiny ossicles of the inner ear.

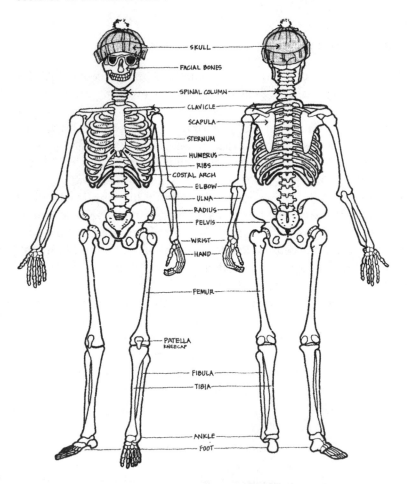

SKULL
FACIAL BONES
SPINAL COLUMN
CLAVICLE
SCAPULA
STERNUM
HUMERUS
RIBS
COSTAL ARCH
ELBOW
ULNA
RADIUS
PELVIS
WRIST
HAND
FEMUR
PATELLA
KNEECAP
FIBULA
TIBIA
ANKLE
FOOT

The skeleton has axial and appendicular components. The axial bones are the pelvis, spinal column, ribs, and skull. Injuries to these structures—except for pelvic fractures—are discussed in the chest, brain, and spine-injury chapters. This chapter covers injuries to the appendicular skeleton, the arms and legs, as well as pelvic fractures.

The upper extremity skeleton consists of the scapula or shoulder blade; the clavicle or collarbone; the upper arm bone or humerus; two bones in the forearm, the radius on the thumb side and the ulna on the little finger side; and 22 bones in the wrist and fingers.

The skeleton of the lower extremity consists of the pelvis; the thighbone or femur; the patella or kneecap; two bones in the lower leg, the tibia and fibula; and 26 bones in the ankle and foot.

Bones connect at joints held together by ligaments, connective tissue, and muscle. Some joints are fixed; others allow varying degrees of movement. Joint surfaces are covered with cartilage to reduce friction and lubricated with joint fluid for smooth movement

FRACTURES AND DISLOCATIONS

A fracture is a break in a bone. Fractures can be open or closed. With open fractures, the skin is broken, exposing the bone to contamination. Closed fractures are covered with intact muscle and skin.

Fractures can also be described as transverse, spiral, oblique, or crushed. This information is usually obtained from an X-ray and has little effect on first aid.

In addition to causing pain, loss of function, and swelling, fractures can be complicated by infection (particularly in open fractures) and damage to blood vessels and nerves. Fractured bone ends can pinch or sever blood vessels, blocking circulation or causing bleeding. Fractures of large, long bones, such as the femur or pelvis, may be accompanied by blood loss that can cause life-threatening shock.

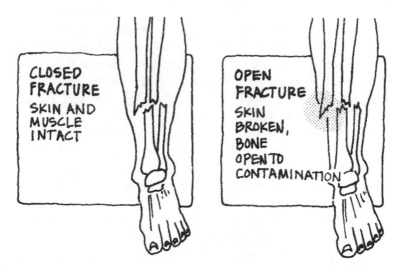

A dislocation is the displacement of a bone end from its normal position at a joint. Dislocations damage the supporting structures at the joint and can disrupt blood vessels and nerves. The ball-and-socket joint of the shoulder is a common site for dislocation. Elbow, finger, and ankle dislocations are also possible. Less common are dislocations to the wrist, hip, and knee.

Signs and Symptoms
Signs and symptoms of both fractures and dislocations include pain and tenderness; crepitus, a grating sound produced by bone ends rubbing together (also a sign of instability and unnatural movement at the fracture site); swelling and discoloration, indicating that fluids are pooling in the damaged tissue; deformity of a limb or joint; and loss of function.

Signs and Symptoms of Fractures and Dislocations
- Pain and point tenderness
- Crepitus
- Swelling and discoloration
- Deformity
- Loss of function or range of motion at a joint (dislocation)
- Loss of function at a bone (fracture)
- Altered circulation, sensation, and movement (CSM)

Assessment of Fractures and Dislocations

The mechanism of injury provides a clue to the extent and location of the injury. Particularly violent incidents, such as falls from a height or direct blows to a joint, are common fracture mechanisms in the outdoors.

Look at the limb for deformity, swelling, or discoloration. Humans are bilaterally symmetrical animals; one side is the mirror image of the other. Comparing an injured with an uninjured limb can reveal a subtle angulation or deformity. If necessary, open zippers or remove clothing to visualize the injury. Feel the limb for localized tenderness, abnormal bumps or protrusions, and swelling.

Assess for circulation, sensation, and movement (CSM). Cold, gray, or cyanotic extremities may be evidence of impaired circulation. Fingers and toes that are warm and the presence of a radial pulse at the wrist or a pedal pulse in the foot indicate good circulation.

Assess for sensation and movement. Test for reaction to touch or pain. Nerve damage may result in loss of strength, inability to move the extremity, numbness, or tingling. A blocked

---

Assessment of Fractures and Dislocations

- Assess the bone or joint.
- Remove clothing; visualize the injury.
- Look for deformity, swelling, discoloration.
- Feel for tenderness, deformity, swelling.
- Assess circulation, sensation, and movement (CSM).

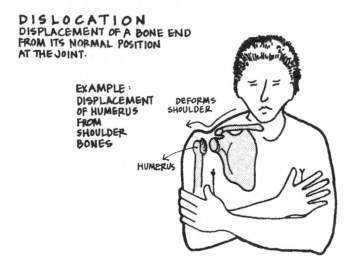

DISLOCATION
DISPLACEMENT OF A BONE END FROM ITS NORMAL POSITION AT THE JOINT.

EXAMPLE:
DISPLACEMENT OF HUMERUS FROM SHOULDER BONES

DEFORMS SHOULDER

HUMERUS

artery with loss of distal circulation is an emergency. After several hours, serious damage may result.

Compartment Syndrome

Compartment syndrome involves increased pressure in a muscle compartment, which is a group of muscles and other tissue surrounded by a collagen-rich membrane called fascia. Bleeding and/or inflammation, secondary to fractures, crush injury, burns, or other trauma, or repetitive activities such as running cause swelling that is trapped by the fascia. Compartment syndrome is most common in the lower leg and forearm, although it can also occur in the hand, foot, thigh, and upper arm.

Signs and symptoms of compartment syndrome include pain, pallor, pressure, and lack of pulse. Pain in the injured extremity is out of proportion to the injury, or stimulated by stretching or movement. The skin is pale or cyanotic. The distal pulse may be diminished or absent. The muscle may feel tight or full.

Treatment Principles. Assess all extremity injuries for compartment syndrome. Acute compartment syndrome is a surgical emergency. There is no effective nonsurgical treatment. Evacuate rapidly.

Treatment Principles for Fractures and Dislocations

Treat fractures and dislocations by immobilizing the injury. Immobilization prevents movement of bones; reduces pain, swelling, and the possibility of further injury; and prevents a closed fracture from becoming an open fracture.

Immobilize the Injury. Any time there is loss of function to a limb or joint, the injury should be immobilized in a splint. If it is not clear whether the injury is a sprain or a fracture, immobilize. Likewise, if you are not sure whether there is a fracture or a dislocation at a joint, immobilize. Immobilize the bones above and below a dislocated joint, and immobilize the joints above and below a fractured bone.

Clean and Dress Wounds. Clean and dress all wounds before splinting. Treat an open fracture as a contaminated soft-tissue injury. Irrigate, but do not scrub, exposed bone ends. Keep

---

Treatment Principles for Fractures and Dislocations

- Immobilize the injury.
  —Bones above and below dislocations
  —Joints above and below fractures
- Clean and dress wounds.
- Remove jewelry, watches, and tight clothing.
- Manage pain with local application of ice, elevation, and compression.
- Assess circulation, skin temperature, and sensation before and after splinting.
- Assess for other injuries.
- Treat for shock.

---

bone ends that cannot be reduced moist with a dressing soaked in disinfected water. An infected fracture is a serious problem that can result in long-term complications.

Splint Before Moving. Splint the injury before moving the patient. If you must move the patient due to risk management concerns, a quick splint fashioned from a foamlite sleeping pad can stabilize the injury. Strap an injured arm to the body. Tie injured legs together.

Remove Jewelry, Watches, and Tight Clothing. Remove jewelry and watches, and loosen clothing that might compromise circulation should swelling occur. If you are managing a splint in cold weather, hot water bottles or chemical heat packs tucked into the splint can provide warmth.

Manage Pain. Use local ice, elevation, compression and non-prescription medications to manage pain (see Chapter 5).

Assess Circulation, Sensation, and Movement. Before and after the splint is applied, assess circulation, sensation, and movement (CSM) in fingers or toes. Repeat this assessment periodically during transport.

Assess for Other Injuries. A fracture or dislocation warrants a full patient assessment for other injuries.

Treat for Shock. A fracture in and of itself does not cause shock. However, damage to nearby tissues, organs, and blood vessels may be a life-threatening problem. Splinting is the basic treatment for shock because it reduces pain and continued injury. Be especially alert for shock with femur and pelvic fractures, multiple fractures, and open fractures.

Angulated Fractures, Dislocations, and Traction-in-Line

Years ago, in basic first aid, we learned to splint fractures and dislocations in the position in which they were found. We were concerned that moving bones to straighten bent extremities would injure blood vessels and nerves. In practice, however, we found that gentle traction and straightening of a fracture can reduce pain and make splints more stable.

Medical opinion now favors straightening with gentle traction-in-line for femur fractures, fractures that are difficult to splint or transport due to angulation, and any fracture or dislocation with impaired distal circulation, sensation, or movement. The current wisdom is that the danger of muscle, nerve,

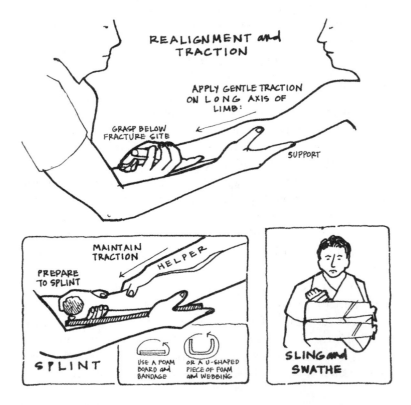

or blood-vessel injury from gentle traction-in-line is less than the damage, discomfort, and pain that results from an injury splinted in an awkward position for long periods.

To straighten a fracture, apply gentle traction-in-line and realign the bone ends. To do this, grasp the limb below the fracture site while another person supports the limb. Align the limb with a gentle pull applied on the long axis of the bone. If resistance or increasing pain occurs, stop and splint in the deformed position.

Dislocations. Consensus opinion in wilderness medicine supports reducing dislocations in the field if prompt transport is not possible or circulation is impaired. The first responder should use judgment and discretion when transport to a medical facility is possible within a few hours. Early reduction decreases pain; is easier if done before swelling, stiffness, and muscle spasms develop; makes immobilization and transportation easier; and reduces risks of long-term circulation and nerve injury.

The scope of practice for a wilderness first responder includes use of traction-in-line to reduce anterior shoulder, patella, and finger or toe dislocations. These tend to be amenable to field reduction with low risk of harm to the patient. Dislocations of the elbow, wrist, knee, ankle, and hip can be complex injuries. Unless CSM is complicated, it is recommended that these injuries be immobilized and promptly evacuated.

Dislocations are relocated with a variety of traction-in-line techniques, depending on the location of the injury. We recommend that you contact a physician or a reputable wilderness medical program for advice and training on specific relocation techniques.

SPLINTING

In the wilderness, improvised splints are the rule, and they may remain in place for days. Splints should pad, support, and immobilize the limb, and insulate the extremity from cold. They should be lightweight to make transporting the patient easier, and allow access to feet or hands to check circulation. There are many commercial splints on the market, but in the backcountry, two commonly available items easily meet these specifications. They are the foamlite pad used for insulation under sleeping bags, and the triangular bandage.

Basic Splinting Techniques

Two basic splinting techniques cover most first aid situations. One is to make a foamlite tube to splint an arm or leg. The other is to fashion a sling and swathe to immobilize injuries to the upper extremities. For both splinting methods, support the foot or hand, but provide access to fingers and toes to assess for CSM.

Foamlite Tube. To make a foamlite tube, roll a foam sleeping pad into a U-shaped tube and trim to fit the limb. Secure with cravats (triangular bandages), elastic bandages, bandannas, sling webbing, or tape. To make the assembly supportive and comfortable, generously pad and firmly (but not tightly) compress it around the limb. Upper extremity injuries are often further supported with a sling and swathe.

Sling and Swathe. The sling and swathe immobilizes arm, shoulder, and collarbone injuries using two triangular bandages, fabric strips, bandannas, or cravats.

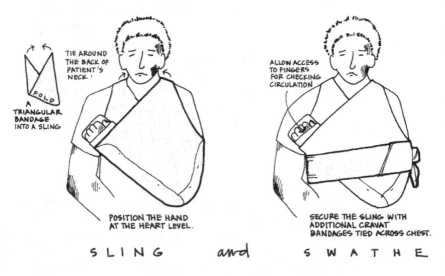

TIE AROUND THE BACK OF PATIENT'S NECK :

A TRIANGULAR BANDAGE INTO A SLING

POSITION THE HAND AT THE HEART LEVEL.

ALLOW ACCESS TO FINGERS FOR CHECKING CIRCULATION

SECURE THE SLING WITH ADDITIONAL CRAVAT BANDAGES TIED ACROSS CHEST.

S L I N G   *and*   S W A T H E

First, clean and dress any open wound. Then use soft material to pad the injury. Add a firm supporting layer outside the soft padding, such as a foamlite pad, Crazy Creek chair, or Therm-A-Rest pad. Sticks, tent poles, or the stays from a backpack can provide additional support. Secure with tape, webbing, or cord.

Qualities of a Good Splint

- Rigid; supports the injury
- Pads the injury
- Insulates from cold
- Lightweight
- Offers access to distal circulation
- Immobilizes the joint above and below a fracture
- Immobilizes the bones above and below a joint injury

Specific Splinting Techniques

Hand. The hand and fingers should be splinted in the "position of function," the position of the hand when holding a glass of water. Fingers can also be "buddy-taped" to each other to reduce range of motion, yet still allow some degree of function. If the injury is confined to the fingers, the wrist need not be splinted. If the injury involves the bones at the base of the fingers, splint the wrist as well.

Wrist and Forearm. Splint injuries to the wrist and forearm with a foamlite stabilizer and/or a sling and swathe. Elevating the hand above the level of the heart may help reduce swelling and pain.

Elbow. An elbow dislocation or fracture is often a complicated and painful injury. Several nerves and arteries pass around the elbow joint and may be damaged by displaced bone ends. The simplest splint for the elbow is the sling and swathe. Splint elbow injuries in the position in which you find it. If the elbow is at an awkward angle, a sling and swathe will not work well. Try a foamlite pad stabilized with a tent pole or the stay from a backpack, bent to the angle of the joint. If possible, bandage the whole arm to the trunk for greater stability.

Upper Arm. The radial nerve and brachial artery lie close to the humerus and can be injured by a fracture. Damage to the artery is most common with elbow dislocations, but damage to the nerve is most common with midshaft fractures. Check the pulse at the wrist. The ability to bend back the hand tests the radial nerve. The humerus can be splinted with a combination

WRIST SPLINT

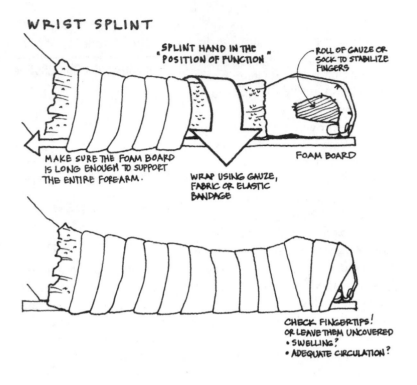

SPLINT HAND IN THE "POSITION OF FUNCTION"

ROLL OF GAUZE OR SOCK TO STABILIZE FINGERS

MAKE SURE THE FOAM BOARD IS LONG ENOUGH TO SUPPORT THE ENTIRE FOREARM.

WRAP USING GAUZE, FABRIC OR ELASTIC BANDAGE

FOAM BOARD

CHECK FINGERTIPS! OR LEAVE THEM UNCOVERED
• SWELLING?
• ADEQUATE CIRCULATION?

SPLINT MATERIALS

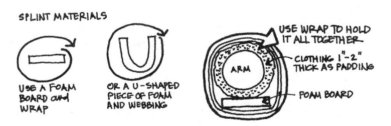

USE A FOAM BOARD and WRAP

OR A U-SHAPED PIECE OF FOAM AND WEBBING

USE WRAP TO HOLD IT ALL TOGETHER

CLOTHING 1"-2" THICK AS PADDING

ARM

FOAM BOARD

of a foamlite splint and sling and swathe. Wrap foamlite on the inside of the arm, over the elbow, and up the outside of the arm for added stability. The patient may be more comfortable if the sling and foamlite cup the elbow without putting pressure on the humerus.

Shoulder. The humerus fits into a shallow socket in the scapula, forming the shoulder joint and allowing for a wide range of motion (ROM). This ROM also makes the joint susceptible to injury. Most dislocations are anterior, with the head of the humerus displaced out of the socket toward the chest.

The signs of dislocation are drooping shoulder, a depression on the front of the shoulder, and loss of function or ROM at the joint. A sling and swathe provides a simple and effective splint. If the shoulder is immobile at an awkward angle, padding may be necessary to support the arm away from the chest.

One technique that may reduce an anterior shoulder dislocation is passive hanging-arm traction. The patient is positioned prone with the dislocated arm hanging loosely. The technique is passive and may work with only the weight of the arm, though 5 to 10 pounds of weight on the wrist may help relax the muscles and allow the shoulder to relocate.

PASSIVE HANGING TRACTION

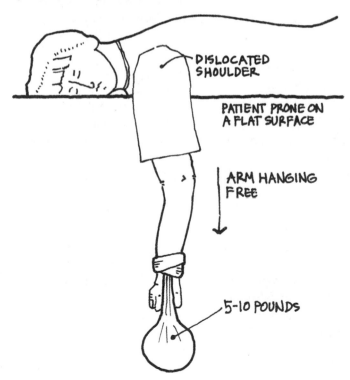

DISLOCATED SHOULDER

PATIENT PRONE ON A FLAT SURFACE

ARM HANGING FREE

5-10 POUNDS

Collarbone. The clavicle acts as a strut, propping the shoulder. It can be fractured by a direct blow to the shoulder or a blow transmitted up an extended arm. A broken collarbone is a common mountain-biking injury. Deformity and tenderness can often be found by feeling the entire clavicle from sternum to shoulder. Typically, a patient with an injured clavicle is unable to use the arm on the injured side. Splint with a sling and swathe, immobilizing the shoulder and arm.

Pelvis. The pelvis is a bowl-shaped structure consisting of three bones fused with the sacrum, the lower portion of the vertebral column. The upper part of the femur meets the pelvis at a shallow socket and forms the hip joint.

A broken pelvis is a serious injury. It takes considerable force to break a pelvis; such force can cause associated internal injuries, including rupture of the bladder and blood loss. Immobilize the trunk and legs. A backboard, litter, vacuum mattress, or improvised litter is necessary to immobilize the pelvis and carry the patient. A garment or piece of fabric wrapped supportively around the pelvis at the level of the hips may help stabilize the pelvis.

Femur and Hip. A dislocated hip is usually the result of a high-velocity mechanism, such as a fall from height. A leg with a dislocated hip is generally shortened, with the foot and knee turned in. If the hip is dislocated for more than a few hours, the blood supply to the head of the femur can be compromised and permanent damage to the bone can occur. Splint hip fractures or dislocations with a U-shaped foamlite tube, immobilizing the entire leg and the pelvis.

Muscles surrounding the fracture of long bones such as the femur may contract, causing the bone ends to override. This increases pain and soft-tissue damage, as well as the possibility of artery and nerve injury. Spasm of the large thigh muscles is a concern in fractures of the femur. A femur fracture can bleed into the surrounding tissues, causing shock. Spasms and overriding bone ends may cause the thigh to appear shortened and swollen.

Splinting a fractured femur with a traction device has been a tool for managing femur fractures; it has been taught on wilderness medicine courses for years. However, trends in practice note that traction splints are not recommended for fractures close to the knee or the hip, that they create a risk of injury to the ankle, and finally that there is a lack of medical evidence that traction improves patient outcomes. In addition, improvised traction splints are challenging to build, particularly so that they maintain constant traction. Many emergency medical services, and NOLS Wilderness Medicine, no longer advocate traction splints for femur fractures. The foundation for immobilization of a femur or thigh injury is a well-padded and firm full-length leg splint that starts at the hip and includes the foot and ankle. If the thigh is angulated, attempt gentle traction-in-line to straighten before splinting.

Knee. Most knee injuries can be wrapped with an Ace bandage, taped, or stabilized with a foamlite splint in such a way that the patient can walk. If the patient can tolerate bearing weight on the injury, in general this will not cause further damage. A grossly unstable knee with major ligament rupture is accompanied by severe pain, inability to move the joint or bear weight, swelling, and obvious deformity. This injury requires a simple splint and a litter evacuation. In some cases, it may be difficult to tell if the femur, the tibia, or the knee is injured. Assume the worst and splint the entire leg.

Lower Leg. The tibia is the "shin bone," running just under the skin from knee to ankle, while the smaller fibula runs lateral to it. The lower ends of the tibia and fibula are the prominent knobs on the sides of the ankle The thin layers of skin over the tibia make open fractures particularly common. Splint both the knee and the ankle in a roll of foamlite.

Ankle. It can be challenging to differentiate between a fracture of and a sprain to the ankle. Both can be immobilized with a stirrup of foamlite and wrapped with clothing for insulation and padding.

SIMPLE LEG SPLINT

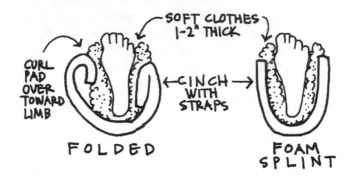

CURL PAD OVER TOWARD LIMB

SOFT CLOTHES 1-2" THICK

←CINCH→ WITH STRAPS

FOLDED

FOAM SPLINT

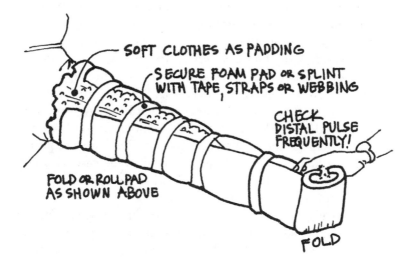

SOFT CLOTHES AS PADDING

SECURE FOAM PAD OR SPLINT WITH TAPE, STRAPS OR WEBBING

CHECK DISTAL PULSE FREQUENTLY!

FOLD OR ROLL PAD AS SHOWN ABOVE

FOLD

FINAL THOUGHTS

In NOLS's experience, fractures and dislocations are not common in wilderness activities, but they do occur, and the first responder should be prepared. A careful assessment, gentle traction-in-line, immobilization, and pain management are the cornerstones of our treatment. Most of us, conscious of weight and bulk when we travel in the wilderness, don't carry prepared commercial splints. We know that we can create what we need from materials at hand such as clothing, sleeping pads, packs, stays, tent poles, bandannas, and natural materials such as sticks. Practice improvising splints from the material you commonly have with you in the wilderness.

Evacuation Guidelines
- Evacuate all musculoskeletal injuries showing loss of function, irreducible dislocations, and any first-time dislocation.
- Rapidly evacuate all open fractures and any musculoskeletal injury with altered CSM.

CHAPTER 7 | SOFT TISSUE INJURIES

INTRODUCTION

Outside the wilderness, we give little thought to the consequences of soft tissue injuries. Small wounds do not disrupt our lives, and infection is an unusual aftermath. On an expedition, however, even relatively minor injuries can have serious consequences. Cut or blistered feet can result in litter evacuations, and hand wounds can end climbing trips. Infection is a real and ever-present risk.

Responding with the proper first aid is essential to expedition members' health and safety. Soft tissue wounds comprise 30 percent of injuries on NOLS courses, with similar patterns seen in other outdoor injury data. In addition to controlling bleeding, first aid for soft tissue injuries in the wilderness includes cleaning the wound, monitoring for signs of infection, and making decisions about what warrants evacuation.

SKIN

The skin is the single largest organ of the body. It protects the internal organs by providing a watertight shell that keeps fluids in and microorganisms out. Glands in the skin regulate body temperature by producing sweat which, when it evaporates,

LAYERS OF THE SKIN :

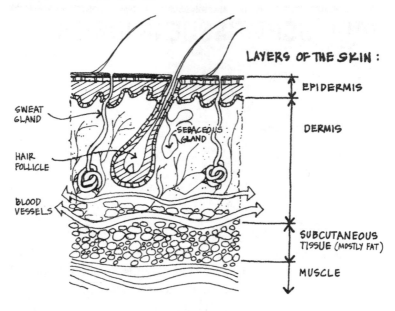

LAYERS OF THE SKIN :

EPIDERMIS

DERMIS

SWEAT GLAND

SEBACEOUS GLAND

HAIR FOLLICLE

BLOOD VESSELS

SUBCUTANEOUS TISSUE (MOSTLY FAT)

MUSCLE

cools the body. Nerves near the skin's surface send messages to the brain about heat, cold, pressure, pain, and body position.

The skin is composed of three layers. The innermost layer is subcutaneous tissue consisting mostly of fat, acting as an insulator and a reservoir for energy. Beneath the subcutaneous tissue lies muscle.

The second layer is the dermis, which contains sweat glands, sebaceous (oil) glands, hair follicles, nerves, and blood vessels. Sweat glands are found on all body surfaces, especially on the palms of the hands and soles of the feet. Sweat glands routinely secrete 0.5 to 1 liter of sweat per day and can produce up to 1 liter per hour during strenuous exercise. The sebaceous glands produce sebum (oil) and lie next to the hair follicles. Sebum waterproofs the skin and keeps the hair supple. Blood vessels in the dermis provide nutrients and oxygen to each cell and remove waste products such as carbon dioxide.

The outermost layer of the skin is the epidermis, made up primarily of dead cells held together by sebum. These dead cells continually slough and are replaced by more dead cells.

CLOSED WOUNDS

Soft-tissue injuries are classified as open or closed. With closed injuries, the skin remains intact; open injuries involve a break in the skin's surface.

Closed injuries include contusions (bruises) and hematomas. With both, tissue and blood vessels beneath the epidermis are damaged. Swelling and discoloration occur because blood and plasma leak out of the damaged blood vessels. With contusions, blood is dispersed within the tissues. Hematomas contain a pool of blood—as much as a pint surrounding a major bone fracture. Depending on the amount of blood dispersed, reabsorption can take from 12 hours to several days. In some cases, the blood may have to be drained by a physician to enhance healing.

Treatment for Closed Wounds
First aid can do little for a bruise. Icing for 20-40 minutes every 2-4 hours may decrease swelling and pain.

OPEN WOUNDS

Open injuries include abrasions, lacerations, puncture wounds, and major traumatic injuries such as avulsions, amputations, and crushing wounds.

Abrasions. Abrasions occur when the epidermis and part of the dermis are rubbed off. These injuries are commonly called "road rash" or "rug burns." They usually bleed very little but are painful and may be contaminated with debris.

Abrasions heal more quickly if treated with anti-microbial ointment and covered with a dressing to keep the wound surface clean and moist.

Lacerations. Lacerations tend to be produced by sharp objects. The cut may penetrate some or all the layers of the skin, and the edges may be straight or jagged. If long and deep enough to cause the wound to gape, the laceration may require sutures, a task for a physician. Sutures are also often indicated if the cut is on the face, hands, or over a joint, or if it severs a

OPEN INJURIES

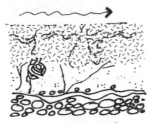

ABRASION
EPIDERMIS / DERMIS
RUBBED OFF.

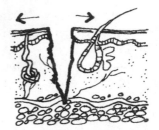

LACERATION
CUTS PRODUCED BY
SHARP OBJECTS.
EDGES CAN BE CLEAN
OR RAGGED.

AVULSION
THE TEARING OFF OF A
FLAP OF SKIN OR ENTIRE
LIMB.

PUNCTURE
POINTED OBJECT
PENETRATES SKIN AND
POSSIBLY AN UNDERLYING
ORGAN OR ARTERY.

tendon, ligament, or blood vessel. Lacerations on the hands or over a joint may be sutured to prevent the wound from being continually pulled apart by movement. Lacerations on the face are usually sutured to decrease scarring.

Puncture Wounds. Pointed objects cause puncture wounds. Although the skin around a puncture wound remains closed and there is usually little external bleeding, the object may have penetrated an artery or organ, causing internal bleeding.

An impaled object through the cheek causing an airway obstruction must be removed. In addition, if the object prevents transport, cannot be stabilized, is loose enough to simply fall out, or prevents bleeding control, it may need to be removed. Otherwise, leave it in place if removing the object could cause more soft-tissue injury and increase bleeding by releasing pressure on compressed blood vessels.

Tetanus is a rare but serious complication. It is a good idea to make sure your tetanus booster is up to date before you take off into the backcountry.

Major Traumatic Injuries. Major traumatic injuries include avulsions, amputations, and crushing injuries.

Avulsion. An avulsion is a "tearing off" that can range in severity from a small skin flap to the near amputation of an entire limb. Skin tends to separate along anatomical planes, such as between subcutaneous tissue and muscle. To treat a small to moderate-sized avulsion, clean under the skin flap and reposition it over the wound.

Amputation. Amputation is the complete severance of a part or extremity. The stump of a cleanly severed extremity may not bleed profusely because the severed blood vessels respond by retracting and constricting. If blood vessels are partially torn, however, they cannot constrict, and bleeding may be massive. If direct pressure does not stop the stump from bleeding, a tourniquet may be necessary.

After treating the patient, rinse the amputated body part with clean water, wrap it in moist sterile gauze and place it in a plastic bag. Then place the bag in cold water or on ice. Do not bury the part in ice, as this may cause cold injury. Make certain that the wrapped part accompanies the patient to the hospital. Reattachment may be possible if you can get to a hospital quickly.

Crushing Injuries. Crushing injuries can cause extensive damage to underlying tissue and bones, and large areas may be lacerated and avulsed. Consider what underlying body parts may be damaged, and conduct a focused exam to find out if any bones have been fractured, if an internal organ has been crushed, or if compartment syndrome is present.

Treatment for Open Wounds
The principles for treating open wounds are to control bleeding, clean and dress the wound, and monitor for infection.

Control Bleeding. Controlling bleeding is the first priority when treating open wounds. Death can come quickly to a patient with a tear in a major blood vessel. Life-threatening bleeding generally means that blood is spurting, soaks clothing, pools on the ground, or is associated with missing body parts.

The main techniques for controlling bleeding are: direct pressure, which can be augmented with elevation; wound packing; and pressure dressings and tourniquets.

Direct Pressure. Applying pressure to torn blood vessels will control most bleeding. Using your hand and a piece of fabric— preferably sterile gauze—apply direct pressure to the wound. The important word is "direct"—the pressure is most effective if applied to the source of the bleed. Three fingers' pressure (hard enough to make your fingers uncomfortable) with the dominant hand, with the non-dominant hand on top to support, seems to work best. If a dressing becomes soaked with blood, leave it in place and apply additional dressings on top. Removing the dressing disturbs the blood clots that are forming.

Controlling Bleeding
- Direct pressure
- Elevation
- Wound packing
- Pressure dressings
- Tourniquets

Elevation. Assuming there are no injuries, such as a fracture, that will be made worse by movement, elevation of an extremity may help decrease the bleeding. Direct pressure and elevation together can control almost all bleeding.

Wound Packing. If a wound is large or gaping you can pack (stuff) the wound with hemostatic gauze, plain gauze, or a clean cloth, and then apply direct pressure. Make sure your wound packing is not so large and bulky that it prevents "direct" pressure. Wound packing may be helpful for groin or armpit injuries where a tourniquet is difficult to apply.

Pressure Dressings. After bleeding is controlled a bulky dressing, firmly secured with roller gauze, Ace wrap, or a strip of cloth or cravat, can provide pressure on the wound and free your hands for other tasks. Check the CSMs to make sure you have not inadvertently made a tourniquet.

Tourniquets. Tourniquets are rarely needed outside a combat situation, but in a case of obvious massive bleeding, or bleeding that can't be controlled by direct pressure, they are the appropriate tool. A commercial tourniquet is best, but in a pinch, a tourniquet can be improvised.

How to Apply an Improvised Tourniquet

1. Once you've determined that a tourniquet is necessary, apply it as close to the injury as possible, between the wound and the heart. Use a bandage that is 3 to 4 inches wide. Never use wire, rope, or any material that will cut the skin.
2. Wrap the bandage snugly around the extremity several times, then tie an overhand knot.
3. Place a small stick or similar object on the knot, and tie another overhand knot over the stick.
4. Twist the stick until the bandage becomes tight enough to stop the bleeding. There should be no pulse and no bleeding distal to the wound. Tie the ends of the bandage around the extremity to keep the twists from unraveling.
5. Using a pen, write "TK" on the patient's forehead and the time the tourniquet was applied. Once it is in place, do not remove the tourniquet. It should remain in place until the patient arrives at the emergency room.
6. There are ongoing arguments about tourniquet release in wilderness medicine. Definitive statements are likely to remain elusive. Check with your physician advisor about this issue.
7. Patients treated with a tourniquet should be rapidly evacuated.

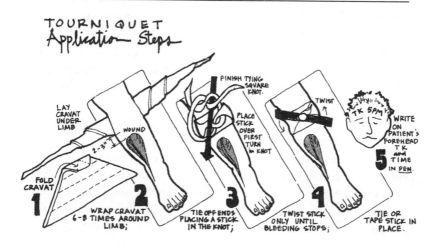

TOURNIQUET
Application Steps

LAY CRAVAT UNDER LIMB

FOLD CRAVAT

1 WRAP CRAVAT 6-8 TIMES AROUND LIMB;

WOUND

2-3"

FINISH TYING SQUARE KNOT.

PLACE STICK OVER FIRST TURN in KNOT

3 TIE OFF ENDS PLACING A STICK IN THE KNOT;

TWIST

4 TWIST STICK ONLY UNTIL BLEEDING STOPS;

TK 5PM WRITE ON PATIENT'S FOREHEAD TK and TIME IN PEN.

5

TIE OR TAPE STICK IN PLACE.

Clean the Wound. Consider any wound, even a minor finger cut or a blister, as potentially infected. On wilderness expeditions, wound cleaning is a priority.

Wash Your Hands and Put on Gloves. Wash your hands using soap and water to prevent contamination of the wound. Put on medical gloves.

Scrub and Irrigate the Wound. Scrub the skin around the wound, being careful not to flush debris into the wound. Clip long hair, but don't shave the skin. Then, irrigate an open wound with water that has been disinfected and is safe to drink. Many wounds can be cleaned simply by irrigating with clean water; usually a half to a full liter. If the wound is obviously dirty or contaminated, a suitable irrigation solution is 1-percent povidone-iodine (usually one part 10-percent povidone-iodine diluted with ten parts water) to resemble the color of dark tea. Medical science tells us that the volume of water is the most important factor in cleaning the wound. A 35cc syringe is a useful tool for pressure irrigating wounds. Remove large pieces of debris with tweezers that have been boiled or cleaned with povidone-iodine.

Rinse with Disinfected Water. After cleaning the wound, rinse the solution with liberal amounts of disinfected water. (See Chapter 24, "Hygiene and Water Disinfection.") Check for further bleeding and apply direct pressure if blood clots were broken loose during the cleaning process and bleeding has resumed.

Dress and Bandage the Wound. Dressings are sterile gauze placed directly over the wound, held in place by bandages. Both come in many shapes and sizes. Some are semi-occlusive (Telfa) or occlusive (Second Skin, Opsite, Tegaderm); some are fabrics designed to absorb fluid and wound exudate; some are simple gauze.

Cleaning Wounds

- Wash your hands with soap and water.
- Put on medical gloves.
- Scrub and irrigate the wound.
  —Scrub the area around the wound.
  —Use sterilized tweezers to remove debris.
  —Use pressure irrigation.
- Rinse thoroughly with disinfected water.
- Dress and bandage the wound.
- Check circulation, sensation, and movement.

Antibiotic ointment, such as Polysporin or Bacitracin, can be applied to a gauze dressing rather than directly to the wound. The ointment-impregnated gauze may help prevent infection and keep the wound moist. Apply the bandage to secure the dressing neatly and in such a way that blood flow distal to the injured area is not impaired. After applying the bandage, check CSMs distal to the injury.

Wounds heal best if moist, not wet or dry. A wound may continue to weep blood or fluid, soaking the dressing. Change these sodden dressings to keep the wound clean and moist, rather than dirty and wet. Dressings may need to be changed multiple times in an extended-care scenario.

Do not close wound edges until the wound has been thoroughly cleaned. Generally, the edges of a small wound will come together on their own. If the skin is stretched apart, butterfly bandages or Steri-strips can hold the edges together. If the injury is over a joint, the extremity may require splinting to prevent the edges from pulling apart. Contaminated wounds should be packed open.

Physicians don't agree on how long a wound can be kept open until it is stitched and will evaluate a wound for sutures based on how old it is, the viability of the edges of the wound, its depth, location, and other factors. A wound that will not close on its own or with a bandage can usually be stitched as much as a day or two later. By itself, the need to use sutures to close a wound does not constitute an emergency. Reasons to expedite an evacuation for an open wound include obvious dirt or contamination; animal bites; wounds that open joint spaces; established infection; wounds from a crushing mechanism; any laceration to a cosmetic area, especially the face; wounds with a lot of dead tissue on the edges or in the wound itself; and wounds that obviously need surgical care, such as open fractures and very deep, gaping lacerations.

Animal bites create a concern for infection because of the microbial flora in animal mouths and the crushing, penetrating, and tearing mechanism of the wounds.

After the Bandage Is Applied. Dressings should ideally be changed daily and the injured area checked for signs of infection. Check circulation, sensation, and movement of the body part distal to the injury. Can the patient tell you where you are touching? Can they flex and extend the extremity? Does the area distal to the injury have good blood perfusion? Any negative answers to these questions may indicate nerve, artery, or tendon damage that will require evacuating the patient rapidly.

Infection
The media occasionally tell dramatic tales of aggressive drug resistant infections and "flesh-eating bacteria." But aside from those stories, on a daily basis outside the wilderness we give little thought to the potential for wounds to be contaminated and colonized by microbes. Before modern medicine understood infection and practiced clean wound care, infections were common and dangerous. In the wilderness, we have less-than-ideal

---

Signs and Symptoms of Infections

MILD/MODERATE INFECTIONS
- Redness and swelling
- Pus, heat, pain

SERIOUS INFECTIONS
- Red streaks radiating from the wound
- Fever and chills
- Swollen lymph nodes

KEY POINTS
- Any soft tissue problem is at high risk for infection in a wilderness environment.
- Any area of redness should be watched closely during the first 12 to 24 hours.
- Always think, "Is this an infection?"
- Oral antibiotics should be started early.
- Additional measures, including applied heat and elevation/immobilization, are important.

---

circumstances for cleaning wounds. Nevertheless, our efforts are essential in preventing wound infection.

Assessment for Infection. Redness, swelling, pus, heat, and pain at the site; faint red streaks radiating from the site; fever; chills; and swollen lymph nodes are all signs of infection.

It may be difficult to decide if local swelling without an obvious wound is due to a muscle strain, bug bite, or infection. The possibility of a deep infection is a concern. History may help rule out the muscle strain.

The four cardinal signs of a soft-tissue infection are redness, swelling, warmth, and local pain. An increase in a wound of pain, warmth, swelling, and redness over 12 to 24 hours suggests infection. Drawing a circle around the swollen area with a pen will help you determine if the infection is spreading or resolving.

Treatment of Infection. An infection localized to the site of the injury can be treated in the field. If the edges of the wound are closed, pull them apart and soak the area in warm antiseptic solution or warm water for 20 to 30 minutes, three to four times a day. If the infection starts to spread—as evidenced by fever, chills, swollen lymph nodes, or faint red streaks radiating from the site—or if the wound cannot be opened to drain, evacuate the patient. If you have oral antibiotics and a protocol for their use, start them early in suspected wound infections.

Treatment for Infected Wounds

- Soak in warm antiseptic solution.
- Pull wound edges apart and clean wound.

Blisters

Blisters, a common backcountry occurrence, can be debilitating. Layers of skin rubbing against each other on the inside of the boot can cause an irritation known as a "hot spot." If the skin layers separate and fill with lymph fluid, a blister may form. A number of things go on inside our boots to form blisters. Pressure on skin and underlying soft tissue reduces blood flow and affects cell metabolism; tight boots or pressure points can exacerbate the problem. Shearing forces from many steps can mechanically separate and damage layers of skin. Wet skin may shear more easily; moist skin resists blisters. Hot skin may also shear more easily. Underlying soft and connective tissue can help an area of skin resist blistering; an area without much soft-tissue padding, such as the heel or the palms of our hands, may be more vulnerable.

The First Step: Prevention. Prevent blisters by making sure boots fit properly, wearing two pairs of socks to decrease friction on the skin, checking feet frequently at rest breaks, changing to dry socks, and stopping at the first sign of rubbing.

Hot Spots. These are not benign; they are an indication of skin damage. They are not a warning but already a problem. Pad with Moleskin or other medical tapes as a buffer against further rubbing. Paper tape or a lubricant under the tape can prevent the skin from tearing when the tape is removed (the stickier the tape, the more the risk for tearing.) Many of the modern blister prevention products will work well.

Small Blisters. Clean the blister and surrounding skin to prevent infection and help the tape stick. Bandage open blisters with a Moleskin donut hole filled with 2nd Skin or antibiotic ointment. Cover closed blisters with 2nd Skin, Blist-o-Ban, or similar product. Cover with duct, medical, or athletic tape, or Moleskin.

Larger Blisters. If the blister is nickel sized or larger, or obviously tense and ready to rupture, drain it. Begin by carefully washing your hands and putting on medical gloves. Clean the area around the blister to decrease the risk of infection. Use a needle that has been soaked in an antiseptic solution, such as povidone-iodine, or heated until it glows red and then allowed to air-cool. Insert the needle at the base of the blister, allowing the fluid to drain from the pinprick. After draining the blister, apply an antibiotic ointment and cover the area with gauze. As with an intact blister, center a doughnut-shaped piece of Moleskin over the drained blister and gauze. Follow up by checking the blister every day for signs of infection.

FINAL THOUGHTS

NOLS has had great success in reducing the number of people who need to be evacuated for preventable wound infections by focusing on initial wound cleaning, good dressing and bandaging, and recognition and early intervention for infections. These simple skills are at the core of wilderness medicine.

Evacuation Guidelines
- Evacuate an infection without improvement within 12 to 24 hours.
- Evacuate any patient with a wound that cannot be cleaned or closed in the field or is not healing.
- Rapidly evacuate a wound that is heavily contaminated, opens a joint space, involves underlying tendons or ligaments, was caused by an animal bite or a crushing mechanism, is on the face, has an impaled/imbedded object, or shows evidence of serious/systemic infection.

CHAPTER 8

BURNS

INTRODUCTION

In the wilderness, the obvious mechanisms for a burn are the sun, stoves, lanterns, and fires. Improper stove use has caused stoves to flare or pressure caps to release and flame, burning unwary cooks. However, other than sunburn, the most common causes of burns on NOLS expeditions are scalds from spilled hot water.

Minor burns may seem no more than a trivial nuisance, but they represent a potential site of infection. Burns of joints, feet, hands, face, and genitalia are particularly serious, due to the complexity of these structures and, in the case of the face, the critical importance of the airway. Anywhere on the body, a large burn compromises the body's ability to prevent fluid loss, and may rapidly cause shock.

TYPES OF BURNS

There are four types of burns: thermal, chemical, radiation, and electrical.

Thermal Burns

Thermal burns are caused by flames, flashes of heat (as in explosions), hot liquids, or contact with hot objects. The degree of associated tissue death depends on the intensity of the heat and the length of exposure. Water at 140°F (59°C) will burn skin in 5 seconds; water at 120°F (48°C) in 5 minutes.

Chemical Burns
Chemical burns are caused by contact with alkalis, acids, or corrosive material. Backcountry chemical burns are rare, but leaking batteries or spilled stove fuel are possible causes.

Radiation and Electrical Burns
Radiation burns in the wilderness are most commonly caused by the sun, and electrical burns by lightning.

ASSESSMENT OF BURNS

The assessment of a burn includes describing the depth and extent of the injury.

Depth of the Burn
Burns are classified by the depth of the injury as either superficial, partial-thickness, or full-thickness.
   Superficial. These burns injure only the epidermis. A superficial burn is red and painful, blanches with pressure, and does not blister. The area heals in 4 or 5 days with the epidermis peeling.
   Partial-Thickness. Deeper burns injure both the epidermis and the dermis, and can be painful. The skin appears red, mottled, wet, and blistered, and blanches with pressure. Blisters can develop quickly after the injury but may take as long as 24 hours to form. The burn takes from 5 to 25 days to heal, longer if it becomes infected.
   Full-Thickness. These burns penetrate deep and injure the epidermis, dermis, and subcutaneous tissue. The skin appears leathery, charred, pearl gray, and dry (or lighter and firm if it's a thermal burn). The area is sunken and has a burned odor. The skin does not blanch and is not painful because blood vessels and nerve endings are destroyed. Painful superficial or partial thickness burns may surround the full-thickness burn area.

ASSESSMENT of BURNS :

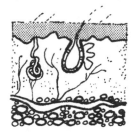

SUPERFICIAL
EPIDERMIS ONLY BURNED
- SKIN RED, PAINFUL

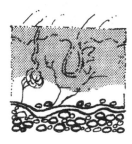

PARTIAL THICKNESS
EPIDERMIS AND DERMIS BURNED
- SKIN BLISTERED (MAY TAKE 24 HOURS +)
- RED, MOTTLED, WET, PAINFUL

FULL THICKNESS
EPIDERMIS, DERMIS AND
SUBCUTANEOUS TISSUE BURNED
- LEATHERY, DRY, CHARRED
- PEARLY GRAY in COLOR

Full-thickness burns destroy the dermis and, if large, require skin grafts to heal.

Extent of the Burn: The Rule of Palms
The extent of burns can be determined by the rule of palms. The area created by holding together the patient's palm and fingers represents 1 percent of their body surface area. Using the patient's palm as a size indicator, estimate the percentage of body area involved.

Location of the Burn

In addition to cosmetic concerns, burns to the face and neck create potentially dangerous airway problems. Burns to the hands and feet are worrisome due to possible loss of function. Burns to the genitals are serious for obvious reasons. Circumferential burns of extremities can produce a constriction that impairs circulation distal to the burn.

TREATMENT FOR BURNS

Thermal, electrical, radiation, and chemical burns are all treated essentially the same way. First, the source of the burn must be eliminated. Then, the airway should be checked. The burn itself is then cooled, assessed, cleaned, and dressed.

TREATMENT FOR THERMAL BURNS

Put Out the Fire. "Stop, drop, and roll" is the sequence to follow if someone catches fire. Stop the person from running. Make them drop to the ground and roll, or roll the person in a sleeping bag or jacket to put out the flames.

Quickly remove the patient's clothing and any jewelry. These retain heat and cause continued burning. Hot water spilled on legs clothed in polypropylene or wool can cause serious burns, as can water spilled into boots, because the boot and sock retain and concentrate the heat.

Check the Airway. Inhalation burns are life threatening and must be recognized early.

Cool the Burn. Smaller burns can be cooled by pouring cool water (not ice-cold) or applying cool wet cloths on the burned site. Avoid hypothermia. Never put ice directly on the site, as it may cause frostbite. Ice also causes blood vessels to constrict, which deprives the burned area of blood, and therefore oxygen and nutrients. Cool a burn for approximately 10 minutes. The cessation of pain is a good endpoint.

Assess the Depth and Extent of the Burn. Most burns are combinations of partial and superficial injuries. Assess the surface area of each burn type using the rule of palms. Monitoring and re-assessment of burns is important; as with frostbite, the depth of the injury may not be immediately apparent and may reveal itself over time.

    Clean and Dress the Burn. Clean the burn with cool, clean water and apply antibiotic ointment. Embers or smoldering clothing on the surface should be removed; do not attempt to remove melted material from the skin. Moist dressings are fine for small burns (< 3 percent of body surface area). Use dry dressings on extensive burns. Change the dressing once a day and monitor the site for signs of infection. Blisters should be kept intact. If they do rupture, gently wash them with antiseptic soap and water, rinse well, pat dry, and cover with sterile gauze.

TREATMENT FOR INHALATION BURNS

Inhalation burns are caused by breathing hot air, gases, and / or particles. The cilia (hairlike structures lining the upper airways) and mucous membranes lining the respiratory tract may be destroyed. The mucous membranes swell, and fluid leaks into the lungs. The body is unable to expel mucus because the cilia are damaged. Mucus collects in the upper airway, decreasing exchange of carbon dioxide and oxygen. Oxygenation is impaired when carbon monoxide from burning material competes with oxygen for binding sites on red blood cells.

    If you suspect an inhalation burn, check the mouth, nose, and throat for signs of soot, redness, or swelling. Are the facial hairs or nasal hairs singed? Check for signs of respiratory distress, such as coughing or noisy, rapid breaths.

    Inhalation burns always require evacuating the patient to a medical facility. Signs and symptoms of respiratory distress may not become apparent for 24 to 48 hours.

TREATMENT FOR CHEMICAL BURNS

Flush chemical burns with any available water for a minimum of 20 minutes. Brush off any dry chemical before rinsing the burn. Remove clothing, jewelry, and contact lenses, as these may retain the chemical and continue to burn the victim.

Speed is important. The longer a chemical stays on the body, the more damage it causes. Looking for specific antidotes wastes time. Use plain water to flush, then wash the burn with mild soap and water.

Rinse a chemically burned eye with water for at least 20 minutes. After flushing the affected eye, cover it with a moist dressing. After 20 to 30 minutes, remove the dressing. If the patient complains of changes in vision, reapply the dressing and evacuate.

Treatment for Burns

- Remove the source of the burn:
  —For thermal burns, stop, drop, roll.
  —For dry chemical burns, brush off dry chemicals.
  —For wet chemical burns, flush with water for 20 minutes.
- Remove clothing and jewelry.
- Assess the airway.
- Cool the burn.
- Assess the depth and extent of the burn.
- Clean the burn.
- Apply a dressing.

TREATMENT FOR RADIATION BURNS

Most skin damage is caused by short wavelengths of ultraviolet radiation (UVA and UVB). UVB causes more sunburn than UVA, but both wavelengths damage skin. The only known beneficial effect of solar radiation on skin relates to the metabolism of vitamin D. Long-term exposure to the sun increases your risk of skin cancer.

Two-thirds of ultraviolet radiation is received during the hours of 10:00 A.M. to 2:00 P.M. At high altitude, the thin atmosphere filters out less ultraviolet radiation and the skin is damaged more quickly. Snowfields reflect 70 to 85 percent of the ultraviolet radiation. Water reflects 2 percent when the sun is directly overhead and more when the sun is lower. Grass reflects 1 to 2 percent. Mountaineering at high altitudes, especially on snow, increases the risk of sun-related problems. Clouds filter out infrared heat radiation and your skin feels cooler, but ultraviolet radiation continues to pass through and the risk of sun exposure still exists.

Sunburn

People with fair skin are susceptible to burning. Darker skin contains more of the protective pigment melanin but does not eliminate the chance of sunburn or provide protection against the cumulative effects of sun exposure.

Unprotected skin can receive superficial or partial-thickness burns from the sun. Exposure to UV radiation often causes fever blisters or cold sores in people with a herpes simplex (viral) infection. These infections can be quite painful. A patient with extensive sunburn may complain of chills, fever, or headache.

Phototoxic Reactions. A phototoxic reaction is an abnormally severe sunburn related to the ingestion of a drug, plant, or chemical, or the application of a drug, plant, or chemical to the skin. Certain drugs, such as sulfonamides (Bactrim, Septra), tetracyclines (Vibramycin), oral diabetic agents, and tranquilizers (Thorazine, Compazine, Phenergan, Sparine) increase the skin's sensitivity to sunlight. Plants that may cause phytophotodermatitis from the interaction of a chemical on the surface of the plant and sunlight include: carrots, celery, citrus fruits (most commonly limes), and wild parsley.

Treatment of Sunburned Skin. Cool, wet dressings will relieve some of the pain. Aspirin, ibuprofen, or related nonsteroidal anti-inflammatory drugs are recommended. Anesthetic sprays and ointments may relieve the pain but increase the risk of a phototoxic reaction.

Prevention with Sunscreens. Exposure to the sun in small doses promotes tanning, which protects the skin from burns. Unfortunately, degenerative changes still occur in the skin, so it is best to use sunscreens or sunblocks and to wear broad-brimmed hats, long-sleeve shirts, and long pants.

Sunscreens are rated by their sun protection factor (SPF). The SPF number is a guideline for the length of time a person wearing the sunscreen can spend in the sun. SPF is based on the minimal "erythemal dose," or the length of time before the exposed skin becomes red. For example, a person without sunscreen may be able to spend 30 minutes safely in the sun. Applying a sunscreen with an SPF of 10 should allow the same person

---

Tips for Preventing Sun-Related Injury: Don't Sunburn!
1. Apply sunscreen 30 minutes before going out, and reapply it frequently.
2. Apply sunblock to your lips, nose, and other sensitive areas.
3. Wear a hat with a brim.
4. Wear sunglasses with 100 percent UV protection, even on cloudy days.
5. Minimize sun exposure between 10:00 A.M. and 2:00 P.M.
6. Wear a long-sleeve shirt and pants.
7. Examine your skin, and see a physician if you notice a mole changing shape, color, or size, or if you have a "sore" that won't heal.

---

to spend 10 times as long in the sun, or 300 minutes before the skin turns red. This system assumes that the sunscreen is not washed off by water or sweat and is used in adequate amounts.

Creams that completely block ultraviolet radiation (zinc oxide, A-Fil, red veterinarian petrolatum) are good for areas that are easily burned, such as the nose, ears, and lips. Use a sunscreen that guards against both UVB and UVA radiation— the label should explain the coverage of the sunscreen. Most people do not apply enough sunscreen and do not apply it often enough. Sunscreens should be still applied on cloudy or overcast days, as the ultraviolet radiation that penetrates cloud cover is often great enough to burn the skin. Sunscreens work better if applied when the skin is warm and allowed to soak in for half an hour before sun exposure. It's a good habit to apply sunscreen well before you are exposed.

Snow Blindness (UV Photokeratitis)
Burning of the cornea and conjunctiva by the sun is called snow blindness. The urban version of this injury is the eye irritation a welder can suffer. Affected people aren't actually blind, but they're reluctant to open their eyes because of the pain. The eyes feel dry, as if they are full of sand. Moving, blinking, or opening the eyes is painful. The eyes are red and tear excessively. This can happen with as little as an hour of exposure to bright sunlight. Symptoms may not develop for 8 to 12 hours after the eyes have been exposed to the sun.

Treatment. Snow blindness heals spontaneously in several days. Cold compresses, pain medication, and a dark environment relieve the pain. Don't rub the eyes or put anesthetics in them, as these can damage the cornea.

Sunglasses, especially those with side blinders, decrease the ultraviolet radiation received by the eyes and prevent snow blindness. If you lose your sunglasses, make temporary ones from two pieces of cardboard with slits cut in them to see through. Wear sunglasses even when it's cloudy.

FINAL THOUGHTS

The American Burn Association and the American College of Surgeons classify burns by depth and extent. They recommend treating partial and full thickness burns greater than 10 percent of the body surface area at a dedicated burn center. We often evacuate smaller burns due to patient discomfort, worry about infection, inadequate amounts of first aid materials to handle daily dressing changes, and inability to use the injured body part.

A patient with burns of the face may also have inhalation burns. Partial- and full-thickness burns of the hands and feet may require special treatment to preserve function, and burns of the groin may produce enough swelling to prevent urination. Burns completely encircling a limb may cut off circulation. Burns, like other soft-tissue wounds, must be kept clean to reduce the risk of infection.

Burns are serious injuries, more easily prevented than treated. Keep safety in mind at all times, especially when around fires and stoves.

Clothing provides portable shade and simple sunburn prevention. A brimmed hat shades the face and neck. Long-sleeve shirts and pants protect skin from the sun. Develop the habit of putting on sunscreen early and often.

Evacuation Guidelines
Evacuate all full-thickness burns. Consider evacuating partial-thickness burns, especially to the hands, feet, face, armpits, or groin, for pain management and wound care.

- Rapidly evacuate any patient with partial- or full-thickness burns covering more than 10 percent of total body surface area (TBSA); any patient with partial- or full-thickness circumferential burns; and any patient with signs and symptoms of airway burns.

ENVIRONMENTAL INJURIES

The wilderness environment that gives us so much enjoyment can also threaten our health with heat and cold, dangerous creatures and plants, altitude, and lightning. NOLS incident data shows that sound leadership and outdoor skill keeps us healthy in the wilderness. This section discusses treatment principles to guide our first aid for heat illnesses, frostbite, hypothermia, altitude illness, submersion, and unwanted interactions with noxious animals, insects, and plants. The experienced outdoor leader knows it is easier to stay warm than to warm the hypothermic patient, easier to stay cool than to treat heatstroke in the field, easier to avoid snakebite than to deal with an envenomation. In this vein, the discussions of these topics share tips for the most important first aid skill, prevention.

CHAPTER 9 | COLD INJURIES

INTRODUCTION

On a snowy subzero morning in early November, after 2 days of searching, a lost hunter was found in the Wind River Mountains south of Lander, Wyoming. His nose, hands, feet, and stomach were frostbitten, and he showed limited signs of life. After a several hour evacuation by snow litter and four-wheel drive, rescuers delivered him to the emergency room with a rectal temperature of 74°F (23°C).

His ordeal was not yet over. The hypothermia had caused his heart to stop, and only after 3 hours of warming and CPR did he begin to recover. The media presented his story as a "miraculous" survival, which is accurate, but the miracle was founded on the skill and teamwork of the rescuers and medical providers.

THE PHYSIOLOGY OF TEMPERATURE REGULATION

Humans are warm-blooded animals; we maintain a relatively constant internal temperature regardless of the environmental temperature. The constant temperature allows human cells, tissues and organs, and especially the biological catalysts known as enzymes, to operate at peak efficiency only within narrow temperature limits. If your temperature rises 2°F above the normal 98.6°F (37°C), you become ill. If it rises 7°F, you become critically ill. If your temperature decreases 2°F you feel cold. A 7°F decrease puts your life in jeopardy.

Humans are adapted to live in tropical climates; our heat-loss mechanisms are highly developed. Our insulation mechanisms, on the other hand, are less efficient. To adapt structurally to cold, our bodies would have to be covered with thick insulating hair and develop greater reserves of fat. Rather than remaining angular and cylindrical, which promotes heat loss, our body shape would become rounder and shorter to prevent heat loss. This would especially affect our ability to tolerate near-freezing temperatures in our fingers and toes.

We generate heat as one product of the process that converts oxygen and food into the chemical energy that powers body functions, but this by itself is not sufficient to keep us warm all winter.

Human beings can live in the cold because our intellectual responses enable us to deal effectively with environmental stress. We compensate for our physical deficiencies (e.g., lack of thick fur) with behavioral responses such as eating, drinking, and creating microclimates through the use of clothing, fire, and shelter. Much of what students learn on NOLS courses is how to live comfortably in extreme environmental conditions by employing skill, disciplined habits, and quality equipment. The diminished intellectual response evident in early stages of hypothermia dangerously impairs our ability to maintain the behaviors that allow us to cope with the environment.

Mechanisms of Heat Production

The three main physiological means for producing heat are metabolism, exercise, and shivering.

Resting Metabolism. Our resting or "basal" metabolic rate is like a constant internal furnace, generating heat as one product of the biochemical reactions that keep us alive. Metabolism is not an efficient means to convert the energy potential in food into work. As a result, much of the energy from metabolism is lost as heat. Because of the heat-generating effect of metabolism, our basal metabolic rate increases slightly when we are exposed to cold for long periods—but not enough to satisfy the body's entire heat requirement in winter conditions.

Exercise. Exercise is an important method of heat production. Muscles, which make up 50 percent of our body weight, produce 70 percent of the heat generated during work. Short bursts of hard physical effort can generate tremendous amounts of heat, while moderate levels of exercise can be sustained for long periods. However, physical conditioning, strength, stamina, and food and water are necessary to sustain activity. Food is the fuel for metabolism. Nutritionally sound rations and good cooking skills are critical to health on wilderness expeditions, particularly in cold climates.

Shivering. Shivering—a random quivering of muscles—produces heat at a rate five times greater than the basal metabolic rate. Shivering occurs when temperature receptors in the skin and brain sense a decrease in body temperature and trigger the shivering response.

As with all forms of work, the price of shivering is fuel. How long and how effectively we shiver is limited by the amount of carbohydrates stored in muscles and by the amount of water and oxygen available. In order to shiver, we have to pump blood into the muscles. One side effect is that warm blood flowing close to the surface reduces our natural insulation and can increase heat loss.

Shivering also hinders our ability to perform the behavioral tasks necessary to reduce heat loss and increase heat production. It is difficult to zip up your parka, start your stove, or ski to camp during violent shivering. Vigorous physical activity can override the shivering response. If we don't capture the heat produced by vigorous exercise in insulating clothing, we can cool past the point of shivering without experiencing the response.

Mechanisms of Heat Loss

The core of the body contains the organs necessary for survival: heart, brain, lungs, liver, and kidneys. The shell consists of the muscles, skin, and superficial tissues. The ebb and flow of blood

RADIATION
TRANSFER OF HEAT FROM
A HOT OBJECT TO A COLD
OBJECT, WITHOUT DIRECT
CONTACT.

↑ HEAD WITHOUT HAT
ESPECIALLY GOOD AT
RADIATING HEAT

EVAPORATION
THROUGH
SWEAT, BREATHING

CONDUCTION
TRANSFER OF HEAT
THROUGH DIRECT
CONTACT.

HOT ←→ COLD

CONVECTION
HEAT LOST TO
MOVING AIR OR
WATER.

MECHANISMS OF Heat Loss

between core and superficial tissues is a constant process. As our temperature rises, blood volume shifts and carries heat to the outer layers of the skin. As we cool, less blood flows to the periphery, preserving heat for the vital organs.

Our mechanisms for heat loss are so well-developed that we lose heat in all but the hottest and most humid conditions. On a warm day, if we did not lose most of the heat our bodies produced, our body temperature would rise. The primary means of heat loss is through the skin. Warm, flushed skin can dispose of heat through conduction, convection, radiation, or evaporation.

The circulatory system controls heat by regulating the volume of blood flowing to the skin and superficial muscles. When we are resting comfortably, only a small percentage of blood flows directly to the skin. During heat stress, however, the blood vessels open up and blood flow to the skin may increase a hundredfold. During cold stress, blood is shunted from the periphery to the core, reducing the heat lost to the environment.

Constricted blood vessels can reduce blood flow to the skin by 99 percent.

Conduction. Conduction is the transfer of heat through direct contact between a hot and a cold object. Energy as heat moves from the warmer object to the colder. We lose heat when we lie on cold ground. We gain heat when we lie on a hot beach or rock. The rate of heat transfer is determined by the temperature difference between the two objects, the surface area involved, and the effectiveness of the insulation between the body and the surface. The more efficient the insulation, the less heat is transferred. Warm air trapped in clothing is an effective insulator. Water, metal, and snow are good conductors.

We reduce conductive heat loss every night by sleeping with a foam pad between our body and the ground. If we wake up cold, we often add insulation to that barrier before we put on more clothing. Damp cotton conducts heat. If we're cold and wearing a damp cotton shirt, we'll take it off. On winter expeditions, we place extra insoles in our boots, and in camp we stand on foam pads to reduce conduction between our feet and the snow.

Convection. Convective heat transfer is the transfer of heat due to the movement of fluids and gases. When we're in direct contact with cold moving air or water, heat escapes from the surface of the body by convection. The rate of heat transfer depends on the temperature difference between the warmer and the cooler body, the surface area in contact, and the speed at which the air or water is moving. Moving air, besides cooling us directly, strips away the microclimate of air heated by the body. The loss of this insulating layer next to the body further accelerates heat loss. Hence the term "wind chill."

To discover the cooling power of moving water, place your fingers in a bowl of cold water. Slowly swirl your fingers. The increase in heat loss is immediately perceptible. Immersion in cold water is a profound threat to temperature regulation.

Heat is transferred by convection through the body by the blood. As we cool and the body shunts blood away from the skin, the superficial tissues—especially in our fingers and toes— no longer gain heat from the blood, which reduces their feeling and function, and increases the likelihood of frostbite.

We reduce convective heat loss by wearing wind-resistant clothes such as tight-weave nylon jackets and pants, and hoods to protect the vulnerable head and neck.

Radiation. Radiation is emission of energy in the form of electromagnetic waves. With an average normal body temperature of 98°F (37°C), humans emit infrared radiation, losing heat in the process. Likewise, we receive radiative heat input from fires, from the sun directly, and from its reflection off snow, or, to a lesser extent, water and the ground.

Radiative heat loss makes clear nights colder than cloudy nights. Cloud cover reflects much of the Earth's radiative heat back to the ground, reducing the severity of the nighttime temperature drop. Reflected radiation bouncing off the walls and snowfields of a cirque during bright sunshine increases warmth, as well as the possibility of sunburn.

The skin acts as a radiator, and higher radiative heat loss occurs from uncovered skin, commonly on the hands, face, and head. Clothing reduces radiative heat loss.

Evaporation. When perspiration evaporates from the skin's surface, the change in state from liquid to gas transfers heat away from the body. Evaporative heat loss accounts for 20 percent of the body's total heat loss in normal conditions—much more when we are under heat stress or working hard. We use this to our advantage to cool ourselves in hot environments.

Sweating accounts for roughly two-thirds of evaporative heat loss. The remaining one-third is lost through breathing. Inhalation humidifies air and warms it to body temperature. During exhalation, evaporation of moisture from the surface of the lungs and airways uses heat and cools the body. The rate and depth of breathing and the humidity of the air determine the amount of heat and moisture lost. The colder and drier the air and the faster the breathing rate, the greater the heat loss.

We reduce evaporative heat loss by controlling our work rate, using techniques such as the rest step when mountaineering (walking with flat feet, transferring weight slowly and smoothly from one leg to the other), and avoiding hard breathing and sweating. Sweating in cold environments wets insulation and cools the body, and should be avoided.

HYPOTHERMIA

A constant balance of heat gain and loss is required to maintain a stable body temperature. The adjustments the body makes are designed to keep our vital organs—heart, brain, lungs, kidneys, and liver—within a temperature range in which they operate effectively. If core temperature rises above normal, potentially life-threatening conditions such as heatstroke or high fever develop. When core temperature drops below normal, hypothermia may result.

Hypothermia can develop whenever heat loss exceeds heat gain, and is as common during the wind, rain, and hail of summer as it is during winter. Immersion in cold water can cause hypothermia. If body temperature drops as low as 80°F (26.4°C), death is likely.

Signs and Symptoms of Hypothermia

MILD HYPOTHERMIA
- Shivering, numb skin with goosebumps
- Minor impairment of muscular performance, e.g., stiff and clumsy fingers
- Mental deterioration begins: poor decisions, confused and sluggish thinking

MODERATE HYPOTHERMIA
- Stumbling, apathy, lethargy
- Obvious mental status changes; irritability, forgetfulness, and complaining
- Obvious muscular incoordination: stumbling, falling, and clumsy hands

SEVERE HYPOTHERMIA
- Energy reserves are depleted, shivering may cease.
- Obvious mental deterioration occurs (e.g., incoherence, disorientation, irrational behavior).
- As the body becomes cooler, heart and respiratory rate and blood pressure fall.
- Severe muscular rigidity may occur.
- The pulse may be undetectable, and the patient may appear to have stopped breathing or to have died.

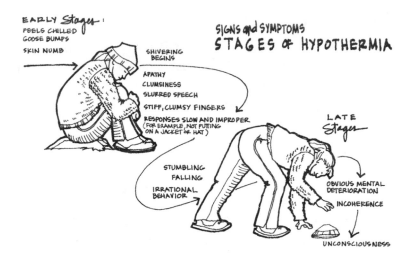

EARLY Stages:
FEELS CHILLED
GOOSE BUMPS
SKIN NUMB

SHIVERING
BEGINS

SIGNS and SYMPTOMS
STAGES OF HYPOTHERMIA

APATHY
CLUMSINESS
SLURRED SPEECH
STIFF, CLUMSY FINGERS
RESPONSES SLOW AND IMPROPER
(FOR EXAMPLE, NOT PUTTING
ON A JACKET OR HAT)

LATE
Stages

STUMBLING
FALLING
IRRATIONAL
BEHAVIOR

OBVIOUS MENTAL
DETERIORATION
INCOHERENCE

UNCONSCIOUSNESS

Signs and Symptoms of Hypothermia

As body temperature falls, mental functions decline and the patient loses the ability to respond appropriately to the environment. Responses are slow and/or improper, such as neglecting to change into dry clothes or put on a rain jacket or hat. Muscular functions deteriorate until the patient is too clumsy to walk or stand. Biochemical processes become slow and deficient as the body cools.

Recognizing Hypothermia (Assessment)

Hypothermia is easily overlooked. In cities, it has been mistaken for alcohol intoxication, stroke, and drug overdose. It may be associated with illnesses such as diabetes and other metabolic disturbances, or with the elderly and the homeless. In the wilderness, hypothermia has been confused with fatigue, irritability, dehydration, and mountain sickness.

You can measure the patient's temperature to detect hypothermia. Conventional thermometers may read down to only 94°F (34°C). Choose a low-reading hypothermia-specific thermometer for your medical kit. Oral or axillary (armpit) temperatures may not reflect the status of the core organs, so the most accurate results would be obtained via rectal temperature. However, obtaining a rectal temperature on a cold and confused patient can be awkward. In addition, undressing the patient to obtain a rectal reading may cause further cooling. For all these reasons, obtaining a rectal temperature is not practical and is rarely done in the wilderness.

Early signs and symptoms of hypothermia can be difficult to recognize. The patient does not feel well. You may assume that they are tired, rather than hypothermic. Yet this is the stage at which successful warming in the wilderness is possible. This patient may not be hypothermic by medical definition; that is, their core temperature may not yet have dropped significantly. The person may only be wet, cold, and unhappy. We need to recognize and address this as possible hypothermia in its early stage, when it is easiest to treat.

Hypothermia in its later stages may be more obvious. The patient is grossly uncoordinated with a clearly altered mental status. This stage of hypothermia is much harder to treat in the wilderness. Warming can be a long and complex process that takes hours, and it may be impossible in the backcountry.

Assessment of Hypothermia

MILD TO MODERATE
- Awake
- Shivering
- Able to walk
- Alert (altered mental status possible)

SEVERE
- Altered mental status
- No shivering
- Unable to walk

Because of this difficulty, if you suspect hypothermia, treat it immediately and aggressively, whether you can obtain a temperature or not. The most important diagnostic tool in the backcountry is the first responder's awareness of the possibility of hypothermia and attention to the patient's mental state. Anyone in a cool or cold environment is at risk for hypothermia. Persons with altered mental status (confused, slurred speech, disoriented) in the outdoors may be hypothermic.

Treatment of Mild to Moderate Hypothermia

A mildly hypothermic patient may be warmed in the field. In the absence of a serious underlying medical condition, the chances for successful warming are good. Although we can't change the weather, we can replace wet clothing with dry, protect the

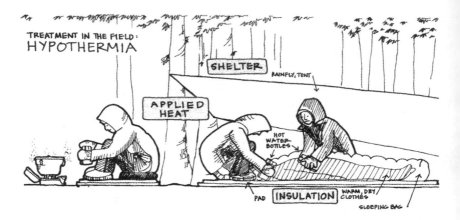

patient from the wind, add layers of insulation, hydrate and feed the patient, and apply heat. Mild or moderately hypothermic patients who can shiver and still produce heat will warm themselves if their body heat is captured by warm, dry, windproof insulation.

Change the Environment
Find shelter. Get out of the wind. Insulate the patient from cold ground. Remove the patient from water. We tend to cool slowly, so it is not necessary to do these tactics in haste at the expense of scene risk management, but they should be done promptly.

Prevent further heat loss
- Dress the patient in dry clothing, including a hat to reduce heat loss from the head and neck. For mild hypothermia, this and a hot drink are often all the treatment that's needed.
- A sleeping bag in a "hypothermia wrap" is the backcountry responder's tried and true warming tool. Place the patient into a sleeping bag with a foam pad underneath. If you have extra sleeping bags, use them. The patient should be in dry clothing, as even damp undergarments can slow the rate of warming since the patient must first use energy to dry the clothing.

- This whole package is wrapped "burrito style" in a tarp or plastic sheet to insulate from wind and moisture loss.
- If you are without a sleeping bag, dress the patient in dry clothes for insulation, and wind or waterproof clothing as a vapor barrier.
- Fires can be an excellent source of heat.

In a harsh environment, especially if the patient is wet, your best or only treatment option may be to wrap the patient and transport to a controlled environment. If dry clothes are not immediately at hand, a wet patient may need to be wrapped in a vapor barrier before insertion in a sleeping bag to keep insulation dry until a proper hypothermia wrap can be crafted. The hypothermia wrap with hot water bottles is a more effective practice than putting another person in the bag. It can be hard to close a sleeping bag tightly around two people. In addition, the warmer is not available for other tasks such as setting up camp and preparing food, and can quickly become cold and fatigued. Experts disagree on the amount of heat actually transferred body to body—some think it's low. As such, the value of a warm person in the sleeping bag may be to heat the insulation, rather than to transfer heat directly to the patient. The warm person may also suppress shivering in the cold person, making them feel more comfortable, but at the same time, the cold person forfeits this effective means of heat production.

Add Heat
Heat packs or hot water bottles may be helpful sources of heat. Apply the hot water bottles to yourself first to make sure they are not too hot, then wrap these carefully so as to avoid burning the patient. The first hot water bottle usually goes into the patient's hands to hold on the chest. This may warm the core, as well as the hands. The next hot water bottle goes by the feet to prevent frostbite.

Add Calories
Warm drinks are a source of heat, fluid, and sugar. The patient must be alert and able to hold the drink and consume it under

their own power. Warm drinks and simple foods, such as candy bars, can be followed by a good meal after the patient is warmed. A fatigued or dehydrated patient is a strong candidate for another episode of hypothermia. Keep the patient insulated and resting until energy and fluid reserves have been replenished. It's best to keep the warmed patient in the sleeping bag for a good night's sleep, and to give them a hot meal and several liters of water.

Exercise

Movement produces heat. In a patient who can stand, balance and is alert, light exercise when they are well-insulated can capture the heat produced and be a valuable warming tool. If the patient is in moderate to severe hypothermia, movement can trigger afterdrop, a further lowering of core temperature and a cause of cardiac events. These patients should be handled gently.

Be Persistent: *Warming Takes Time.* Individuals such as the hunter described in the introduction have recovered from prolonged, profound hypothermia. Newspaper headlines occasionally describe "frozen" and "dead" people who were successfully warmed. The adage to remember about hypothermia treatment is that "the victim is never dead until they are warm and dead."

Treatment of Severe Hypothermia

A severely hypothermic patient produces little or no heat, and in the absence of external heat sources may cool further. There may be complications from an underlying medical condition or trauma and complex disturbances in the body's biochemical balance. A cold heart is susceptible to abnormal rhythms such as ventricular fibrillation, a random quivering of the heart that interferes with its ability to pump blood. Jarring or bouncing, almost inevitable in transport from the backcountry, can trigger this arrhythmia. Attempts at care can lead to further harm; victims who seem fine when pulled from water can suddenly deteriorate, especially if they are allowed to walk or are warmed aggressively. A severely hypothermic patient has significantly reduced blood flow from their extremities, which has the effect of trapping cold blood away from the core. A sudden change in activity level or posture can allow that cold blood to enter the body core, causing a temperature afterdrop. Conversely, shock may result from blood vessels opening after the pressure of the water is removed. Avoid by handling the victim gently and keeping them horizontal.

Field warming of severe hypothermia is unrealistic. Evacuation of a severely hypothermic patient must occur simultaneously with attempts to prevent further cooling. Use a hypothermia wrap. Apply heat to the patient during transport to prevent further cooling. Monitor ABCs and vitals.

It may be difficult to find the pulse or respiration rate of a severely hypothermic patient. The heart rate may be twenty to thirty beats per minute and the breathing rate only three to four times a minute. Take your time during assessment. Check the heartbeat and breathing for at least 1 minute, carefully watching for the rise and fall of the chest, listening for any breath sounds, and feeling for the pulse at the neck with warm fingers. Ideally, use a cardiac monitor to assess heart rhythm. If in doubt, withhold chest compression and perform rescue breathing.

FROSTBITE

Frostbite is the freezing of tissue, most commonly seen on fingers, toes, and ears. Fluid between cells can freeze, and the formation of ice crystals draws water out of the cells. Mechanical cell damage also occurs as the crystals rub together. Blood clots form in small vessels and circulation stops, further damaging cells.

A second phase of injury occurs during warming. Damaged cells release substances that promote constriction and clotting in small blood vessels, impairing blood flow to the tissues and causing further damage. Frostbite is not

Causes of Frostbite
- Cold stress
- Low temperatures
- Moisture
- Poor insulation
- Contact with supercooled metal or gasoline
- Interference with circulation of blood:
  —Cramped position
  —Tight clothing (gaiters, wristwatches, etc.)
  —Tight boots
  —Dehydration

life threatening, but tissue damage from frostbite can result in loss of function and amputation.

For first aid purposes, frostbite is classified as superficial (also known as frostnip), partial thickness, and deep or full thickness. However, the degree of damage can be difficult to assess until the frostbite has thawed.

Assessment of Frostbite

In frostnip or superficial frostbite, only the outer layer of skin is frozen. It appears white and waxy, or possibly gray or mottled. High winds together with cold temperatures can lead to frostnip on exposed areas of the face, nose, ears, and cheeks.

After the nipped area is warmed, the layer of frozen skin becomes red. Over a period of several days the dead skin peels.

Partial-thickness frostbite has progressed into the underlying tissues. It may feel hard on the surface, soft and resilient below. Blisters usually appear within 24 hours after warming.

The most serious form is deep or full-thickness frostbite. The injury extends from the skin into the underlying tissues and muscles. The external appearance is the same as frostnip and partial-thickness frostbite, but the frozen area feels hard with no underlying resilience. After thawing, the area may not blister or may blister only where deep frostbite borders on more superficial damage.

Signs and Symptoms of Frostbite

All forms of frostbite can look similar:
- The skin is cold, waxy, and pale or mottled.
- There can be tingling, numbness, or pain.
- The tissue may be soft if partially frozen, or hard if frozen.
- Blisters may form if the frostbite has been thawed.

Differentiating partial-thickness from deep frostbite before thawing is difficult, and the extent of the injury may not be apparent for days. Blisters containing clear fluid, extending to the tips of the digits and forming within 48 hours of warming, suggest partial-thickness frostbite. Blood-filled blisters that don't reach the tips of the digits, delayed blisters, or the lack of blisters indicate deep frostbite.

Treatment of Frostbite

Frostnip or small areas of partial-thickness frostbite can be warmed by skin-to-skin warming (discussed below). Larger areas of possible partial-thickness frostbite and all full-thickness frostbite should be treated with rapid warming by immersion in warm water between 99° to 102°F (37° to 39°C). Dangerous folk remedies for frostbite include rubbing the frozen part with snow, massaging the area to restore circulation, and exposing it to an open flame. Many people, including the author, have traveled long distances with frozen feet in order to reach a place where warming could be done once and done well. Tissue damage seems to be related to the length of time the tissue stays frozen, but how long the tissue can be kept frozen without increasing the damage is a matter of controversy. Do not keep tissue frozen any longer than necessary.

There are several practical problems with keeping a frost-bitten extremity frozen while evacuation takes place. Unintentional slow warming is common and often unavoidable. If the injury occurred from exposure to extreme cold, lack of proper clothing, or in conjunction with hypothermia, the frostbitten area may warm slowly as the underlying problem is corrected. The activity of traveling may generate enough heat to begin thawing. Thus, while warming in warm water is ideal, skin-to-skin warming may be most practical.

Skin-to-Skin Warming. If the injury is confined to a small area of the body, such as tips of toes or fingers, slow thawing is likely unavoidable. Fast warming is preferred, so skin-to-skin warming, hands under armpits, or feet on your companion's belly should be started.

Rapidly Warm in Warm Water. The ideal treatment for frostbite—best done in a hospital—is rapid warming in water between 99° and 102°F (37° and 39°C). Ideally, use a thermometer to ensure proper water temperature. For a rough estimate, 105°F (40°C) is hot tap water. Cooler water will not thaw frostbite rapidly. Hotter water is very painful and may burn the patient.

Water temperature should remain constant throughout the procedure. This requires a source of hot water and a container large enough to hold the entire frozen part. Do not pour hot water over the frozen tissue. Rather, immerse the frozen area, being careful not to let it touch the sides or bottom of the container. When the water cools, remove the frostbitten part, quickly warm the water, and re-immerse the part.

Thawing frozen fingers generally takes 45 minutes. There is no danger of over-thawing, but under-thawing can leave tissue permanently damaged. A flush of pink indicates blood returning to the affected site. Warming frostbite is generally very painful. NSAIDs (non-steroidal anti-inflammatories) such as aspirin or ibuprofen are appropriate for pain relief. If hypothermia is present, it takes priority in treatment.

Post-thaw Care. Air-dry the extremity carefully; don't rub. Swelling will occur, along with blister formation. Inserting gauze between the fingers or toes keeps these areas dry as swelling occurs. Blisters should be kept intact. Thawed tissue is delicate, and seemingly minor trauma can cause damage. NSAIDs may relieve pain and inflammation. Prevent freezing after thawing. The freeze–thaw–freeze sequence will produce permanent tissue damage.

NONFREEZING COLD INJURY

A nonfreezing cold injury (NFCI) results from exposure to continued wet, cold conditions that many outdoor recreationists avoid. Expeditions and military operations that spend extended periods in the field will often find periods with these conditions unavoidable. Understandably, much of what we know about nonfreezing cold injury—immersion foot or trench foot—comes from the military. In World War I, when the term "trench foot" was coined, the British Army experienced 29,000 immersion-foot casualties in the winter of 1915–1916; frostbite and immersion-foot casualties for U.S. forces in Europe in World War II totaled 90,000.

Nonfreezing injury is a local injury that occurs most commonly to the feet in cold, wet conditions, when blood vessels constrict in response to heat loss, reducing blood flow to the extremity and depriving cells of oxygen and nutrients. The ensuing injury may range from a few weeks of sore feet to permanent

---

Signs and Symptoms of Nonfreezing Cold Injury
• The skin is cold, swollen, shiny, and/or mottled.
• Tingling, numbness, or pain may be present.
• Capillary refill time is slow.
• After warming, skin may be warm, red, swollen, and painful.
• In severe cases, blisters, ulcers, and gangrene may develop.

---

muscle and nerve damage. In some cases, victims experience months of pain, disability, and even amputation.

It is common to hear that at least 12 hours of exposure to cold, wet conditions is necessary to produce the injury. However, it can happen more quickly, over a long, wet, cold hiking day or in a multi-hour river crossing. These episodes of short-onset nonfreezing cold injury could be due to individual susceptibility or the culminating event of long-term exposure. Sadly, as little as an afternoon's lapsed attention can undo days of diligent attention to foot care.

Assessment of Nonfreezing Cold Injury
Stay alert to subtle forms of nonfreezing cold injury that do not necessarily look mottled, gray, or waxy. You may not always see poor capillary refill or altered skin color and temperature; you may see only cool, pale extremities, mild swelling, and complaints of numbness or tingling. Pain is unusual in the field, becoming more common after blood flow has returned to the extremity after expedition's end.

Nerves are most susceptible to injury from reduced blood flow, so be suspicious of any numbness, tingling, or pain in your feet in cool conditions. Damaged nerves in the feet cause many of the long-term effects of immersion foot: pain, numbness, chronic tingling, and itching.

The patient may not notice the constricted condition of the feet until after the trip. People returning from prolonged wet and cold conditions should avoid long, hot showers or baths. The rapid warming can surprise the unwary with swollen, painful, and red feet.

Treatment of Nonfreezing Cold Injury

- Warm nonfreezing cold injuries slowly at room temperature.
- Elevate the feet to reduce the swelling.

In serious cases, swelling, pain, and blister formation prevent walking. Bed rest to avoid trauma is often necessary until the injury heals. NSAIDs are recommended because of their anti-inflammatory properties.

Chilblains and Pernio

The nonfreezing cold injuries chilblains and pernio—red, itchy, rash-like lesions on the skin—tend to occur on the extremities, especially the hands and feet, and are more common in cold, wet conditions than cold and dry conditions.

The chilblain usually is swollen and tender, itchy, and reddish to purple in color. It has a nodular, bump-like appearance. Pernio, sometimes called the long-term effect of chilblains, can look like chilblains except that there is more chance of blisters with a dark crust. Both pernio and chilblains can cause persistent itching, numbness, and pain. As with any cold injury, prevention beforehand is better than treatment after the fact.

Prevention of Cold Injury

Prolonged cold, wet conditions make some degree of nonfreezing cold injury inevitable. The best footwear-gaiter system is of little help. Prevention depends on consistent good habits with gear, vigilance, and ongoing assessment.

Many of our techniques to prevent NFCI arise from experience both in the military and on NOLS expeditions living for weeks in cold and damp conditions. In World War I, the British significantly reduced immersion-foot casualties (without making major footwear changes) by using techniques that we still follow today: wearing well-fitting boots with heavy wool socks; keeping the body warm; removing wet socks and drying and massaging the feet twice a day; not sleeping in wet footwear; drying wet socks against the skin; keeping feet out of water or mud as much as possible; watching carefully and reacting

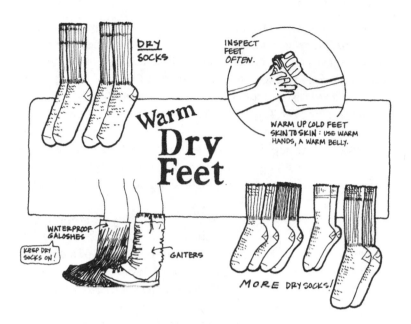

promptly to any numbness or tingling; and keeping footwear loose to allow for circulation.

What follows are suggestions accumulated over the years from NOLS instructors.

Dry Your Socks. Drying socks is a continual activity on wilderness trips. During the day, we stick wet socks under our shirts to dry them against the skin and at night we drape them over our chests and bellies in our sleeping bags. We'll hang them in the sun and dry them over a fire. Keep one pair of dry socks in a dry place, such as in a sleeping bag or a small plastic bag.

Sleep with Warm, Dry Feet. Even after a long, cold, wet-feet day, sleeping with dry feet every night helps to prevent nonfreezing cold injury, so go to bed with warm, dry feet and keep them that way all night long.

Use the Environment to Your Advantage. Travel early. Stop before nightfall, leaving time to care for your feet. In spring and summer, use the hardened overnight snowpack to stay on top of the snow. Stop when the snowpack becomes wet and soft, and dry your feet and socks in the afternoon sun. Choose campsites with good sun exposure and campfire possibilities.

Look at Your Feet. Local cold injuries are as much a leadership problem as a medical one. Messages sent to the brain from the feet may be faulty due to nerve damage, so when the conditions are ideal for non-freezing cold injury to occur, daily or twice daily visual foot checks must be part of the routine.

Give Your Feet Top Priority. In some places where people hike and ski, it is impossible to have dry feet all day. The best footwear won't keep you dry in soaking wet tundra or through multiple river crossings. On these days, if your socks are damp and your feet cool, stop, warm your feet, and, if possible, change into dry socks.

Warming cool feet on a companion's belly or stopping to change socks in the middle of the day should be routine tasks, not impositions. When you get to camp, get out of your wet boots immediately. Change into a pair of dry socks and begin to actively dry your wet or damp socks. Warm your feet promptly. Don't wait until bedtime.

For outdoor leaders, role modeling good foot care on the trail and in camp is essential. Frostbite is the most well-known cold injury, and many people are not well-informed on the subtleties of nonfreezing cold injuries. Novices often assume that some degree of cooling is unavoidable and acceptable, and inadvertently cross a line from extremity cooling to a cold injury.

Use Foot Powder. Foot powder does not seem to help prevent immersion injury, other than as a discipline in conjunction with changing socks. People with a tendency toward athlete's foot (a fungal infection) have found medicated foot powders helpful.

Keep Your Core Warm. Poor nutrition, dehydration, wet socks, inadequate clothing, and constriction of blood flow by shoes, socks, gaiters, or tight clothing are all predisposing factors.

Use Proper Equipment. Footwear is important. Waterproof or dryable boots, gaiters, galoshes or nylon overshoes can help keep feet dry. Avoid a tight fit with your boot and sock system. Bring multiple pairs of socks.

FINAL THOUGHTS

The possibility of cold injury is our constant companion on wilderness trips. It's a threat not only in the mountains or in winter conditions but anytime the environment is cool and wet—be it a fall rainstorm, a cold desert night, or immersion in a cool ocean, river, or lake. Prevention is better than any treatment. Choose effective insulating material such as wool and synthetic parkas, and waterproof, windproof pants. To live comfortably as you travel through the wilderness, use these items properly, eat and stay hydrated, and hone your camping and navigation skills.

A common thread in many nonfreezing cold injury and frostbite scenarios is people who tolerate cold feet, wait too long before intervening, and are surprised when they discover that they have been injured. If your feet are not definitely warm, you're doing something wrong. Novices may believe that they have to tolerate some level of cold extremities as an unavoidable consequence of camping. Although there is some truth to this, a novice lacks the experience to know how much one can tolerate before an injury occurs, and even an expert can be fooled. Don't be one of those people who rationalize not taking care of their feet by saying, "My feet are cold, but not that cold."

Evacuation Guidelines
Hypothermia:
- Mild hypothermia can be treated in the field. People with severe hypothermia need to be gently and rapidly evacuated for hospital warming.

Frostbite and nonfreezing cold injuries:
- Isolated, small (less than the size of a quarter) thawed areas of frostbite can be kept in the field if subsequent freezing can be prevented. In general, people with larger areas of partial- or full-thickness cold injuries should be evacuated. The pain from nonfreezing cold injury usually dictates evacuation.

CHAPTER 10 | HEAT ILLNESS

INTRODUCTION

Our bodies produce heat constantly. When heat production exceeds heat loss, body temperature rises. To survive in a hot environment, human beings must eliminate enough heat to keep the body temperature within acceptable limits—97° to 100°F (35° to 37°C). Vital organs are irreversibly damaged when the body temperature stays at or above 107°F (41.5°C) for any length of time.

Outdoor leaders should be knowledgeable about the causes, recognition, and treatment of heat illness. Preventing heat illness—like preventing hypothermia, frostbite, altitude illness, and dehydration—is a 24-hour-a-day leadership task.

PHYSIOLOGY OF HEAT ILLNESS

The body generates 2,000 to 5,000 kilocalories (kcal) of heat per day. Every metabolic function, blink of the eye, and beat of the heart produces heat. Basal metabolism alone would raise the body temperature 1.5°F per hour if heat were not dissipated.

As discussed in Chapter 9 ("Cold Injuries"), the four main mechanisms by which the body loses heat are radiation, evaporation, convection, and conduction. Of these, radiation and evaporation are the body's primary avenues of heat loss.

Radiation. Under heat stress, the body increases heart rate and cardiac output, and directs more blood to the skin. Normally, one-third to one-half liter of blood per minute is shunted to the skin. The body can increase skin blood flow to four liters per minute when it is heat stressed. Shunting blood to the body's surface warms the skin and thus increases the amount of heat radiated into the environment. Radiation accounts for about 65 percent of heat lost when air temperature is lower than body temperature. Conversely, in hot environments, radiation is a major source of heat gain. The body can gain up to 300 kcal per hour when exposed to the sun.

Evaporation. Sweat dripping from your skin does not cool. Sweat cools when metabolic heat changes the sweat from liquid to vapor, carrying that heat away from the body. Sweat dripping from your skin is not being evaporated, and does not cool as efficiently. A heat-acclimatized person in a dry environment can sweat as much as 2 liters per hour, for a potential total loss of 1 million kcal of evaporated heat.

Acclimatization. Acclimatizing to heat is as important for the prevention of heat illness as acclimatization to altitude is for the prevention of altitude illness. Acclimatizing to heat entails increasing the rate of sweating, decreasing the sweating threshold, improving vasodilation, and decreasing electrolyte loss in the sweat. When acclimatized, we sweat faster and sooner, and lose fewer electrolytes in the sweat.

To become acclimatized to a hot environment, the body requires 1 to 2 hours of exercise in the heat daily for approximately 10 days to 2 weeks. To remain acclimatized requires 1 to 2 hours of exercise per week.

Predisposing Factors in Heat Illness. Increased heat production, decreased heat dissipation, and a lack of salt and water are the basic factors that produce heat illness.

Other factors in the development of heat illness are age, general health, use of medications or alcohol, fatigue, and a prior history of heat illness. Patients with underlying illness or injury may not be able to tolerate heat. Children don't tolerate heat as well as adults. Individuals with compromised heart function are less able to adjust when stressed by heat. Fatigue and lack of sleep increases the risk of heat illness. Antihistamines, antipsychotic agents, thyroid-hormone medications, amphetamines, and alcohol are among the drugs that have been implicated in the development of heat illness. Some interfere with thermoregulation; others increase metabolic activity or interfere with sweating.

HEAT ILLNESS

Heat illnesses range from heat syncope and cramps to heat exhaustion and heatstroke. Signs and symptoms of these illnesses, like those of hypothermia and altitude illness, may be subtle and remain unrecognized until a sudden collapse occurs.

Heat Syncope

Heat syncope is fainting due to heat stress. Shunting of blood to the periphery decreases blood flow to the brain as vessels dilate and blood pools in the large leg veins. Standing for long periods of time ("soldier-on-parade" syndrome) is a common cause of heat syncope.

Assessment and Treatment for Heat Syncope. Prior to fainting, the person may complain of tunnel vision, vertigo, nausea, sweating, or feeling weak.

Heat syncope is self-limiting; causal factors abate when the patient becomes horizontal. Move the patient into the shade and off hot ground; leave the patient lying flat with legs elevated, and the signs and symptoms will usually promptly resolve.

Heat Syncope

SIGNS AND SYMPTOMS
- Tunnel vision, vertigo, nausea, sweating, weakness
- Sudden fainting

TREATMENT
- Lie flat, elevate legs.
- Hydrate.

Exercise-Associated Muscle Cramps

Exercise-associated muscle cramps (heat cramps) are painful muscle contractions that follow exercise in hot conditions. We don't know what causes the cramps. They may be due to dehydration, electrolyte imbalance in the muscle, neuromuscular fatigue, or any combination of these causes. People who sweat profusely and drink only water to replace lost fluids are more susceptible to heat cramps.

Assessment and Treatment for Heat Cramps. Calf, abdominal, and thigh muscles can be affected, and muscle spasms in the abdomen can be severe. Treat by moving the patient to a cool spot. Mix one-quarter to one-half teaspoon of salt in a liter of fluid and have the patient drink it slowly. Tums can be helpful as a source of calcium. Gentle limb straightening or massaging the muscles can help relieve the cramps.

Heat Cramps

TREATMENT
- Rest, lie flat, elevate legs.
- Hydrate.
- Straighten limbs gently.

Heat Exhaustion

Heat exhaustion is just what the term says: fatigue from the stress of coping with a hot environment. The work of heat dissipation, along with stress from coping with sunlight and heat, exhaust the patient. Heat exhaustion does not imply low fluid volume from dehydration, although dehydration can occur alongside heat exhaustion.

Assessment for Heat Exhaustion. The patient complains of weakness, fatigue, headache, vertigo, thirst, nausea, vomiting, muscle cramps, and faintness. The body temperature is often slightly elevated, but it may be normal or even slightly lower than normal. Skin signs are variable; pale and cool, or flushed (warm and red), and clammy. Pulse and respiratory rate are elevated. Urine output may be decreased due to dehydration.

Treatment for Heat Exhaustion. Provide a cool environment, lay the patient flat, remove excess clothing, and shade the patient or move them out from direct heat. Active cooling is not necessary.

Hydrate. If the patient is mentally alert enough to hold a glass and drink, allow them to drink. Water, a dilute solution of sugar drinks with a teaspoon of salt, or a sports drink is fine.

Monitor. Watch the patient, who often gets better when you remove the heat stress and assist with rest and hydration.

Assessment of Heat Exhaustion and Heatstroke

HEAT EXHAUSTION
- Heart rate elevated
- Respiratory rate elevated
- Skin variable; pale and cool, or flushed (warm and red), clammy
- Headache, nausea, weakness, fatigue
- Temperature normal or slightly elevated

HEATSTROKE
- Heart rate elevated
- Respiratory rate elevated
- Skin hot (color and moisture can vary)
- Altered mental status
- Temperature >104°F (40°C)

Heatstroke

Heatstroke is a life-threatening emergency. Patients have exaggerated heat production and an inability to cool themselves. The reason why this happens is not well understood. There are two broad classifications of heatstroke: classic and exertional. Classic heatstroke affects the chronically ill, the elderly, and infants. It develops slowly and is common during heat waves. Exertional heatstroke is more likely to affect healthy, fit individuals and to develop rapidly during exercise or hard physical work.

Assessment for Heatstroke. In contrast to heat exhaustion, the onset of exertional heatstroke is usually rapid. The patient develops an altered mental status. The pulse and respiratory rate are elevated. Skin temperature tends to be hot, color and moisture can vary. The patient may or may not be sweating. Signs and symptoms include confusion, drowsiness, disorientation, irritability, anxiety, and ataxia, as well as the signs and symptoms of heat exhaustion. Heatstroke victims usually have a rectal temperature above 104°F (40°C).

The boundary between heat exhaustion and heatstroke may not be clear. Some authorities consider heat exhaustion an early stage of heatstroke; others consider it a distinct illness. Regardless, if a patient has altered brain function and a history of exposure to heat, they should be treated for heatstroke.

Treatment for Heatstroke. Treatment of heatstroke is rapid cooling. Both the temperature reached and the length of time it is sustained can affect the long-term outcome of the disease.

Provide a Cool Environment, Lay the Patient Flat, Remove the Patient's Clothing, Cool with Water and Fanning. Shade the patient or move them away from direct heat. Lay the patient flat and remove their clothing. Spray the patient with water and fan the body to enhance evaporation. Apply cool cloths to the patient's trunk, armpits, abdomen, and groin, where large blood vessels lie near the skin surface.

Immersion in cool or cold water is the most effective cooling method, as long as the patient is protected from drowning. There is a theoretical concern that cold water immersion will trigger shivering and thus heat production, but this is uncommon and the value of the rapid cooling outweighs this risk. There is also a theoretical concern that the patient can become hypothermic, but this is also uncommon and unlikely.

Monitor Temperature. Document how long the temperature was elevated, how high it was, and how long it took to cool the patient. Body temperature may remain unstable even after cooling.

Evacuate. Any patient you suspect of having heatstroke should be evacuated immediately for further evaluation. Evacuate a heatstroke patient, keeping a close watch on temperature. Internal organ damage may not present itself for several days following the episode of heatstroke.

Treatment of Heat Exhaustion and Heatstroke

HEAT EXHAUSTION
- Cool environment.
- Rest, lie flat.
- Hydrate.

HEATSTROKE
- Cool immediately (cool water and fan).
- Evacuate.

Risk Factors for Exertional Heatstroke
- Overweight
- Overdressed
- Fatigue
- Dehydration
- Alcohol use
- Medications
- Exertion
- High humidity
- High temperature
- Not acclimatized
- Young athlete

FINAL THOUGHTS

Prevention of heat-related illness eliminates the need for treatment. Leaders need to be alert for signs of developing heat illness in their groups. Environmental risk factors of high heat and humidity, coupled with dehydration, exertion, overdressing, and the cumulative stress of several days in the heat should raise caution flags. The vague symptoms of fatigue, headache, weakness, irritability, and malaise should be recognized as indicators of dehydration and heat illness.

Tips for Preventing Heat Illness
- Shade the head and back of the neck to decrease heat gain from the sun.
- Drink lots of fluids. A simple indicator of hydration is the color of your urine. The urine should be clear to pale yellow. Dark urine indicates dehydration.
- Make sure your diet contains an adequate amount of salt. The average American diet contains 10 to 12 grams of salt per day, which should be adequate for exercising in hot environments.
- Wear loose-fitting, light-colored clothes. This maximizes heat loss by allowing convection and evaporation to take place.
- Exercise cautiously in conditions of high heat and humidity. Air temperatures exceeding 90°F (32°C) and humidity levels above 70 percent severely impair the body's ability to lose heat through radiation and evaporation.
- Know the warning signs of impending heat illness—dark-colored urine, dizziness, headache, and fatigue.
- Acclimatize. It takes 10 days to 2 weeks to acclimatize to a hot environment.

Evacuation Guidelines
- Heat syncope, cramps, and exhaustion can often be treated in the field.
- Rapidly evacuate any person who has altered mental status associated with suspected heat illness.

CHAPTER 11 | ALTITUDE ILLNESS

INTRODUCTION

Each year, thousands of people trek in Nepal, South America, and Africa at altitudes over 13,000 feet (3,900 meters). In the United States, thousands of people climb Mount Rainier's 14,408 feet (4,391 meters) and hundreds attempt Denali's 20,320 feet, (6,193 meters). Skiers in the Rocky Mountains often ski above 10,000 feet (3,000 meters) within 24 hours of leaving low elevations. Studies show that signs and symptoms of altitude illness can affect up to 40 percent of these people.

Taking the time to acclimatize to altitude will lower, but not eliminate, the risk of experiencing altitude illness. NOLS expeditions have managed life-threatening cerebral edema at 21,000 feet (6,400 meters) on Cerro Aconcagua in Argentina and in the Himalayas, and pulmonary edema at 11,000 feet (3,300 meters) in Wyoming's Wind River Range. If you travel in mountains, you need to know how to prevent, recognize, and treat altitude illness.

Definitions of Altitude

- High altitude: 8,000–14,000 feet (2,400-4,200 meters)
- Very high altitude: 14,000–18,000 feet (4,200-5,400 meters)
- Extreme altitude: above 18,000 feet (5,400 meters)

CAUSES OF ALTITUDE ILLNESS

As elevation increases, atmospheric pressure (barometric pressure) falls. Normally, oxygen diffuses from the lung into the blood along a pressure differential, from higher gas pressure in the lung to lower gas pressure in the blood. At altitude, diminished barometric pressure reduces the pressure of oxygen in the lung and thus decreases the amount of oxygen diffusing into the blood. For example, in an average healthy person at sea level, blood is 95 percent saturated with oxygen. At 18,000 feet (5,400 meters), because of the reduction in atmospheric pressure, blood is only 71 percent saturated; that is, it is carrying 24 percent less oxygen. This reduction in the amount of oxygen in the blood underlies all forms of altitude illness.

ADAPTATION TO ALTITUDE

The body undergoes numerous physiological changes at higher elevations in order to increase oxygen delivery to cells and improve the efficiency of oxygen use. These changes usually begin almost immediately and continue to occur for several weeks. People vary in their ability to acclimatize to the physiological stresses of altitude. Some adjust quickly; others fail to acclimatize, even with gradual exposure over a period of weeks.

Increased Respiratory Rate. During the first week of acclimation, a variety of physiologically beneficial changes take place. Respiratory rate and depth increase in response to lower concentrations of oxygen in the blood, causing more carbon dioxide to be lost and more oxygen to be delivered to the lungs. The increased respiratory rate begins within the first few hours of arriving at altitudes as low as 5,000 feet (1,500 meters).

The lost carbon dioxide causes the body to become more alkaline. To compensate for the body's increasing alkalinity, the kidneys excrete bicarbonate—an alkaline substance—in the urine. This compensation occurs within 24 to 48 hours after hyperventilation starts.

Increased Heart Rate. Heart rate increases to meet the physiological stress of lower blood oxygen concentration. Except at extreme altitudes, heart rate returns to near normal after acclimatization.

Increased Red Blood Cell Production. As acclimatization continues, the bone marrow increases red blood cell production. New red blood cells become available in the blood within 4 to 5 days, increasing the blood's oxygen-carrying capacity. An acclimatized person may have 30 to 50 percent more red blood cells than a person at sea level.

Acclimitization to Altitude

EARLY CHANGES
- Increased respiratory rate
- Increased heart rate

LATER CHANGES
- Increased red blood cell production
- Increased 2, 3-DPG production
- Increased number of capillaries

Increased 2, 3-DPG Production. Within the blood cells 2, 3-diphosphoglycerate (DPG) increases. This compound helps oxygen combine with hemoglobin. Production of myoglobin, the intramuscular oxygen-carrying protein, also increases.

Increased Number of Capillaries. In response to altitude the body develops more capillaries, the small blood vessels from which oxygen diffuses into cells.

ALTITUDE ILLNESS

Anyone who ascends to high altitude will become hypoxic, the condition of having insufficient oxygen in the blood. Altitude illness results from hypoxia, but why some people become ill at altitude and others don't is not fully understood. Most people who become ill do so within the first few days of ascending to altitude.

The three common types of altitude illness are acute mountain sickness (AMS), high-altitude pulmonary edema (HAPE) and high-altitude cerebral edema (HACE). AMS is the most common and while it can make you miserable, it is not life threatening. HAPE is less common, more serious, and causes the greatest number of altitude illness–related deaths. HACE is rare but can be sudden and severe.

Factors That Affect the Incidence and Severity of Altitude Illness
- Rate of ascent—the faster you climb, the greater the risk.
- Altitude attained (especially sleeping altitude)—the higher you ascend, the greater the risk.
- Length of exposure—the longer you stay high, the greater the risk.
- Inherent physiological susceptibility—some people are more likely to become ill, and we don't know why.
- Ascending in the presence of signs and symptoms of altitude illness—if you are not acclimatizing, stop ascent until you adjust.

Treatment of altitude illness is based on four principles: (1) stop ascent when symptoms develop; (2) descend if there is no improvement or condition worsens; (3) descend immediately if there is shortness of breath at rest, loss of coordination, or altered mental status; and (4) don't leave people with altitude sickness alone. The definitive treatment of all forms of altitude illness is descent.

ACUTE MOUNTAIN SICKNESS (AMS)

Acute mountain sickness is a headache in conjunction with recent altitude gain, and one or more of the following symptoms: nausea, loss of appetite, fatigue, insomnia, and disturbed sleep.

Signs and Symptoms of AMS

Signs and symptoms tend to start 6 to 36 hours after arrival at an altitude to which we are not acclimatized. Symptoms can be worse in the morning, probably due to the normal decrease in the rate and depth of breathing during sleep, which lowers blood oxygen saturation. A common symptom of AMS is a headache. Malaise, an uneasy feeling, drowsiness, and low energy occur. Loss of appetite and nausea commonly accompany AMS and contribute to the overall sensation of feeling lousy. Persons with AMS

Signs and Symptoms of AMS
- Headache
- Malaise
- Loss of appetite
- Nausea, vomiting
- Disturbed sleep

may develop edema, an excess of fluid seen as puffiness, especially in the face and hands. During sleep, a person's rate and depth of respiration may gradually decrease until breathing ceases entirely for 5 to 50 seconds. This phenomenon, called Cheyne-Stokes respiration, contributes to disturbed sleep.

Treatment of AMS
Follow the treatment principles for altitude illness. Stop ascending until signs and symptoms resolve, descend if there is no improvement with rest, and descend immediately if signs of severe AMS appear. Light activity around camp is fine, as long as the theme is rest and acclimatization, not more fatigue. Stay hydrated. Aspirin, acetaminophen, or ibuprofen may ease the headache. Descend if symptoms worsen, or signs of HACE, such as ataxia, loss of balance, or HAPE, such as shortness of breath, become apparent.

Treatment of AMS
Treatment Principles for Altitude Illness (AMS)
1. Don't go up until the symptoms go down.
   - Stop ascent until signs and symptoms resolve.
   - If the patient does not improve over 24-48 hours, descend to the last camp the patient slept at without signs or symptoms.
   - Descend immediately at the first sign of severe AMS.
2. Acclimatize.
   - Light exercise.
   - Maintain adequate hydration.
3. Pain medications such as NSAIDs for headache are okay. Avoid sedatives.
4. Monitor for shortness of breath, ataxia, altered mental status.

HIGH-ALTITUDE PULMONARY EDEMA (HAPE)

HAPE is abnormal fluid accumulation in the lungs at altitude. HAPE rarely occurs below 8,000 feet (2,400 meters). HAPE is dangerous in part because it can be insidious in development, yet abrupt in onset. In other words, it can start slowly and be mistaken for fatigue or mild respiratory illness. By the time it presents as HAPE, patients can quickly become very ill.

Signs and Symptoms of HAPE

The symptoms of HAPE result from a decreasing ability of the lungs to exchange oxygen and carbon dioxide. The symptoms usually begin 24 to 96 hours after ascent. The patient complains of a dry cough, shortness of breath, and more fatigue than expected. The heart and respiratory rates increase.

Signs and Symptoms of HAPE

- Shortness of breath on exertion, progressing to shortness of breath at rest
- Fatigue
- Dry cough, progressing to wet, productive cough
- Increased heart rate and respiratory rate
- Rales (sounds of fluid in the lungs)

As HAPE worsens, the shortness of breath, weakness, and fatigue occur at rest or with light exercise. The patient complains of a productive cough, headache, and loss of appetite. The heart and respiratory rates remain elevated. The nail beds become cyanotic. Rales (rattles) in the lungs can be heard with a stethoscope.

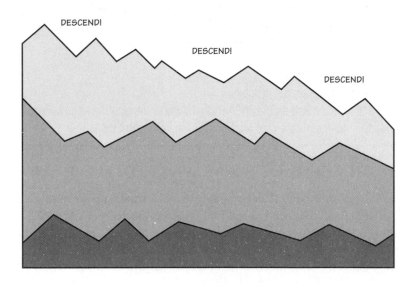

As HAPE becomes severe, rales can be heard without a stethoscope. The patient coughs up frothy, blood-tinged sputum. The patient becomes ataxic, lethargic, or develops an altered mental status.

Treatment of HAPE
- Descend until symptoms abate— at least 2,000 to 3,000 feet.
- Oxygen may be helpful.

HAPE, like AMS, can become worse at night due to Cheyne-Stokes respirations. HAPE is a life-threatening illness.

Treatment of HAPE

Descend to a lower altitude as quickly as possible. Exercise can make HAPE worse; ideally the patient is carried. Immediate descent is essential. Descend until the symptoms abate.

If you are unable to descend immediately, but have oxygen available, give the patient oxygen at a flow rate of 4 to 6 liters per minute. If the condition does not improve, increase the flow of oxygen. Descend as soon as possible.

HIGH-ALTITUDE CEREBRAL EDEMA (HACE)

HACE is a severe form of altitude illness caused by swelling of the brain. HACE generally occurs above 12,000 feet (3,600 meters).

Signs and Symptoms of HACE

HACE presents with signs and symptoms of AMS as well as a change in mental status and ataxia. The patient may become

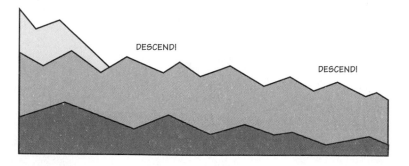

confused, disoriented, or slip into unresponsiveness. Headache may or may not be present.

Ataxia. Ataxia is a sign—some experts say the most useful sign—of severe AMS or HACE. The test is simple. Have the patient try to walk a straight line over unobstructed ground. If the patient wobbles or falls, they have ataxia.

Treatment of HACE
Descend. Unlike AMS, HACE will not improve with time and acclimatization. Descend to a lower elevation as soon as you notice any ataxia or change in mental status. Give oxygen if available.

Hyperbaric Bags. Portable hyperbaric chambers are used in the treatment of altitude illness. These bags are made of nonpermeable nylon and are inflated with a foot pump to greater than atmospheric pressure. increase oxygen diffusion into the blood. They simulate a descent of several thousand feet.

Hyperbaric bags are temporary treatment for emergencies, intended for use during evacuation to lower altitudes or if you are unable to descend immediately.

Signs and Symptoms of HACE
- Signs of acute mountain sickness
- Neurological signs and symptoms such as vision disturbances, seizures, hallucinations
- Ataxia
- Possible headache
- Altered mental status
- Nausea and vomiting

Treatment of HACE
- Descent
- Oxygen

DESCEND!

MEDICATIONS AND ALTITUDE

Several medications are used for the prevention and treatment of altitude illness, including acetazolamide (Diamox) and dexamethasone (Decadron). Discussing these drugs is beyond the scope of this text. Check with your physician advisor for recommendations on their use.

FINAL THOUGHTS

Acclimatization is key. A slow rate of ascent is a sound, but not foolproof, way to prevent acute altitude illness. General recommendations for an ascent profile include 1,000 to 1,500 feet (300 to 600 meters) per day above 10,000 feet (3,000 meters) with frequent rest days.

Acclimatization
- Ascend slowly.
- Climb high, sleep low.
- Hydrate.

Climb high and sleep low. The sleeping altitude is important. It is best not to increase the sleeping altitude by more than 2,000 feet (600 meters) at a time. Set up camp at lower elevations and take day trips to high points. Ferry loads up to a high camp and then return to the low camp to sleep as you acclimatize.

Avoid sleeping pills, which decrease the respiratory rate, aggravating the lack of oxygen.

Be aware of the influence of ego, peer pressure, and schedules on your rate of ascent. If you are not acclimatizing well, stop, rest, and allow time to adjust. Pushing higher and denying the signs and symptoms of altitude illness is asking for trouble for you and your companions.

Evacuation Guidelines
- Evacuation and/or rapid descent for patients with severe altitude illness (HAPE or HACE).
- Evacuate any patient unable to acclimatize.

CHAPTER 12 | POISONS, STINGS, AND BITES

INTRODUCTION

A poison is any substance—solid, liquid, or gas—that impairs health when it comes into contact with the body. Poisoning ranks fifth in causes of accidental death in the United States, responsible for approximately 5,000 deaths a year. Approximately one million cases of nonfatal poisoning from substances such as industrial chemicals, cleaning agents, medications, and insect sprays occur each year in the United States.

Virtually any substance can be poisonous if consumed in sufficient quantity. For example, vitamins can be healthy supplements at recommended dosing, but highly toxic in overdose. A snakebite that delivers enough venom to kill a child may only produce illness in an adult.

In the wilderness context, poisoning is commonly thought of as envenomation from snakes, spiders, or scorpions. Venomous animals have specialized glands that produce toxic substances for use against adversaries and prey, delivering the venom through injection with fangs or stingers, secretion onto the skin, or as saliva administered through bites. Most animal venoms are complex mixtures of toxic and carrier (nontoxic) substances. The toxins in venoms vary in potency, effect, and chemical makeup. They may impair nerve function, destroy cells, or affect the heart or blood.

171

Much information has been disseminated about the treatment of serpent, spider, and scorpion bites, and much of that information is inaccurate. Outside the United States, there are snakes, spiders, and insects that carry deadly venoms. In the United States, however, snakes and spiders cause relatively few deaths each year. This is not to understate the potency of these poisons, but rather to emphasize that ill-informed and misguided treatment can be as harmful to the patient as the venom.

POISONS

Poisons enter the body through ingestion, inhalation, absorption, and injection.

Ingested Poisons

Examples of ingested poisons include drugs, toxic plants, and bacterial toxins on contaminated food. Mistaking poorly labeled fuel bottles for water bottles has led to accidental ingestion of gasoline. Drugs, including nonprescription medications, can be accidentally or intentionally ingested in harmful amounts. In the backcountry, people have died after mistakenly eating poisonous plants and mushrooms. An expert should identify any vegetation you intend to eat. Save samples for later identification.

Treatment of Ingested Poisons. Three principles guide the treatment of ingested poisons: call a poison control center, consider inducing vomiting, and evacuate.

If you can, contact poison control and seek advice. They will want to know what substance was ingested, how much was ingested, the time of ingestion, when the victim last ate, and the person's age, sex, and weight.

Inducing vomiting for an ingested poison is no longer recommended in the frontcountry. The risks of airway obstruction outweigh the benefit, which is presumed low, of removing the poison before it is absorbed. In the wilderness, where access to poison control may be delayed, vomiting may help if it is tried early, usually within 30 minutes of ingestion. The wilderness traveller commonly self-induces vomiting by tickling the back of the throat to stimulate the gag reflex.

Do not induce vomiting if the patient has a seizure disorder or if the patient has an altered mental status, as the airway may become obstructed with vomit. Do not induce vomiting for ingested corrosive chemicals or petroleum products. Vomiting can increase the corrosive damage, as these chemicals burn both on the way down and

---

Treatment of Ingested Poisons
- Call poison control.
- Consider inducing vomiting.
- Evacuate.

---

on the way back up the esophagus. Vomiting also increases the chances these substances will enter the lungs, where they are extremely harmful and can cause chemical pneumonia. There is no proven value to diluting an ingested poison with water or other liquids.

Activated Charcoal. Activated charcoal isn't the charcoal from a fire but rather a special preparation sold over the counter, usually packaged in 4-ounce plastic bottles or tubes. The patient drinks the slurry, which binds the poison and allows it to be excreted without being absorbed into the body. Activated charcoal is controversial, used less and less, and should be used only after consultation with a physician. Because of its weight and bulk, and the infrequency of poisoning in the backcountry, wilderness kits rarely include it. You may find it in a well-stocked base camp or boat medical kit.

Inhaled Poisons

Carbon monoxide, the most frequently inhaled poison in the United States, is an odorless and colorless gas produced from incomplete combustion. Portable stoves, lanterns, and heaters are all sources of carbon monoxide, and unfortunate campers have died from their use in tents and other poorly ventilated spaces.

Carbon monoxide is a gas that combines with hemoglobin in the blood, displacing oxygen and reducing the oxygen-carrying capacity of the blood. The signs and symptoms are not always obvious, and because the gas is colorless and odorless, exposure can be undetected and thus quite dangerous. At high altitudes, where less oxygen is available, the potential for poisoning increases. Signs and symptoms of carbon monoxide poisoning range from light-headedness and headache,

Carbon Monoxide Poisoning

SIGNS AND SYMPTOMS

- Lightheadedness, dizziness, throbbing headache
- Nausea and vomiting
- Irritability, impaired judgment
- Level of responsiveness deteriorates
- Seizures, respiratory failure, coma

TREATMENT

- Move patient to fresh air.
- Maintain airway.
- If possible, administer oxygen.

weakness, nausea, vomiting, loss of manual dexterity, confusion, and lethargy to coma, seizures, and death. A cherry-red coloring of the skin and mucous membranes is a very late sign of carbon monoxide poisoning and may not occur until after the person has died.

Treatment of Inhaled Poisons. The immediate treatment for any inhaled poisoning is to remove the patient from the source of the poison. Maintain the airway and move the patient to fresh air. Although not readily available in the wilderness, administration of oxygen is standard treatment. A patient who experiences a notable disturbance in alertness or coordination, complains of breathing difficulty, or becomes unresponsive should be evacuated to a physician for evaluation.

Prevent inhaled poisoning by keeping tents or snow shelters well ventilated during cooking or, better yet, by cooking outside.

Absorbed Poisons

Poisons can be absorbed into the body through the skin or mucous membranes. Pesticide sprays absorbed through the skin are a common source of poisoning. Toxins secreted into the skin by sea cucumbers and some species of exotic reptiles and amphibians can cause serious reactions.

Treatment of Absorbed Poisons. If the poison is dry, brush it off, then flush the area with large volumes of water. If the poison is wet, flush the site thoroughly with water, then rinse with water. Exceptions are lye and dry lime, which react with water to produce heat and further corrosion. Do not rinse lye or dry lime; rather, brush the powder off the skin.

Treatment of Absorbed Poisons

- Dry poisons: brush off, then rinse with water.
- Wet poisons: rinse thoroughly with water.

Injected Poisons

Poisons that enter the body by injection, such as the venoms of stinging insects and reptiles, are often complex systemic poisons with multiple toxins. The injected poisons that most concern us in the wilderness are the venoms of snakes, bees, wasps, spiders, and scorpions.

Bees and wasps cause more deaths in the United States than snakes—approximately 100 deaths a year, usually from the acute allergic reaction known as anaphylaxis.

Venomous Snakes. Imagine trying to catch a small mammal for dinner, equipped only with a long, limbless body. You might evolve the ability to leap quickly to your victim. You might also evolve a venom to immobilize the victim. This is how a rattlesnake makes its living: striking quickly and accurately, and immobilizing or killing its victims with venom.

Approximately 45,000 snakebites occur in the United States each year, 8,000 of them from venomous snakes. Half a dozen people a year die from these bites, most of them young, elderly, or infirm. Bites commonly occur on the arms below the elbow, and on the legs below the knee. In most cases, the snake is provoked by being handled, antagonized, or inadvertently stepped on.

Prevent snakebite by watching closely where you step. Never reach into concealed areas. Shake out sleeping bags and clothing before use. One NOLS student was bitten on the hand when he attempted to pick up a rattlesnake. Never handle snakes, even if you think they are dead.

Two families of medically important venomous snakes in North America are the Elapidae, represented by the coral snake, and Crotalidae (pit vipers), represented by the rattlesnake, copperhead, and cottonmouth or water moccasin. Elapidae venom primarily affects the nervous system, causing death by paralysis and respiratory failure. Crotalidae venom is a complex mix of substances affecting the nerves, the heart, blood clotting, and other functions.

Coral Snake. The coral snake averages 23 to 32 inches in length and is thin and brightly colored, with adjacent red and yellow bands. It is the creature referred to in the old North American rhyme "red and yellow kill a fellow, red and black, venom

CORAL SNAKE

THIN, BRIGHTLY
COLORED

23-32" LONG

↳ ADJACENT RED/YELLOW BANDS

SYMPTOMS:

- *LITTLE PAIN OR SWELLING*

- *NEUROTOXIC VENOM POISONING MAY LEAD TO DROWSINESS, WEAKNESS AND OTHER SYMPTOMS and PROGRESS TO POSSIBLE RESPIRATORY FAILURE.*

lack." Coral snakes live in the southern and southwestern states, inhabiting dry, open, brushy ground near water sources. They are docile and bite only when provoked. Their short fangs generally limit their bites to fingers, toes, and loose skin folds.

The signs of systemic poisoning by the neurotoxic venom, which may appear several hours after the bite, include drowsiness, weakness, nausea, rapid pulse, and rapid respiration progressing to respiratory failure. To slow venom absorption, and in contrast to the treatment recommended for rattlesnake bites, the limb is splinted and wrapped distal to proximal with gauze or an elastic bandage. This wrap is firm, but a pulse should still be present in the foot or wrist.

Rattlesnakes, Copperheads, and Water Moccasins. These pit vipers have triangular heads, thick bodies, and pits between the eyes and nostrils. Coloring and length vary with the species. Most are blotched and colored in earthy browns, grays, or reds. The number of rattles a rattlesnake might have varies with its age and stage of molt. Rattles are thought to have evolved as a warning device to prevent hoofed mammals from stepping on the snake.

The pit viper's two fangs retract when the mouth is closed and extend during a strike. These snakes periodically shed their

RATTLESNAKES

GENERAL CHARACTERISTICS:

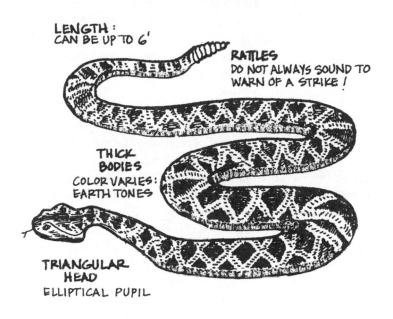

LENGTH:
CAN BE UP TO 6'

RATTLES
DO NOT ALWAYS SOUND TO
WARN OF A STRIKE!

**THICK
BODIES**
COLOR VARIES:
EARTH TONES

**TRIANGULAR
HEAD**
ELLIPTICAL PUPIL

MECHANISMS OF A RATTLESNAKE BITE:

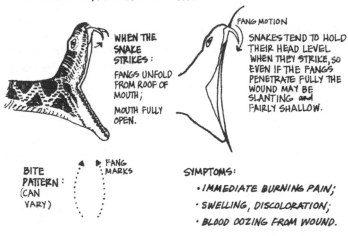

**WHEN THE
SNAKE
STRIKES:**

FANGS UNFOLD
FROM ROOF OF
MOUTH;

MOUTH FULLY
OPEN.

FANG MOTION

SNAKES TEND TO HOLD
THEIR HEAD LEVEL
WHEN THEY STRIKE, SO
EVEN IF THE FANGS
PENETRATE FULLY THE
WOUND MAY BE
SLANTING and
FAIRLY SHALLOW.

**BITE
PATTERN:**
(CAN
VARY)

FANG
MARKS

SYMPTOMS:
- IMMEDIATE BURNING PAIN;
- SWELLING, DISCOLORATION;
- BLOOD OOZING FROM WOUND.

Signs and Symptoms of Pit Viper Poisoning

- Swelling, pain, and tingling at the bite site
- Tingling and a metallic taste in the mouth
- Fever, chills, nausea, and vomiting
- Blurred vision and muscle tremors

fangs. At times, two fangs are present on each side. One is potent, the other not. Venom release is under the snake's control; a pit viper can apparently adjust the volume of venom injected to match its victim's size. The age, size, and health of the snake affect venom toxicity. The same factors affect the victim's response to the venom.

Multiple strikes are possible, and depth of the bite varies, as does the amount of venom injected. Fang marks are not a reliable sign of envenomation, as 20 to 30 percent of bites do not envenomate. Pain at the site with rapid swelling and bruising is a better sign that venom has been injected.

Signs and Symptoms of Venomous Poisoning. The wide array of signs and symptoms of venomous poisoning reflect the complex suite of toxins in the venom and include swelling, pain, and tingling at the bite site, tingling and a metallic taste in the mouth, fever, chills, nausea and vomiting, blurred vision, blood filled blisters, and muscle tremors.

Gently clean the wound with an antiseptic soap and apply a sterile dressing. Remove rings and other constrictive items. The goal of treatment is safe and rapid transport to a hospital for evaluation. Keep the affected limb at heart level or below. Keep the patient quiet, hydrated, and comfortable during evacuation. Activity and anxiety accelerate the absorption of the venom. Ideally you should immobilize and carry the victim. Walking is acceptable if the patient feels up to it and if no other alternative is available.

A healthy adult may become ill from an envenomation but probably will not die. The patient is often at greater danger from the effects of treatment by misinformed rescuers. Pressure bandages, tourniquets, electric

Treatment of Rattlesnake Bites

- Clean wound with antiseptic soap.
- Remove rings and other constrictive items.
- Keep limb at or below level of heart.
- Keep patient quiet, hydrated, and comfortable.
- Evacuate.

shock, ice, and incision of the area can permanently damage tissue that might otherwise remain unaffected. Pressure bandages are appropriate treatment for a coral snake bite and some exotic snakebites, but not for rattlesnake envenomations, in which local concentration of venom can cause tissue damage.

Non–North American Snakebite. World-wide, snake bite is a significant public health problem causing tens of thousands of deaths. Snakes outside of North America that are significant sources of envenomation include vipers such as death adders and rattlesnakes, but are primarily elapids: cobras, mambas, and kraits; Australian brown snakes, tiger snakes, and taipans. The potent neurotoxic venoms of some of these snakes can result in altered mental status, unresponsiveness, blurred vision, paralysis, seizures, and respiratory and heart failure.

Treatment is the same as for pit vipers, with the exception of the use of immobilization and a pressure bandage, described earlier for the coral snake, on the bitten extremity for an elapid bite. In Australia, the wound is not washed, to allow for an assay that can identify the venom.

Bee and wasp stings. The venom apparatus of most species of bees, located on the posterior abdomen, consists of venom glands, a venom reservoir, and structures for injection. The stinger and venom are used in defense and in subjugation of prey.

Multiple stings are more dangerous than single stings, and those occurring close together in time are more dangerous than those occurring over a longer duration. Multiple stings, which often result from disturbing a nest, can be life threatening.

Stings from bees and wasps usually cause instant pain, swelling, and redness. If the stinger remains in the skin, scrape or flick it out. A barb prevents the bee from withdrawing the stinger, so the bee's muscular venom reservoir left behind attached to the stinger continues to inject until the stinger is scraped away.

Gently clean the wound with an antiseptic soap. Ice or cool compresses may help relieve pain and swelling. The patient should avoid scratching stings, as this can cause secondary infection. Applying meat tenderizer to relieve the pain is a

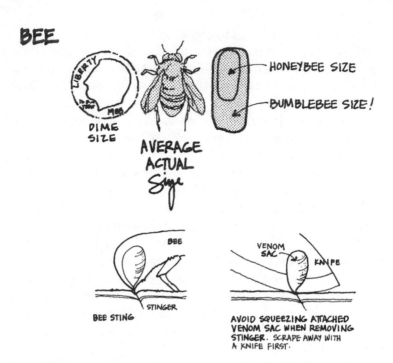

BEE

DIME SIZE

HONEYBEE SIZE

BUMBLEBEE SIZE!

AVERAGE ACTUAL Size

BEE

BEE STING

STINGER

VENOM SAC

KNIFE

AVOID SQUEEZING ATTACHED VENOM SAC WHEN REMOVING STINGER. SCRAPE AWAY WITH A KNIFE FIRST.

folklore remedy not supported by any scientific study.

Bee and wasp stings cause more anaphylactic reactions than do the stings of any other insect. Individuals who are allergic to the sting of one species of bee or wasp may also be allergic to that of different species.

Treatment of Bee Stings
- Scrape or flick off stinger.
- Clean wound with antiseptic soap.
- Ice or cool compress may relieve pain.
- If necessary, treat for anaphylaxis.

Arachnids. Arachnids are wingless, mostly terrestrial, and have four pairs of legs. Spiders, scorpions, tarantulas, and ticks are arachnids. There are over 30,000 spider species worldwide. They live in a variety of habitats, and all are carnivorous.

Poisonous spiders inject venom through hollow fangs. The venom is primarily for subduing and killing prey, and secondarily for defense. The venoms are fast-paralyzing agents that also contain enzymes to predigest prey, which is then sucked up.

Widow Spiders. The black widow spider has a sinister name, yet kills at most four to six people a year in the United States. A member of the genus *Latrodectus*, the venomous adult female is 4 centimeters long and is shiny black with a red "hourglass" marking on the bottom of the abdomen. The adult male is smaller, brown or grey, and not venomous. There are five species of "widow" spiders; only three are black, but all have some type of red marking on the underside of the abdomen. Black widows are typically found under stones and logs. They are common in desert overhangs, crawl spaces, outhouses, and barns; they are rare in occupied buildings.

The black widow usually bites only when its web is disturbed. The bite is not initially painful—a pinprick sensation with slight redness and swelling, followed by numbness. Ten to sixty minutes may pass before the onset of toxic symptoms. The venom is primarily a nerve toxin that stimulates muscle contraction, causing large muscle cramps. The abdomen may become board-like and excruciatingly painful. Weakness, nausea, vomiting, and anxiety are common. Systemic signs include hypertension, breathing difficulty, seizures, and cardiac arrest in the very young or very old.

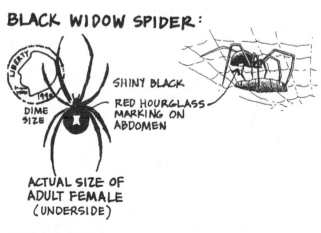

BLACK WIDOW SPIDER:

SHINY BLACK

RED HOURGLASS
MARKING ON
ABDOMEN

DIME
SIZE

ACTUAL SIZE OF
ADULT FEMALE
(UNDERSIDE)

• FEMALE ADULTS VENOMOUS;

• LOOK FOR DISTINCTIVE RED HOURGLASS
MARKING ON THE UNDERSIDE OF
ABDOMEN!

The pain generally peaks in 1 to 3 hours and can continue over several days. The natural course of the illness is general recovery after several days. Local cleansing and ice may retard pain and venom absorption. Antivenom—a medication containing antibodies against specific poisons, especially those in the venom of snakes, spiders, and scorpions—is available, as are agents to counteract muscle spasms.

Recluse Spiders. The brown recluse spider, *Loxosceles reclusa,* is rare in the western US; it is most abundant in the South and Midwest. It has a violin-shaped mark on its head. The spiders average 1.2 centimeters in length with a 5-centimeter leg span. Unlike the black widow, both sexes are dangerous.

Brown recluse spiders live in hot, dry, undisturbed environments such as vacant buildings and woodpiles. They are nocturnal hunters of beetles, flies, moths, and other spiders, and they are most active from April to October, hibernating in fall and winter. They attack humans only as a defensive gesture.

The venom of the brown spider causes cell and tissue injury. Signs and symptoms vary from a transient irritation to painful and debilitating skin ulcers. Although the bite can be sharply painful, it is often painless. Nausea and vomiting, headache, fever, and chills may be present. In severe envenomations, redness and blisters form within 6 to 12 hours. Within 1 to 2 weeks, an area of dying skin—a necrotic

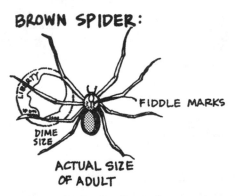

BROWN SPIDER:

FIDDLE MARKS

DIME SIZE

ACTUAL SIZE OF ADULT

• VIOLIN SHAPED MARKS ON TOP OF HEAD
• BOTH MALE and FEMALE ADULTS VENOMOUS

ulcer—forms and may leave a craterlike scar. Clean the bite site with an antiseptic soap and evacuate the patient to a physician.

Brown-spider and brown recluse bites are rare, especially outside their home range; yet they are a source of myth and frequent misdiagnosis. Likewise, the hobo spider (genus *Tegenaria*) has developed a reputation, probably undeserved, as a source of necrotic spider bites.

Tarantulas. Except for some species found in the tropics, tarantulas are not dangerous. The tarantula's fangs are too weak to penetrate very deeply, and the effects of the rare bite are limited to a small local wound.

Scorpions. Grasslands and deserts are the primary habitats for the more than 600 species of scorpions, some of which carry deadly venoms. In North America, most species are relatively

SCORPIONS

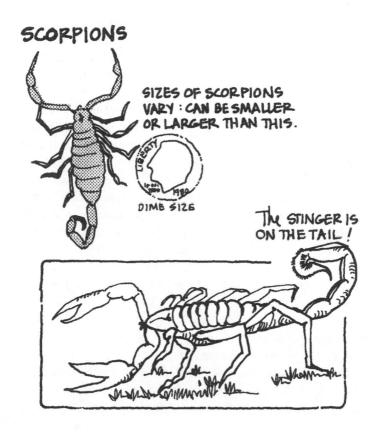

SIZES OF SCORPIONS VARY : CAN BE SMALLER OR LARGER THAN THIS.

DIME SIZE

The STINGER IS ON THE TAIL !

harmless, their stings producing effects similar to those of bee stings. Only one type of North American scorpion, a small yellowish species of the genus *Centruroides*, is dangerous. It lives in Mexico, Arizona, and New Mexico, and has been reported in southern Utah. Fatalities from its venom occur mostly in the young and the old.

Treatment of Spider Bites and Scorpion Stings
- Clean wound with antiseptic soap.
- Ice or cool compress may relieve pain.
- If systemic symptoms of envenomation develop:
  —ABCs and supportive care.
  —Evacuate to antivenom.

Scorpions feed at night on insects and spiders, injecting their prey with multiple toxins from a stinger at the tip of the tail. Scorpions like to hide in dark places during the day; beware when reaching into woodpiles or under rocks. Develop a habit of shaking out shoes, clothes, and sleeping bags when in scorpion country.

A scorpion sting produces a pricking sensation. Typical symptoms include burning pain, swelling, redness, numbness, and tingling. The affected extremity may become numb and sensitive to touch.

Treat the sting by applying ice or cool water to relieve the local symptoms. Clean the wound with an antiseptic soap. Severe poisoning signs and symptoms include impaired speech resulting from a sluggish tongue and tightened jaw, muscle spasms, nausea, vomiting, convulsions, incontinence, and respiratory and circulatory distress. Immobilize the extremity and transport the patient to a hospital. A *Centruroides* antivenom is available.

Ticks. Ticks, relatives of spiders and scorpions, are divided into two major families: hard ticks and soft ticks. Most common in the Rockies is the hard tick, genus *Dermacentor*. Like all ticks, it requires blood meals to molt from larva to nymph and from nymph to adult. The various diseases the tick carries are transmitted between hosts during the blood meal. These diseases include tick fever, relapsing fever, spotted fever, tularemia, babesiosis, and Lyme disease.

Preventing exposure is essential in tick-infested areas. Topical tick insecticide is available; look for the chemical ingredient permethrin. A visual inspection of all body parts at least

TICKS

DIME SIZE

ACTUAL SIZE OF ADULT

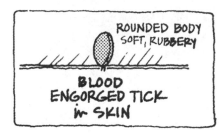

ROUNDED BODY
SOFT, RUBBERY

BLOOD ENGORGED TICK in SKIN

GENUS *DERMACENTOR*
COMMON WYOMING TICK

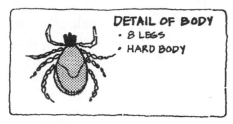

DETAIL OF BODY
• 8 LEGS
• HARD BODY

LIFE CYCLE of the TICK:

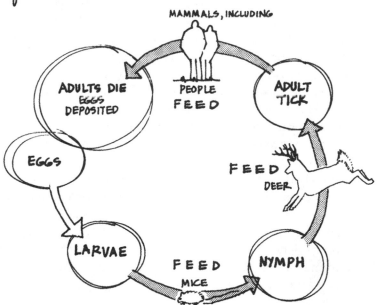

MAMMALS, INCLUDING
PEOPLE FEED

ADULTS DIE
EGGS DEPOSITED

ADULT TICK

EGGS

FEED
DEER

LARVAE

FEED
MICE

NYMPH

Treatment of Tick Bites

• Promptly remove the tick with a gentle, steady pull.
• Clean the bite site with soap and water.
• In cases of rash, fever, flu symptoms, or muscle aches following a tick
  bite, the patient should be seen by a physician.

---

twice daily is recommended, as adult ticks generally stay on the body for a few hours before attaching. Even after a tick has attached itself, prompt removal may prevent the transmission of disease.

To remove a tick, grasp it as close to the skin as possible with tweezers or gloved fingers. Pull the tick out with steady pressure. Clean the bite site thoroughly with an antiseptic soap. Traditional tick removal methods (a hot match head, nail polish, or alcohol) may induce the tick to regurgitate into the wound, or kill the tick without removing it. Avoid these methods.

Diagnosis of tick-caused illness in the field is difficult. If a rash, fever, flu symptoms, or muscle aches and pains accompany a tick bite, a physician should see the patient.

Insects. The bites of mosquitoes, blackflies, midges, horseflies, and deerflies tend to be relatively minor. Usually only localized irritation occurs, although anaphylaxis is a possibility. This group is more significant for its capacity to act as vectors of diseases such as malaria, and dengue and yellow fevers. Worldwide, only the mosquito transmits more disease than the tick.

To help reduce mosquito and other insect bites, use the following chemical and nonchemical precautions:

- Wearing protective clothing and avoiding mosquito habitat and times of peak mosquito activity.
- Judicious use of DEET or picaridin-based repellents, natural repellents (often made with soybeans or lemon eucalyptus), and insecticides such as permethrin.

Controversy persists over the safety and effectiveness of various repellents. The EPA recommends the following general use information for DEET-based products:

- Read the label carefully before use.

- Apply repellent sparingly. Heavy application and saturation are unnecessary for effectiveness. Repeat applications only as necessary and according to label directions.
- Do not apply over cuts, wounds, irritated skin, eyes, or mouth. Discontinue if skin irritation develops.
- Do not apply to children's hands or allow children to handle the product.
- Avoid DEET use on children under 2, and use only the least concentrated product (10 percent DEET or less).

Hantavirus
Hantavirus is found throughout North America but is most frequently associated with the southwestern states. It is carried by rodents, primarily deer mice, pinyon mice, brush mice, and chipmunks. The virus produces a serious respiratory disease passed from the rodent to humans through inhalation of aerosolized microscopic particles of dried rodent saliva, urine, or feces. You can become infected by touching your mouth or nose after handling contaminated materials. A rodent's bite can also spread the virus.

Symptoms are general and flu-like: fever, headache, muscle aches, and sometimes nausea and vomiting. Hantavirus infections progress to breathing difficulty, which is caused by fluid buildup in the lungs.

To minimize the risk of hantavirus infection, follow these precautions:
- Check potential campsites for rodent droppings and burrows.
- Do not disturb or crawl around in rodent burrows or dens.
- Avoid sleeping near woodpiles, burrows, or dens that may be frequented by rodents.
- Avoid sleeping on bare ground; use a ground cloth or a tent.
- Store foods in rodent-proof containers, and promptly and appropriately dispose of garbage.
- Don't use old cabins until they have been cleaned and disinfected.

FINAL THOUGHTS

Simple Tips for Preventing Poisoning Emergencies
- Read labels for information on toxic substances.
- Cook outside or in well-ventilated tents or snow shelters.
- Identify plants before you eat them.
- Be aware of foot placement.
- Look before you reach under logs or overhangs, or onto ledges.
- Shake out clothing, footwear, and sleeping bags.

Evacuation Guidelines
- Consider evacuation for anyone who has ingested a potentially harmful substance.
- Evacuate rapidly any poisoned patient who has an altered mental status or shows signs of respiratory distress.
- Contact the American Association of Poison Control Centers at 1-800-222-1222 for advice.
- Evacuate all patients bitten by a poisonous snake; expedite evacuation if the patient shows signs of envenomation.
- Rapidly evacuate patients bitten by spiders if slurred speech, difficulty swallowing, blurred vision, seizures, or respiratory or cardiovascular involvement occurs.
- Evacuate any patient with a history of an imbedded tick who develops a fever, rash, and flu-like symptoms.

CHAPTER 13 | LIGHTNING

INTRODUCTION

The incidence of lightning-related deaths in the United States has declined consistently in recent years, testimony to the effect of current public awareness and prevention campaigns. Yet lightning remains a powerful and unpredictable natural force. In the United States, fatalities have recently averaged forty per year, though many more sustain permanent injuries.

MECHANISMS OF INJURY

Injuries can result from the high voltage, secondary heat production, or the explosive force of the lightning. Lightning can injure a person in five ways:

- Direct hit: Actually being struck by lightning.
- Lightning "splash": Lightning hits another object and splashes onto objects or people standing nearby.
- Direct transmission: Being in contact with an object that has been hit directly.
- Ground current: Receiving the ground current as it dissipates from the object that has been hit—believed to be the most common mechanism of injury.
- Blunt trauma from the explosive force of the shock wave.

TYPES OF INJURY

Most victims are splashed by lightning or have contact with ground current. Very few people actually sustain a direct hit. Although a direct hit can deliver 200 to 300 million volts, the duration is short (1 to 100 milliseconds), and full thickness burns are uncommon.

Lightning burns form distinctive patterns. Superficial linear burns follow areas of heavy sweat concentration. A linear burn may begin beneath the breasts, travel from the sternum to the abdomen, then split down both legs; or it may follow the midaxillary line (an imaginary line drawn through the middle of the armpit to the waist).

Lightning-caused punctate burns are circular and small, less than a half-inch (one centimeter) in diameter. Also, featherlike patterns, which are not true burns, leave imprints on the skin. Most lightning burns are superficial or partial thickness, with some of the punctate burns being full thickness.

Lightning strikes may throw victims a considerable distance, causing injury. The cells in the brain controlling breathing and heart function may be injured, causing respiratory and cardiac arrest.

Lightning can knock its victims unresponsive. Some patients will become temporarily paralyzed and have one or

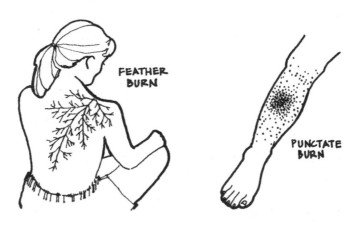

FEATHER BURN

PUNCTATE BURN

both eardrums ruptured. Other signs and symptoms are confusion, amnesia, temporary deafness or blindness, and mottling of the skin. There can be long-term emotional and psychological consequences of lightning injury.

Treatment Principles

Lightning patients should receive a thorough patient assessment. We treat what we find: fractures and burns with standard first aid procedures, cardiac or respiratory arrest with Basic Life Support. It is often stated that CPR has a higher success rate in lightning victims. This may be a myth; regardless, treat cardiac arrest with CPR. The heart may start beating again before respirations begin; if this occurs, cease chest compressions but continue rescue breathing.

Risk Management for Lightning

There is no safe place outdoors in a lightning storm. At best, we can manage the risk by reducing our exposure.

- In urban areas, seek safety in buildings (not small sheds) and vehicles. "When thunder roars, go indoors."
- Outdoor places can carry greater or lesser risk, but there is no safe place in a lightning storm.
- Know the local weather patterns:
  —Plan wisely to avoid being exposed in dangerous places.
  —Pick your campsites with prevention in mind, optimally among a uniform stand of trees or low, rolling hills.
- Know when to seek a better location:
  —Monitor approaching storms. Lightning can strike miles ahead of or behind a storm.
  —Thunder, a clear sign of danger, can be heard for 10 miles in calm air, much less in turbulent stormy air.
  —Flash-bang ranging systems, based on sound traveling 1 mile every 5 seconds (1km/3sec), can be deceptive. To use flash-bang correctly, you must match the flash with the correct bang, and know the speed of the approaching storm.

FREQUENT STRIKES
EXTREMELY
HAZARDOUS

OCCASIONAL
STRIKES
HAZARDOUS

RELATIVELY
SAFE

LARGE CAVE
(NOT SHALLOW) SAFE
ONLY IF WALLS /
ENTRANCE AVOIDED.

SIT ON SOMETHING DRY and
NON-CONDUCTING (FOAM PAD,
ROPE, DRY PACK.)

SQUAT WITH FEET FACING DOWNHILL.
TRY TO KEEP HANDS
OFF THE GROUND!

LIGHTNING Safety

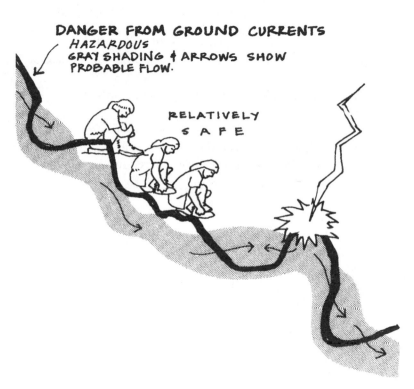

DANGER FROM GROUND CURRENTS
HAZARDOUS
GRAY SHADING & ARROWS SHOW
PROBABLE FLOW.

RELATIVELY
SAFE

- Avoid dangerous locations:
  —Places higher than surrounding terrain: peaks, ridges, hilltops.
  —Isolated tall objects such as lone trees.
  —Open terrain such as meadows.
  —Large bodies of water, especially the shoreline.
  —Shallow overhangs and caves.

Lightning Position

Sitting on something that keeps you off the ground (e.g., sleeping pad, pack, coil of rope) and making yourself as small as possible to minimize contact with the ground may provide some protection against ground current. It does not provide complete safety, so we use it only after we are sure we can't move to a better location. Ground current is most dangerous when there is distance separating body parts touching the ground. The distance creates a potential (voltage) difference lightning can traverse. For that reason, any position that keeps the body compact and that you can comfortably maintain is as good as any other; people most commonly sit on a pad with legs together, minimizing contact with the ground.

—Places previously struck; lightning will strike the same place twice.
—Long conductors: pipes, wires, wire fences, wet ropes.
• When it is impractical to move to a safer location, insulate yourself from ground current, stay low (lightning position), and disperse a group to limit casualties.

Evacuation Guidelines
• All lightning injury patients should be evacuated for further evaluation and treatment.

CHAPTER 14
DROWNING AND COLD-WATER IMMERSION

INTRODUCTION

Sudden immersion in cold water causes a gasp for air, constriction of blood vessels in the extremities, and increased breathing and heart rate. The initial gasp may result in water inhalation, and the urge to breathe rapidly makes it more difficult to hold one's breath.

Heart rhythm abnormalities may cause death, and as strength and coordination diminish, the chance of drowning increases. What's more, as the brain cools, we think less clearly and may do foolish things such as removing a personal flotation device (PFD) or swimming aimlessly.

In the wilderness, we often encounter situations that present the risk of cold water immersion. Water conducts heat twenty-five times faster than air; water colder than 77°F (25°C) presents risk for hypothermia, and this hazard becomes more severe when the temperature drops below 59°F (15°C). In North America, most water remains below 77°F year-round, and many mountain lakes never warm past 59°F, even in mid-summer. We are unable to remain warm at any of these temperatures unless we wear wetsuits or drysuits.

DROWNING

Drowning (the process of experiencing respiratory impairment from submersion in a liquid) is the second-most-common cause of accidental death in children and the third-leading cause of death in young adults. A majority of drowning victims are young males. Alcohol is involved in many drowning accidents. Freshwater drowning, especially in pools, is more common than saltwater drowning.

Submersion injury is a general term for any adverse effect from submersion in water.

ASPECTS OF A TYPICAL DROWNING

Drowning often begins with an unplanned submersion. Victims commonly hold their breath, panic, and struggle while in a near-vertical position, with their head tilted back, accompanied by ineffective downward arm and bicycling leg movements that make little or no forward progress. Hypoxia, loss of responsiveness, and respiratory and cardiac arrest soon follow. Often, victims are first seen floating motionless, sinking silently below the surface, or diving into water and never surfacing.

Treatment of Drowning

For first aid purposes, the type of water (salt, fresh, clean, dirty) does not matter. Airway maintenance and, if necessary, rescue breathing and chest compressions are essential to the treatment of unresponsive drowning victims. If you have any doubts about how long the victim was submerged, attempt resuscitation. Albeit rare, there are case reports of people surviving prolonged submersion in ice water.

The goals of treatment are to remove the victim from the water, protect the cervical spine, prevent cardiac arrest, and stabilize the patient's temperature.

Remove the Victim from the Water. Remove the victim from the water as quickly as possible.

Rescuer safety is a priority. Remember the lifesaving adage: "reach, throw, row, tow, and go." First try reaching for the victim, remaining in contact with the shore or the boat. Second, throw a lifeline. Third, row or paddle to the victim. Attempt a swimming rescue only as a last resort; do not enter the water to attempt rescue if you have not received training.

Handle the Patient Gently. A patient who was submerged in cold water may be hypothermic. Position the patient perpendicular to the beach slope, parallel to the water's edge, to begin treatment (avoid head or legs higher).

Check the ABCs. Assess and check the ABCs. Aggressive initiation of airway, breathing, and circulation measures is the standard treatment in drowning rescue. A key concern with a drowning victim is lack of oxygen (hypoxia) to the brain; airway maintenance and rescue breathing may be critical in avoiding cardiac arrest.

If there is water or vomit in the airway, remove it with suction or use of the recovery position, to facilitate draining and cleaning of the mouth and upper airway. Do not spend time removing white foam from the upper airway. This is likely from the lungs. Give rescue breathing through the white foam. If available, administer oxygen.

Treatment of Drowning

- Remove the victim from the water.
- Handle gently.
- Manage airway and consider rescue breathing.
- Protect the cervical spine.
- Perform a focused exam and history.
- Treat for hypothermia.
- Monitor vital signs.

Protect the Cervical Spine. Unless injury can be ruled out, assume that the victim has a neck injury and use the jaw-thrust technique to open the airway. Neck injuries can be caused by surfing, diving in shallow water, or flipping a kayak or decked canoe in rapids.

Perform a Focused Exam and History. A complete patient exam is warranted to assess for injury.

Treat for Hypothermia. Remove wet clothing, and dry and insulate the patient to prevent further heat loss.

Evacuate the Patient. Outside the wilderness, a physician should evaluate any victim of involuntary submersion. Lung injury from inhaled water may not be immediately evident, although onset of respiratory signs and symptoms usually occurs within 6 hours. In the wilderness we don't evacuate every asymptomatic person who swims through a rapid or takes a dunking during a river crossing and comes up coughing. Monitor for wet lung sounds, productive cough, rapid shallow respiration, cyanosis, inability to take a deep breath, irregular and/or depressed heart rate, or decreased level of responsiveness. Evacuate the victim of a submersion incident if that person required resuscitation, was unresponsive in the water, or exhibits shortness of breath or other symptoms of respiratory difficulty.

IMMERSION HYPOTHERMIA

It's a common misperception that we quickly become hypothermic and drown when immersed in cold water. In fact, while cold water is very uncomfortable and we can quickly cool to the point where meaningful movement is difficult, actual hypothermia takes a while to develop. Dr. Gordon Giesbrecht of the University of Manitoba, Canada, is a leading researcher in immersion hypothermia. Dr. Giesbrecht's simple message is "1 minute, 10 minutes, 1 hour." We need to control our breathing and survive the first minute; gasping when our head is underwater can cause drowning. We have 10 minutes to move carefully and thoughtfully before we will become incapacitated by the cold. We have an hour before we will become unresponsive due to hypothermia. While we still need to promptly rescue people and treat hypothermia, we know we should not panic. We have time to plan correct actions.

Treatment of Immersion Hypothermia
Although there may be subtle differences between hypothermia on land and in the water, these differences are not relevant to field treatment. Treat immersion hypothermia by removing the victim from the water. Handle the patient gently, as rough handling may trigger lethal heart rhythm abnormalities and a phenomenon known as circum-rescue collapse. As much as possible, keep the patient horizontal. Treat the patient for hypothermia as discussed in Chapter 9 ("Cold Injuries"). Dry and insulate the patient; prevent further heat loss; ensure adequate

airway, breathing, and circulation; and place the patient in a sleeping bag, possibly with another person or with hot water bottles as heat sources.

FINAL THOUGHTS

Safety around lakes, rivers, and the ocean begins with respect for the power of moving water and the debilitating effects of cold water. According to the Coast Guard, cold water, failure to wear a personal flotation device (PFD), and the inability to swim are the most common factors in whitewater deaths.

In two out of three drownings, the victims could not swim, had no intention of entering deep water (and thus were ill prepared), and were affected by alcohol or drugs. Most drownings occur 10 to 30 feet from safety; only 10 percent of drownings occur in a guarded pool.

If you are awaiting rescue, assume the HELP (heat escape lessening posture) by bringing your knees to your chest and crossing your arms over them. If you're with a group of people awaiting rescue, everyone in the group should face inward and huddle with arms interlocked. You must be wearing a PFD to assume either of these positions. If possible, get out of the water onto an overturned or partially submerged boat. It is always better to keep as much of yourself or the victim out of the water as possible, even when the wind is blowing.

Risk Factors Related to Drowning

- Age—toddlers and teenage males are at highest risk.
- Location—private swimming pools, small streams, ponds, and irrigation ditches are common drowning sites.
- Gender—males dominate all age groups.
- Alcohol—a factor in one-third to two-thirds of drownings.
- Injury—cervical spine injury, as from diving or surfing.
- Seizure disorder—risk is greatest if poorly controlled; hyperventilation may cause predisposition to seizures.
- PFD—failure to wear one.

DROWNING CHAIN OF SURVIVAL

The links in the drowning "chain of survival" are prevention, recognizing distress, providing flotation, removing the victim from the water and providing care.

1. Prevention begins with maintaining awareness and being conservative in and around water.

Swimming
—Be honest about your swimming ability and know the ability of your group's members.
—Don't underestimate the ability of cold water and current to impair your ability to swim.
—Know how to identify ocean rip currents and how to escape if caught in one.
—Do not swim alone.
—Wade instead of swim; be aware of drop-offs.
—Swim parallel to shore rather than out into deeper water.
—Wear a personal flotation device (PFD) properly.
—Learn to recognize distress in the water.

Backcountry
—Know and practice appropriate stream/river crossing methods.
—Moving water above your knees may be impassable and dangerous.
—Scout the crossing site. Look downstream. Consider other options.
—Use hiking poles as support and consider unbuckling backpack waist and sternum straps.

Boating
—Wear PFDs and avoid alcohol consumption.
—Scout hazards or unknown waterways.
—Be watchful of changes in weather and wind.

2. Recognize distress; in the front country, ask someone to call for help.
3. Provide flotation to prevent submersion.
4. Remove from water, if it is safe to do so.
—Scene safety is paramount; do not enter the water to attempt rescue if you have not received training.
5. Provide care as needed; seek medical attention.

Clothing selection for paddling or other activities around water requires finding a balance between overdressing (and overheating) and adequately protecting the body against sudden immersion in cold water. Extra clothing should be easily accessible in the cockpit of your boat or in your pack, and should be put on if developing conditions increase the likelihood of a cold dunking.

Well-developed safety and rescue programs exist for swimming, sea kayaking, whitewater boating, and sailing. If you're involved in any of these activities, seek out these programs for further training.

Evacuation Guidelines

- Evacuate any person who required resuscitation, was unresponsive in the water, or exhibits shortness of breath related to immersion.

CHAPTER 15 | MARINE ENVENOMATIONS

INTRODUCTION

Injuries from marine organisms rarely result from an aggressive, unprovoked attack. Most injuries occur as a result of accidental contact or when a threatened animal reacts in self-defense. This chapter discusses two broad categories of injuries from aquatic animals: marine-spine envenomations and nematocyst-sting envenomations. Marine-spine envenomations are commonly treated by immersion in hot water. Nematocyst envenomations may be treated with vinegar or immersion in hot water.

Marine-Spine Envenomations

Marine animals with venom known to be harmful to people include the lion fish, scorpion fish, stonefish, sea urchin, starfish, and stingray, which deliver venom through spines; and the cone shell, which injects venom through a proboscis. Envenomation may cause life-threatening injury or mild irritation, depending on the species, the number of punctures, the amount of venom, the health of the victim, and other factors.

Scorpion Fish

There are three genera in this family—stonefish, zebra fish, and scorpion fish—and several hundred species. The stonefish, inconspicuous and possessing a highly toxic venom, is considered to be among the most dangerous of all venomous creatures.

Zebra fish are spectacularly colored; stonefish and scorpion fish are less so. All members of the family are found in shallow waters. Zebra fish are free swimmers; stonefish and scorpion fish often hide in cracks, near rocks, or among plants. The stonefish may bury itself under sandy or broken coral bottoms. A dead stonefish is still dangerous! Its venom remains active for 48 hours after death.

The immediate intense pain of stonefish envenomation peaks in 60 to 90 minutes and can persist for days despite treatment. Stonefish wounds are slow to heal and prone to infection.

Sea Urchins

Sea urchins are nonaggressive, nocturnal, omnivorous feeders that move slowly across the ocean bottom and are often found on rocky bottoms or burrowed into sand and small crevices. The hard spines protecting their vital organs can envenomate victims if the urchin is stepped on, handled, or bumped. Their grasping organs, called pedicellariae, can also envenomate.

Symptoms are usually local and mild; however, infections are possible if pieces of imbedded spines remain in the skin or joint capsules. A physician should evaluate spines imbedded in joints or large fragments left in soft tissues. Severe reactions are rare.

Spines lodged in the skin often turn it a brownish-purple color. This reaction is harmless and can be seen whether or not a spine has broken off and remains imbedded.

Starfish

The venomous crown-of-thorns starfish is found in the Indo-Pacific area, the Red Sea, the eastern Pacific, and the Sea of Cortez. Starfish are predators and scavengers that feed on other echinoderms, mollusks, coral, and worms. The upper surface of the crown-of-thorns starfish is studded with sharp, poisonous spines that can penetrate even the best diving gloves.

Cone Shells

These animals live in shallow waters, reefs, and tide pools; they have beautiful shells that hide a nasty sting. Cone shells project a long proboscis from the narrow end of the shell and inject venom from its tip. Toxicity to humans varies, but it rarely causes death. Do not handle cone shells. Drop them immediately if you see the proboscis. Almost all reported envenomations have come from collectors handling the shells.

The injury resembles a bee sting, with pain, burning, and itching. Serious envenomations produce cyanosis and numbness at the injury site, progressing to numbness around the mouth, then generalized paralysis.

Treatment of cone-shell stings is largely supportive care. Clean and thoroughly irrigate the puncture wound. The benefit of hot-water soaks is unproved, but they may provide pain relief. Likewise, the value of circumferential-pressure bandages is unconfirmed, but they may slow the spread of the venom.

CONE SHELL:

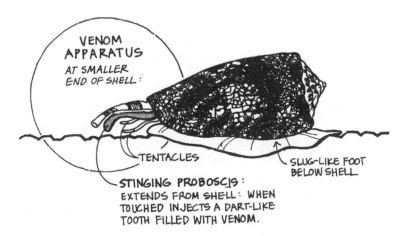

VENOM APPARATUS
AT SMALLER END OF SHELL:

TENTACLES

SLUG-LIKE FOOT BELOW SHELL

STINGING PROBOSCIS: EXTENDS FROM SHELL: WHEN TOUCHED INJECTS A DART-LIKE TOOTH FILLED WITH VENOM.

Stingrays

Stingrays are bottom feeders, often found in shallow waters lying atop or partially buried under sandy bottoms. Most stingray envenomations occur when a swimmer or wader steps on a buried ray. The stingray's tail whips up and its serrated barbs can inflict a nasty wound. Such defensive attacks usually cause wounds to the leg or ankle, and pieces of barbs may remain imbedded in the wound. Wounds often take the form of bleeding soft-tissue lacerations or punctures. Intense local pain may last up to 48 hours.

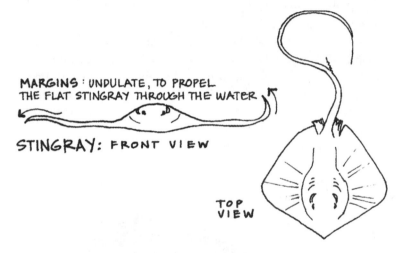

MARGINS: UNDULATE, TO PROPEL THE FLAT STINGRAY THROUGH THE WATER

STINGRAY: FRONT VIEW

TOP VIEW

Signs and Symptoms of Marine-Spine Envenomation. Signs of marine venom injury include local discoloration, cyanosis, and laceration or puncture wound. Symptoms include numbness, tingling, and intense local pain. In serious envenomations, nausea, vomiting, paralysis, respiratory distress, heart rhythm irregularities, and shock can occur.

Treatment of Marine-Spine Envenomation. Treat marine envenomations by controlling bleeding, removing imbedded spines, cleaning the wound, and controlling pain with hot-water soaks.

Immerse the Injury in Hot Water. Immerse the injury in water as hot as the patient can tolerate—usually for 30 to 90 minutes or until the pain is gone. This therapy is thought to inactivate

---

Treatment of Marine-Spine Envenomations

- Control bleeding.
- Immerse the injury in water as hot as the patient can tolerate, usually for 30 to 90 minutes or until the pain is gone.
- Remove imbedded spines.
- Irrigate the wound.
- Clean the wound.
- Elevate the extremity to help control swelling.
- Monitor for signs of infection or envenomation.
- Provide medications for pain.

---

heat-sensitive proteins in the venom. Immersion in a large pot or a plastic bag filled with hot water is best. Hot compresses can also be used.

Clean the wound with irrigation. Remove obvious imbedded spines carefully. Imbedded spines are a source of infection and a continuing source of venom. Their presence also retards healing and may cause further injury. Removing them is often difficult; the spines are brittle and break easily, leaving a foreign body that may cause infection. Use tweezers or fingers (wear gloves) to remove the spines. If the spine is hard to remove, leave it in place and evacuate the patient. Elevate the extremity to help control swelling. Remedies such as meat tenderizer, papain, or mangrove sap are not scientifically confirmed and may irritate the wound. Medications to control pain are appropriate.

Monitor the patient for signs of systemic effects of envenomation. With severe envenomation, signs and symptoms of shock and respiratory distress will develop. In these cases, the treatment is supportive care and evacuation.

NEMATOCYST-STING ENVENOMATIONS

Nematocysts are specialized stinging capsules found in members of the phylum Cnidaria, which includes sea anemones, jellyfish, hydroids such as the Portuguese man-of-war, and corals. The nematocyst discharges an incapacitating venom, allowing the animal to kill and digest its prey.

Nematocyst discharge is triggered by contact with the skin or by changes in osmotic pressure, which can occur when the nematocyst is rinsed with fresh water. Nematocysts are generally found around the animal's mouth or on the tentacles, and nematocysts from dead jellyfish can still envenomate.

Anemones

Stinging cells line the tentacles of these sessile organisms. Contact often occurs from accidentally brushing into the anemone. Anemone nematocysts usually produce only very mild local symptoms.

Jellyfish

These animals vary in size from pinhead to whale-like. Most produce mild local signs and symptoms; however, some produce very potent venom. The box jellyfish (*Chironex fleckeri*) can cause death within 1 minute.

Portuguese Man-of-War

This large colony of animals (not a true jellyfish) usually lives on the surface of the open ocean, its long, transparent tentacles dangling for prey. Winds and currents transport it, and sometimes push the animal or pieces of its tentacles into coastal waters. Contact with pieces of tentacle usually causes only mild, superficial reactions. However, contact with a large number of tentacles from an intact animal can provoke massive envenomation and cause serious reactions.

Fire Coral

Fire corals are so named because they make you feel as if you've touched hot coals. They are found in coral reefs in tropical waters. Their nematocyst sting causes immediate pain, often described as burning, and small raised red areas on the skin. The localized pain usually lasts 1 to 4 days.

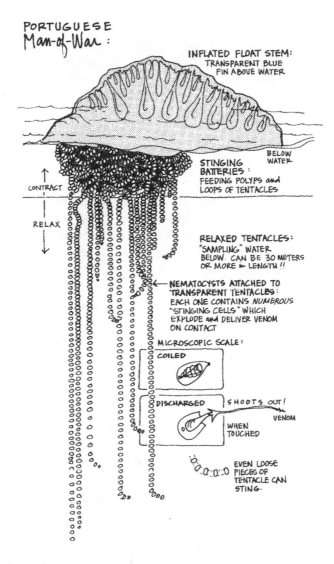

PORTUGUESE
Man-of-War :

INFLATED FLOAT STEM:
TRANSPARENT BLUE
FIN ABOVE WATER

BELOW WATER

STINGING BATTERIES :
FEEDING POLYPS and
LOOPS OF TENTACLES

CONTRACT ↑

RELAX ↓

RELAXED TENTACLES:
"SAMPLING" WATER
BELOW. CAN BE 30 METERS
OR MORE in LENGTH !!

NEMATOCYSTS ATTACHED TO
TRANSPARENT TENTACLES:
EACH ONE CONTAINS *NUMEROUS*
"STINGING CELLS" WHICH
EXPLODE and DELIVER VENOM
ON CONTACT

MICROSCOPIC SCALE:

COILED

DISCHARGED

SHOOTS OUT!

VENOM

WHEN TOUCHED

EVEN LOOSE
PIECES OF
TENTACLE CAN
STING.

Hard Coral

Hard corals are not highly venomous but often have sharp edges that can cause abrasions or even lacerations. The wounds heal slowly and can become infected, especially if pieces of coral are imbedded in the skin. Some species can cause rashes. Vigorous irrigation of the wound helps remove coral pieces.

Sea Cucumbers

These creatures are bottom scavengers found in both shallow and deep water. Sea cucumbers often feed on nematocysts, so they may secrete Cnidarian venom as well. Some species also produce a liquid toxin that causes skin irritations and severe inflammatory reactions (swelling, raised patches, itching, oozing). To treat, rinse the skin thoroughly with water and soak the injured area in vinegar.

Signs and Symptoms of Nematocyst-Sting Envenomations

Signs and symptoms range from mild skin irritations to rapid death, and they vary considerably with the venomous species. In general, contact with a nematocyst produces painful local swelling, redness, and a stinging, prickling sensation that progresses to numbness, burning, and throbbing pain. Pain may radiate from the extremities to the groin, abdomen, or armpit. The contact site may turn a reddish-brown-purple color, marked by swelling. In more serious cases, blisters may occur.

Severe envenomation may produce headache, abdominal cramps, nausea, vomiting, muscle paralysis, and respiratory or cardiac distress.

Treatment of Nematocyst-Sting Envenomations

Treat nematocyst injury first by protecting yourself, and second by inactivating and removing nematocysts from the skin. Rinse the injury with seawater to begin removing remaining nematocysts. Do not scrape, rub, or rinse with fresh water, as this may cause any nematocysts on the skin to release more venom. If you have vinegar (5-percent acetic acid), test a small area for adverse effects—in some species, vinegar may trigger further nematocyst discharge. If it appears to help, soak the injury in vinegar for at least 30 minutes. If vinegar treatment is unavailable or not indicated, soak the injured area in hot water (105°F/41°C) for 30 to 90 minutes. Alcohol, meat tenderizer, and baking soda are less effective, although a baking-soda slurry is effective in treating the sting of the Chesapeake sea nettle.

Treatment of Nematocyst-Sting Envenomations
- Rinse with seawater to remove remaining nematocysts.
- Test a small area with vinegar.
- If vinegar is helpful, soak for at least 30 minutes.
- If vinegar increases nematocyst discharge, immerse the injury in hot water.
- After soaking, remove all visible tentacles.

After soaking, remove all visible tentacles with tweezers. Sticky tentacles may be easier to remove if you first apply a drying agent such as baking soda, talcum powder, or sand. Be careful. Rescuer injury is common both in the water and when removing nematocysts on shore.

FINAL THOUGHTS

Learn to identify marine animals and to understand their habits. When wading, shuffle your feet to alert stingrays to your presence. Touching marine animals or coral formations is not necessary to enjoy them. When swimming and diving, avoid standing or walking on coral reefs or banging against them. A minimum-impact approach protects not only you but also the fragile underwater environment.

Evacuation Guidelines
- Evacuate any patient with a large soft-tissue wound, imbedded spine, unmanageable pain, or systemic signs and symptoms of envenomation.

MEDICAL EMERGENCIES

When we venture into wilderness, we bring with us our clothing and camping gear, our companions, enthusiasms and aspirations, and our medical history. The NOLS incident data shows the variety of illness, from flu-like symptoms to chest pain, allergies to abdominal pain, that can occur in the wilderness. The wilderness first aider isn't expected to know the details of these complex medical conditions. All we need is knowledge of the treatment principles that prepare us to manage this diversity of medical problems and to identify those requiring evacuation to the care of the physician.

This section also provides guidance in addressing mental health concerns that may arise in the wilderness. In most first aid texts and courses, this is an underappreciated topic, yet any seasoned outdoor leader knows that mental health problems arise on our trips and expeditions. The treatment principles will guide your field care of these patients.

CHAPTER 16
ALLERGIES AND ANAPHYLAXIS

INTRODUCTION

The immune system is an extensive array of cells, structures, antibodies, and other elements constantly defending us against foreign substances: microorganisms, pollen, dust, food, cat dander—practically all the pieces of the natural world. Usually the immune system smoothly identifies and neutralizes harmful substances with white blood cells, antibodies, and mild inflammation. It's a wonderful, critical, complex, and efficient system. Among the many things it does is remember a first encounter with a foreign substance, producing antibodies designed to recognize and neutralize the invader the next time it appears.

Normally, this interaction is delicately balanced. An overreaction causes us misery when it triggers an inflammatory response we call an allergy. In an allergic person, reintroduction of the foreign material—an allergen—results in an inappropriately large release of histamine. Histamine causes fluid to leak from blood vessels, resulting in edema and swelling, which can obstruct the airway. It also dilates blood vessels, which can lead to shock.

SIGNS AND SYMPTOMS OF MILD TO MODERATE ALLERGIC REACTIONS

Allergic reactions range from mild to severe, and they can be immediate or delayed. For most people, the allergic response is mild, though often irritating. Hay fever is one example of a mild allergic response, causing sufferers to complain of a runny nose, sneezing, swollen eyes, itching skin, and possibly hives. An allergic reaction may also be local, the result of insect stings or contact with a plant. The local reaction may include redness, swelling, itching, perhaps hives, all staying near the point of contact.

Signs and Symptoms of Mild to Moderate Allergic Reaction

- Local swelling near a sting
- Runny nose, sneezing, swollen eyes, hay fever
- Flushed and itchy skin
- Hives or welts on the skin
- Mild or no breathing difficulty

Treatment of a Mild to Moderate Allergic Reaction

- Remove the allergen from the patient or the patient from the offending environment.
- Administer oral antihistamines.
- Hydrate.
- Monitor for difficulty breathing.

Treatment for Mild to Moderate Allergic Reactions

First remove the allergen from the patient or the patient from the offending environment. It's hard to treat a pollen reaction standing under a tree shedding millions of pollen grains, or to treat an allergy to dust in a dusty cabin. Antihistamines are the usual treatment. The antihistamines treat the underlying mechanism of the reaction: the release of too much histamine. Monitor the patient closely for a developing severe reaction.

SIGNS AND SYMPTOMS OF SEVERE ALLERGIC REACTIONS

An anaphylactic response is a massive generalized reaction of the immune system that is potentially harmful to the body. Common triggers of anaphylaxis are drugs and some foods, as well as bee stings and insect bites. Instead of the mild symptoms of hay fever, anaphylaxis produces rash, itching, hives, flushed skin, and swollen and red eyes; large areas of swelling typically involving the face, lips, and tongue; difficulty swallowing; asphyxiating swelling of the larynx with respiratory distress and inability to speak in more than one- or two-word sentences; gastrointestinal symptoms and signs such as crampy abdominal pain and vomiting; and signs and symptoms of shock. The airway obstruction and shock may be fatal. Onset usually occurs within a few minutes of contact with the triggering substance, although the reaction may be delayed and/or a second reaction can occur after treatment of the first reaction. Any airway swelling; large areas of swelling especially involving the face, neck, or lips; respiratory distress; or shock should be treated with epinephrine.

Signs and Symptoms of Anaphylaxis
- Flushed and itchy skin
- Hives and welts on the skin
- Swollen face, lips, and tongue
- Respiratory distress
- Shock

Treatment of Anaphylaxis
- Remove the allergen from the patient or the patient from the offending environment.
- For large areas of swelling, respiratory distress, or shock, inject epinephrine.
- When the patient can swallow, administer oral antihistamines.
- Watch for a second reaction.
- Evacuate.

Treatment of Severe Allergic Reactions

If you suspect an allergic reaction while the patient can still swallow, administer oral antihistamines. When the reaction becomes severe, the anaphylaxis is treated with immediate administration of epinephrine (a prescription medication) to counteract the effects of the histamine. Fatalities in anaphylaxis are often associated with delayed administration of epinephrine.

Epinephrine reverses vasodilation, increases vasoconstriction and thus supports blood pressure, decreases mucus production, dilates the bronchi, and stabilizes histamine-secreting mast cells (thus decreasing histamine release). Epinephrine is much more powerful than antihistamines and is the gold standard medicine for anaphylaxis. Antihistamines are supportive medications that reduce the allergic response and may prevent ongoing or biphasic reactions.

Epinephrine for anaphylaxis can save a life with low risk of adverse events. States are increasingly enacting legislation supporting administration of epinephrine for anaphylaxis by laypeople. Persons who know that they are vulnerable to anaphylaxis usually carry injectable epinephrine in an auto-injector (Adult dose is 0.3 cc of 1:1000 epinephrine. Infants and children weighing from 10 kg to 25 kg dose is 0.15 mg of 1:1000 epinephrine. Infants less than 10 kg dose is 0.1mg/kg of 1:1000 epinephrine). Those who may need to use, or to assist the patient in using, the auto-injector should familiarize themselves with the particular device; several different models are on the market, and color coding and procedures for use are not standardized.

Evacuation Guidelines
- Evacuate rapidly any patient with a severe allergic reaction. Secondary reactions can occur within 12 to 24 hours.

CHAPTER 17 | RESPIRATORY AND CARDIAC EMERGENCIES

INTRODUCTION

Illnesses of our respiratory and cardiac systems—most critically, our lungs and our heart—are unfortunately common. They range from problems that are manageable in the field, to conditions that we at best recognize and provide supportive care for while we evacuate the patient to the definitive care they need.

RESPIRATORY AND CARDIAC EMERGENCIES

A history of asthma, heart disease, or even a heart attack does not, by itself, prevent someone from paddling a river, climbing a peak, or hiking the Wind River Range. While people with significant lung and heart disease are more unlikely to travel in the wilderness, they do venture outside. Especially at the interface of the front- and backcountry, search and rescue data shows us we need to be prepared to manage these illnesses.

Hyperventilation Syndrome

Hyperventilation syndrome is an increased respiratory rate often caused by an emotional stimulus. The patient becomes apprehensive, nervous, or tense. For example, a person may have a fear of heights, and the thought of rock climbing can trigger a hyperventilation episode; or a climber may fall and suffer a

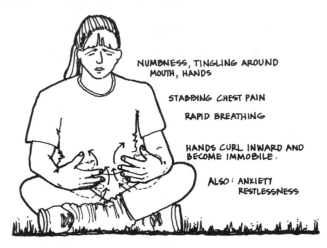

CARPOPEDAL SPASMS
HYPERVENTILATION SYNDROME :

NUMBNESS, TINGLING AROUND
MOUTH, HANDS

STABBING CHEST PAIN

RAPID BREATHING

HANDS CURL INWARD AND
BECOME IMMOBILE.

ALSO: ANXIETY
RESTLESSNESS

minor injury but begin to hyperventilate out of fear and anxiety. Hyperventilation confounds many injuries and illnesses, and can quickly become the major condition affecting the patient.

Signs and Symptoms of Hyperventilation. Signs and symptoms of hyperventilation include a high level of anxiety, a sensation of suffocation without apparent physiological basis, dizziness and/or faintness, dry mouth, rapid and deep respiration, rapid pulse, and sweating.

As the syndrome progresses, the patient may complain of numbness or tingling of the hands or around the mouth. Thereafter, painful spasms of the hands and forearms called carpopedal spasms may occur. The hands curl inward and become immobile, and the patient may complain of stabbing chest pain. Rapid respiration increases the loss of carbon dioxide, which causes the blood to become alkaline, and the alkaline blood causes the carpopedal spasms.

Treatment for Hyperventilation. To treat hyperventilation syndrome, calm the patient and slow their breathing. Coach the patient to breathe slowly. It may take some time before the symptoms resolve. Breathing into a paper bag, once thought to help increase carbon dioxide in the blood, is no longer a recommended treatment.

Pulmonary Embolism

A pulmonary embolism occurs when a clot (usually from a leg vein) breaks loose and lodges in the blood vessels of the lung. Decreased mobility—lying in a tent waiting out a storm or long plane flights—may predispose a person to a blood clot. Smoking and a history of recent surgery or illness that kept the patient in bed are also risk factors. There is an increased tendency for blood to clot in arteries and veins at high altitudes. Dehydration, increased red blood cells, cold, constrictive clothing, and immobility during bad weather have been cited as possible causes.

Signs and Symptoms of Pulmonary Embolism. It can be difficult to distinguish a pulmonary embolism from cardiac, pneumothorax, or other problems; often the first responder only recognizes and reacts to chest pain and difficulty breathing. The patient complains of sudden-onset shortness of breath and pain with inspiration. Respiratory distress may develop, including anxiety and restlessness; shortness of breath; rapid breathing and pulse; signs of shock, including cool, clammy skin, and paleness or cyanosis of the skin, lips, mucous membranes and fingernail beds; and labored breathing using accessory muscles of the neck, shoulder, and abdomen to achieve maximum effort.

Treatment for Pulmonary Embolism. First responders can't dissolve the emboli in the field. If you identify respiratory distress or chest pain, administer oxygen if it is available, and evacuate the patient promptly.

Pneumonia

Pneumonia is a lung infection that can be caused by bacteria, viruses, fungi, and protozoa. The resulting inflammation of the alveolar spaces causes swelling and fluid accumulation, resulting in difficulty breathing. People weakened by an illness, chronic disease, fatigue, or exposure are especially at risk. Pneumonia can be serious and is a leading cause of death.

Signs and Symptoms of Pneumonia. Signs and symptoms of pneumonia are shortness of breath, fever and chills, a productive cough with green-yellow or brown sputum, and pain on inspiration or coughing. The patient may have a recent history of upper-respiratory infection. If you can listen with a stethoscope, lung sounds may be noisy.

Treatment of Pneumonia. Patients with pneumonia should be evacuated. Encourage the patient to cough and breathe deeply to keep the lungs clear. Hydration is important and oxygen, if available, will be helpful. The patient may be more comfortable sitting up.

Asthma

Asthma is a syndrome characterized by narrowing of the airways, increased mucus production, and bronchial edema. Asthma's exact cause is unknown. We do know that allergy and environmental (nonallergic) factors such as molds, cold air, chemical fumes, cigarette smoke, exercise, and infections play a role.

Asthma is usually a reversible condition, unlike other chronic lung diseases such as emphysema and bronchitis, in which the breathing impairment is persistent because of destruction of lung tissue and chronic inflammation. Airway narrowing in asthma can improve spontaneously or in response to medication. A prolonged, severe asthma attack that is not relieved by treatment is an emergency requiring rapid transport.

Signs and Symptoms of Asthma. Signs and symptoms of mild-to-moderate asthma are wheezing, chest tightness, and shortness of breath. The heart and breathing rates are increased. When asthma becomes severe, the patient may be hunched over, bracing the upper body and working to breathe. The patient may be able to speak only in one- or two-word clusters. If you can listen with a stethoscope, lung sounds may be diminished or absent. If the patient becomes sleepy or too fatigued to breathe, the situation is dire.

Signs and Symptoms of Pneumonia

- History of upper-respiratory infection
- Sweating, fever, chills
- Productive cough
- Pain on inspiration or coughing
- Shortness of breath
- Noisy lung sounds
- General illness

Treatment of Pneumonia

- Encourage patients to cough.
- Hydrate.
- Administer oxygen.
- Evacuate.

Treatment of Asthma. People with asthma often have medications, commonly bronchodilators, that they administer as needed with an inhaler. You may need to help the patient relax and use the inhaler properly; shake it first, hold it in the mouth (use a spacer chamber if it is available), have the patient exhale, and then depress the device and inhale the mist deeply, holding the breath for 5 to 10 seconds before exhaling. Ideally the patient has a treatment plan from their physician that describes the dose of their inhaler for mild and moderate episodes of asthma. If the patient doesn't have a plan, a common regimen to stabilize the initial exacerbation is 4-8 puffs every 20 minutes for up to 4 hours. Warm, humidified air, or oxygen if available, can also help relax airways and clear mucus. Severe asthma episodes may require medications (epinephrine and steroids) usually not available in the wilderness, and such patients should be evacuated promptly.

Signs and Symptoms of Asthma

MILD-TO-MODERATE ASTHMA
• Chest tightness
• Wheezing and coughing
• Shortness of breath
• Increased heart and breathing rates
• Increased mucus production
• Fatigue

SEVERE ASTHMA
• Use of accessory muscles to breathe.
• Decreasing breath sounds progressing to absence of sounds.
• Speaking in one- to two-word clusters.
• Sleepiness.
• Cyanosis.

Treatment of Asthma
• Bronchodilators
• Warm, humidified oxygen
• Hydration and rest
• Evacuate if asthma is severe.

Chest Pain and Heart Disease

Heart disease is a leading cause of death in the United States. Atherosclerosis, a common form of heart disease, slowly builds deposits on arterial walls that narrow the artery and impede blood flow. The narrowed artery can spasm, constrict, or lodge a clot, depriving tissue of blood. If this happens in the brain, the result may be a stroke. If it happens in the heart, it causes chest pain (also known as angina pectoris, or just angina) or a myocardial infarction—a heart attack. Angina is pain from diminished

---

Signs and Symptoms of Cardiac Chest Pain

- Persistent chest pain: crushing, tight, pressing, viselike, constricting
- Shortness of breath
- Anxiety and denial
- Pain radiating to arm or jaw
- Nausea and vomiting
- Fainting
- Cool, sweaty skin, pale skin and mucous membranes
- Rapid, slow, weak, or irregular heartbeat
- Back pain
- History of angina, heart attack, or cardiac risk factors

---

blood flow. A myocardial infarction is heart muscle damage from blocked blood flow. Sudden death from a heart that beats erratically, or not at all, can be a result of heart disease.

Signs and Symptoms of Cardiac Chest Pain. Cardiac chest pain is often described as crushing, tight, pressing, viselike, and constricting. It occurs below the breastbone and can radiate into the left arm and jaw, and may be accompanied by shortness of breath, anxiety, sweaty skin, pale skin and mucous membranes, nausea, dizziness, and irregular pulse.

Figuring out whether non-traumatic chest pain is a heart condition can be difficult under the best of circumstances. Inflammation of the stomach or esophagus, chest muscle strains, rib injury, lung problems, bronchitis, and coughing can all cause chest pain. To complicate the situation, women, the elderly, and people with diabetes may have a heart attack with fainting, nausea, back pain, weakness, or shortness of breath, but without chest pain.

Pain brought on by physical or emotional stress and relieved by rest may be angina, while unprovoked and persistent pain may be a myocardial infarction.

Treatment for Cardiac Chest Pain. A patient with chest pain symptoms that cannot be easily attributed to a chest injury, lung problem, stomach upset, or muscle strain should take one adult aspirin every 24 hours and be evacuated. Reduce the demands on the heart by calming the patient and making them rest. Administer oxygen if it is available. If your patient has a history of cardiac chest pain, they may have nitroglycerin, a medication

---

Treatment of Suspected Cardiac Chest Pain

- Reduce anxiety and activity.
- Administer oxygen.
- Support patient with their personal medications.
- Evacuate.

---

often administered by placing a tablet under the tongue. They should take this according to their physician's orders.

Evacuation Guidelines
- Evacuate all patients with suspected cardiac chest pain or cardiac symptoms.
- Rapidly evacuate any patient with a new onset of chest pain that is not clearly musculoskeletal, and any patient with chest pain that is not relieved as expected by rest and nitroglycerin.
- Expedite evacuation if a severe asthma attack is unresponsive to medications.

CHAPTER 18 | ABDOMINAL PAIN

INTRODUCTION

The abdomen contains the digestive, urinary, and reproductive systems, and the major blood vessels supplying the lower extremities. A lot can go wrong in the belly, and assessing the seriousness of a problem can be difficult, even for a physician. As first responders, our role is to decide whether the problem is an "acute abdomen" and, if so, to support and evacuate the patient. Knowledge of the location and function of the abdominal organs, and some of the common abdominal problems, can make this determination easier.

ABDOMINAL ANATOMY AND PHYSIOLOGY

Abdominal and Pelvic Cavities. The abdominal cavity, like the chest, is lined by a slippery membrane called the peritoneum, which covers the organs. The diaphragm separates the chest from the abdomen.

The liver, gallbladder, stomach, spleen, pancreas, appendix, and large and small intestines lie in the abdominal cavity. The kidneys, ureters, adrenals, pancreas, aorta, and inferior vena cava are behind the peritoneum. The vagina, cervix, uterus, ovaries, bladder, lower end of the large intestine, and rectum are located in the pelvic cavity.

227

ORGANS OF THE
ABDOMINAL CAVITY

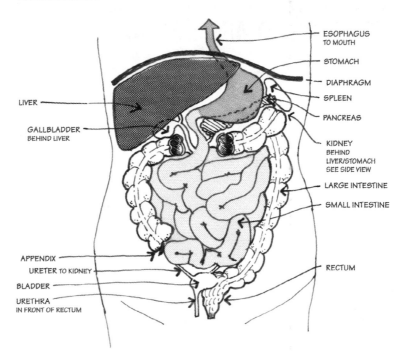

Digestive Tract. The digestive tract processes food to nourish the cells of the body. Secretions within the digestive tract
break down food into basic sugars, fatty acids, and amino acids.
These products of digestion cross the wall of the intestine and
travel through the veins to the liver for detoxification. From
the liver, blood circulates nutrients to the individual cells of the
body.

The digestive tract starts at the mouth, where food mixes
with saliva: a combination of mucus, water, salts, digestive
enzymes, and organic compounds. Swallowed food passes
from the mouth into the pharynx, which divides into the trachea
and esophagus. The trachea lies in front of the esophagus, and
food could easily go into the trachea, but a thin flap of cartilage
called the epiglottis closes the entrance to the trachea with each
swallow.

The esophagus is a muscular tube extending from the larynx to the stomach. Contractions of the esophagus—peristalsis—propel food to the stomach.

Stomach. The stomach is a J-shaped organ, located in the upper-left quadrant of the abdomen. The major function of the stomach is to store food and move it into the intestine in small amounts. Every 15 to 25 seconds, stomach contractions mix food with gastric juice, turning it into a thin liquid called chyme. Water, salts, alcohol, and certain drugs are absorbed directly by the stomach.

Small and Large Intestines. From the stomach, chyme passes into the small intestine, a tube 21 feet (6 meters) long and one inch (2.5 cm) in diameter. Peristalsis moves food through the intestines. Within the first foot of the small intestine, food mixes with secretions from the pancreas and gallbladder. The rest of the small intestine absorbs the products of digestion (proteins, fats, carbohydrates, vitamins, and minerals).

Chyme then passes from the small intestine to the large intestine, a tube five feet (1.5 meters) long and 2.5 inches (6 cm) in diameter. The appendix is located just below the junction of the small and large intestines. The large intestine absorbs water, leaving behind non-digestible parts of food as solid stool. The rectum stores feces, which are moved out of the body by a series of sphincters in the anus, which is the last two inches (5 cm) of the intestinal tract.

Liver. The liver lies beneath the diaphragm in the upper-right quadrant. At 4 pounds in weight, it is the largest solid organ in the abdomen and the one most often injured. The liver performs more than 500 known functions, among them detoxifying the products of digestion; converting glycogen, fat, and proteins into glucose; storing vitamins; and producing bile.

Gallbladder. Bile, essential for fat digestion and absorption, is stored in the gallbladder, a small pear-shaped organ. The gallbladder responds to the presence of food (especially fats) in the small intestine by constricting and emptying bile into the intestine.

Pancreas. An oblong organ located behind the liver, the pancreas contains two types of glands. One produces pancreatic

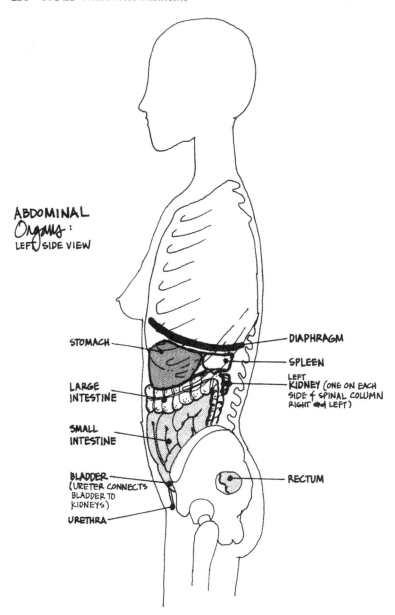

ABDOMINAL
Organs:
LEFT SIDE VIEW

STOMACH

LARGE
INTESTINE

SMALL
INTESTINE

BLADDER
(URETER CONNECTS
BLADDER TO
KIDNEYS)

URETHRA

DIAPHRAGM

SPLEEN

LEFT
KIDNEY (ONE ON EACH
SIDE of SPINAL COLUMN
RIGHT and LEFT)

RECTUM

juice, which aids in the digestion of fats, carbohydrates, starches, and proteins. The juice flows directly into the small intestine via the pancreatic duct. The other gland secretes chemicals, including insulin, that regulate sugar metabolism.

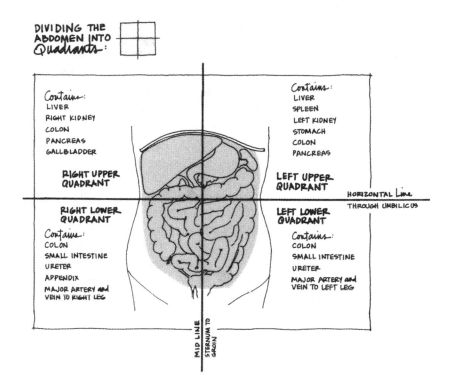

DIVIDING THE ABDOMEN INTO Quadrants:

Contains:
LIVER
RIGHT KIDNEY
COLON
PANCREAS
GALLBLADDER

RIGHT UPPER QUADRANT

Contains:
LIVER
SPLEEN
LEFT KIDNEY
STOMACH
COLON
PANCREAS

LEFT UPPER QUADRANT

HORIZONTAL Line THROUGH UMBILICUS

RIGHT LOWER QUADRANT

Contains:
COLON
SMALL INTESTINE
URETER
APPENDIX
MAJOR ARTERY and VEIN TO RIGHT LEG

LEFT LOWER QUADRANT

Contains:
COLON
SMALL INTESTINE
URETER
MAJOR ARTERY and VEIN TO LEFT LEG

MID LINE
STERNUM TO GROIN

Spleen. The spleen, located in the upper-left quadrant beneath the diaphragm, is the only abdominal organ not involved in digestion. The spleen produces white blood cells and destroys worn-out red blood cells.

Urinary System. The urinary system, composed of kidneys, ureters, bladder, and urethra, discharges waste materials filtered from the blood. The two kidneys rid the blood of toxic wastes, and control water and salt balance. If the kidneys fail to function, toxic waste will concentrate in the blood, causing death.

Urine flows from the kidneys to the bladder via the ureters. The bladder can hold up to 800 milliliters of urine. At 200 to 400 milliliters, we feel the urge to void. The bladder empties to the outside via the urethra.

ABDOMINAL ILLNESS

Many, many illnesses can develop within the abdomen. This section is by no means exhaustive, but it does cover problems that we tend to see in the backcountry. The most important part of this chapter is the final section, which reminds us not to worry about diagnosis but rather to do a sound assessment and decide if the signs and symptoms meet the evacuation criteria.

Kidney Stones

Kidney stones occur when minerals, such as calcium, precipitate from the urine in the kidney. Predisposing factors for kidney stones include urinary tract infections, dehydration, an increase in dietary calcium, too much vitamin D, and cancer.

Signs and Symptoms of Kidney Stones. As a stone passes down the ureter, the patient experiences excruciating pain that comes and goes with increasing intensity. The pain usually begins at the level of the lowest ribs on the back, and radiates to the lower abdomen and the groin. The patient is pale, sweaty, nauseated, and often writhing in pain. There may be pain with urination and blood in the urine. Chills and fever are not present. The duration of the pain depends on the location of the stone. Pain is severe while a stone passes from the kidney to the bladder and may stop after the stone has dropped into the bladder. The pain may last as long as 24 hours, but the duration is usually shorter.

Treatment for Kidney Stones. Drinking copious amounts of water may help the patient pass the stone. Pain medication may help. If pain continues for more than 24 hours or if the patient is unable to urinate, evacuate.

Appendicitis

Appendicitis is an infection of the appendix causing pressure, swelling, and inflammation. The highest incidence of appendicitis occurs in males between the ages of ten and thirty.

Signs and Symptoms of Appendicitis. The classic symptoms of appendicitis are pain behind the umbilicus (the navel), anorexia, nausea, and vomiting. They usually develop gradually over 1 to 2 days. The pain then shifts to the lower right quadrant, halfway between the umbilicus and the right hipbone. The patient may have one or two bowel movements but usually does not have diarrhea. If you apply pressure with your hand over the lower right quadrant, the patient may complain of pain when you remove your hand, known as rebound tenderness. A fever and elevated pulse may be present. Due to pain, the patient may choose to lie on their side or back, with legs tucked in the fetal position. There may also be pain when the patient jumps, walks, or jars their right leg or side.

If the infection remains localized (as an abscess on the appendix), the patient may only run a low fever and complain of not feeling well. The abscess may not rupture for a week or more. If the abscess does rupture, the pain temporarily disappears but soon reappears as the abdominal cavity becomes infected (peritonitis).

Treatment for Appendicitis. Appendicitis is a surgical emergency. The patient must be evacuated.

Peritonitis

Peritonitis is an inflammation of the peritoneum. Causes include penetrating abdominal wounds, abdominal bleeding, or ruptured internal organs that spill digestive juices into the abdominal cavity.

Signs and Symptoms of Peritonitis. Signs and symptoms of peritonitis vary, depending on whether the infection is local or general. The patient lies very still, as movement increases the pain, and may complain of nausea, vomiting, anorexia, and fever. The abdomen is rigid and tender. The infection causes peristaltic activity of the bowel to stop, so the patient has no bowel movements. Shock may be present. The patient appears very sick.

Treatment for Peritonitis. Peritonitis is a severe infection beyond our capability to treat in the wilderness; treat the patient for shock and evacuate.

Hemorrhoids

Hemorrhoids are varicose veins of the anal canal. They may be internal or external. Constipation, straining during elimination, diarrhea, and pregnancy can cause hemorrhoids. External hemorrhoids can be very painful. Internal hemorrhoids tend not to be painful but bleed during bowel movements. The stool may be streaked on the outside with blood. The patient may complain of itching around the anus.

Treatment for Hemorrhoids. Apply moist heat to the anal area. This can be done with a bandanna dipped in warm water. Rest, increased liquid and fruit intake to keep the stools soft, and/or anesthetic ointments (such as dibucaine, Preparation H, or Anusol) may decrease pain and bleeding.

Gastric and Duodenal Ulcers

Decreased resistance of the stomach lining to pepsin and hydrochloric acid, or an increase in the production of these chemicals, may result in ulcers. Stress, smoking, aspirin use, certain bacteria, caffeine or alcohol consumption, and genetic factors are possible causes.

Signs and Symptoms of Ulcers. The patient complains of a gnawing, aching, or burning in the upper abdomen at the midline, 1 to 2 hours after eating or at night when gastric secretions peak. The pain may radiate from the lowest ribs to the back and frequently disappears if the patient ingests food or antacids.

Is it an ulcer, though, or just indigestion? Indigestion symptoms tend to be associated with eating. The patient complains of fullness and heartburn, and may belch or vomit small amounts of food. Indigestion worsens when more food is ingested. As time passes and the stomach empties, symptoms disappear. Indigestion tends to be related to a single meal.

Treatment for Ulcers. The primary treatment for ulcers is to take antacids an hour after meals; eat small, frequent meals; and avoid coffee, alcohol, and spicy foods, which increase the secretions of the stomach. If the ulcer perforates the wall of the stomach, symptoms of peritonitis occur.

ABDOMINAL TRAUMA

Abdominal organs are either solid or hollow. When hollow organs are perforated, they spill their contents into the abdominal cavity. Solid organs tend to bleed when injured. Either bleeding or spillage of digestive juices causes peritonitis.

Blunt Trauma. Inspect the abdomen for bruises, the location of which will suggest what organs may have been damaged. Pain, signs and symptoms of shock, and a significant mechanism of injury to the abdomen are reasons to initiate an evacuation.

Penetrating Wounds. Assume that any penetrating wound to the abdomen has entered the peritoneal lining. Treat the patient for shock and evacuate.

Impaled Objects. In general leave any impaled object in place; if the object prevents transport, cannot be stabilized, is loose enough to simply fall out, or prevents bleeding control, it may need to be removed. If left in place, stabilize the object with dressings. If there is bleeding, apply pressure bandages around the wound.

Evisceration. An evisceration is a protrusion of abdominal organs through a laceration in the abdominal wall. After rinsing the bowel with disinfected water, you may be able to gently "tease" small exposed loops back into the abdomen. If not, cover the exposed bowel with dressings that have been soaked in disinfected water. Keep these moist to prevent the exposed loops of bowel from becoming dry. Change the dressings daily. Treat for shock and evacuate the patient.

ABDOMINAL ASSESSMENT

The first responder needs a few simple skills to evaluate the condition of a patient with an abdominal problem.

1. Inspect the abdomen. Position the patient in a warm place, lying down. Remove the patient's clothing so that you can see the entire abdomen. A normal abdomen is slightly rounded and symmetrical. Look for old scars, areas of bruising, rashes, impaled objects, eviscerations, and distention. Check the lower back for the same.

2. Listen to the abdomen in all quadrants. Place your ear on the patient's abdomen and listen for bowel sounds (gurgling noises). An absence of noise indicates an injured or ill bowel, but without a stethoscope it is difficult to say with confidence that bowel sounds are absent; you can only say that bowel sounds are clearly present.

3. Palpate the abdomen. With your palms down, apply gentle pressure with the pads of the fingers. Make sure your hands are warm and that you palpate all four quadrants. Cold fingers or jabbing can cause the patient to tighten the abdominal muscles, thereby impeding the assessment. The abdomen should be soft and not tender. Abnormal signs include localized or diffuse tenderness and stiff, rigid muscles ("board-like abdomen").

4. Using OPQRST as a memory aid, ask about pain: Where is it located, where does it radiate to, and what is the severity and frequency? What aggravates or alleviates the pain? Are there patterns to the pain (at night, after meals, etc.)? Ask the patient about their past medical history: Any past surgery, diagnoses, treatment, or injuries? Any problems with swallowing, digestion, bowel, bladder, or reproductive organs?

FINAL THOUGHTS

Many medical problems cause acute abdominal pain. Determining the actual source of the pain and the urgency of the condition can be difficult, even for a physician. As the leader of a wilderness trip, your task is not to make a diagnosis; it is to decide whether the pain indicates an "acute abdomen," a possible surgical emergency requiring further evaluation. Perform a thorough assessment and decide if your patient triggers any evacuation criteria.

Evacuation Guidelines

Evacuation is recommended for:

1. Any patient who has:
   • Pain inconsistent with a simple UTI or gastroenteritis
   • Signs and symptoms or the possibility of pregnancy (see chapter 20)
2. A patient with:
   • Persistent or worsening gastroenteritis (crampy, diffuse, or intermittent pain) over 24 hours, spiking fever, bloody diarrhea, or dehydration
   • Inability to tolerate any oral fluids more than 24 hours, especially if accompanied by diarrhea volume losses, or fever

Rapid evacuation is recommended for:

1. A patient with abdominal pain that is:
   • Persistent for 12 hours, especially if constant, localized or worsening
   • Accompanied by guarding, tenderness, distension, rigidity
   • Produced or aggravated by movement, jarring or foot strike
   • Accompanied by blood in the urine, vomit, or feces
   • Accompanied by fever >102°F (39°C)
   • Accompanied by signs and symptoms of shock

| **DIABETES**

Like people with cardiac and respiratory disease, persons with diabetes routinely participate in wilderness expeditions. They minimize the complications—high and low blood sugar—through careful planning and the help of their companions. NOLS founder Paul Petzoldt worked with physicians in the early 1970s to support students with diabetes to attend our remote month-long wilderness expeditions. At that time, this was a bold initiative. Now we know that with control and care, people with diabetes can participate in any activity.

DIABETES

Diabetes is a disease of sugar metabolism, affecting millions of people. It is a complex disease characterized by a broad array of physiological disturbances. In the short term, which is the context of our first aid care, the disturbance in sugar metabolism can manifest itself as too much or too little sugar in the blood. In the long term, these disturbances can lead to complications including high blood pressure and heart and blood vessel disease; they can also affect vision, kidneys, and immune function.

Causes of diabetes include genetic defects, infection, auto-immune processes, or direct injury to the pancreas. The pancreas produces hormones, most notably insulin, which help regulate sugar balance. Insulin facilitates the movement of sugar from the blood into the cells. A deficit of insulin results in an excess of sugar in the blood, disturbing fluid and electrolyte balance. This disorder is known as hyperglycemia (high blood sugar).

In contrast, excess insulin promotes the movement of sugar into the cells, lowers the blood-sugar level, and deprives the brain cells of a crucial nutrient. This disorder is known as hypoglycemia (low blood sugar).

A healthy pancreas constantly adjusts the insulin level to the blood-sugar level. The pancreas of a person with diabetes produces defective insulin or no insulin. To compensate for this, a person with diabetes takes medication to stimulate endogenous insulin, or takes artificial insulin. Treatment plans for people with diabetes also include diet and exercise.

Hyperglycemia

People with diabetes who are untreated, have defective or insufficient insulin, or become ill may develop a high level of sugar in the blood. Consequences of hyperglycemia may include dehydration and electrolyte disturbances as the kidneys try to eliminate the excess sugar, and acid-base disturbances as cells starved for sugar turn to alternative energy sources such as fats and proteins.

Signs and Symptoms of Hyperglycemia. Hyperglycemia tends to develop more slowly than hypoglycemia, but it can come on within a few hours if the patient is ill. The first symptoms are often nausea, vomiting, thirst, and increased urine output. The patient's breath may have a fruity odor from the metabolism of

Signs and Symptoms of Hyperglycemia

- Mental status: may be confused and slow to respond
- Heart rate: weak, rapid
- Respiratory rate: increased
- Skin: warm, dry
- Increased hunger, increased thirst, increased urine output, fatigue
- Breath odor: acetone, sweet
- Persistent high blood-sugar levels

Treatment Principles for Hyperglycemia

- If unable to distinguish between hypoglycemia and hyperglycemia, give sugar.
- Hydrate.
- Do not give insulin.
- Support the patient's sick day plan
- Evacuate.

fats as an energy source. The patient may also have abdominal cramps or pain, and signs of dehydration including dry skin and intense thirst. Unresponsiveness is a late and very serious sign.

Treatment of Hyperglycemia. This patient has a complex physical disturbance and needs the care of a physician. Treatment is supportive: airway maintenance and treatment for shock. Dehydration is a serious and common complication of hyperglycemia. If the patient is alert, give oral fluids.

Hypoglycemia

Hypoglycemia results from the treatment of diabetes, not the diabetes itself. If a person with diabetes takes too much insulin or fails to eat sufficient sugar to match the insulin level, the blood-sugar level will be insufficient to maintain normal brain function.

Hypoglycemia can occur if the person with diabetes skips a meal but takes their usual insulin dose, takes more than the normal insulin dose, exercises strenuously and fails to eat, or vomits a meal after taking insulin.

Signs and Symptoms of Hypoglycemia. Hypoglycemia has a rapid onset, the most prominent symptoms being alterations in mental status due to a lack of sugar to the brain. The patient may be irritable, nervous, weak, and uncoordinated; or, in more serious cases, may become unresponsive or have seizures. The pulse is often rapid, the skin and mucous membranes pale, cool, and clammy.

Treatment for Hypoglycemia. Brain cells need sugar and can suffer permanent damage from low blood-sugar levels. The treatment of hypoglycemia is to administer sugar. The common recommendation is to administer

Signs and Symptoms of Hypoglycemia

- Mental status: confused, disoriented, irritable. Can progress to obvious mental-status changes
- Heart rate: rapid
- Respiratory rate: normal or shallow
- Pale, cool, clammy skin, pale mucous membranes
- Breath odor: no changes

Treatment for Hypoglycemia

- If you are unable to distinguish between hypoglycemia and hyperglycemia, give sugar until the patient becomes awake and alert.

15gr of rapid absorbing glucose. If the patient is awake and able to swallow, sources of a useful amount of sugar include: one small tube cake frosting; one tablespoon of syrup, jam, jelly, table sugar, or honey; two small cookies; or a two inch square piece of unfrosted brownie or cake.

If the patient is unresponsive, establish an airway, place the patient on their side, then place a small amount of sugar paste between the patient's cheek and gum. Raising blood sugar by this route takes time. Expect slow improvement while you diligently monitor the airway.

Hypoglycemia or Hyperglycemia?
Hypoglycemia usually has a rapid onset; the patient's skin can be pale, cool, and clammy. They may have pale mucous membranes and obvious disturbances in behavior or altered mental status. Hyperglycemia typically has a gradual onset. Often, the patient may be confused and slow to respond with flushed, dry skin, or has a history of recent illness. Suspect hyperglycemia in a person with diabetes who is ill, especially if it is associated with vomiting. A fruity breath odor may be present. A patient with hypoglycemia will respond to sugar; a hyperglycemic patient will not, but the extra sugar will cause no harm and so can be administered safely.

Ask any patient with diabetes, "Have you eaten today?" and "Have you taken your insulin today?" If the patient has taken insulin but has not eaten, you should suspect hypoglycemia. The patient will have too much insulin, not enough sugar, and a blood-sugar level that is too low to sustain normal brain function. If the patient has eaten but has not taken insulin, hyperglycemia should be suspected. This person has more sugar in the blood than can be transported to the cells.

Persons with diabetes can be very knowledgeable about their reactions and intuitively know if they are getting into trouble. Many people with diabetes measure their blood-sugar levels daily and check their urine for ketones. If you're on a wilderness trip with a person with diabetes, learn their medication and eating routines, method of measuring blood sugar, and daily fluctuations in blood-sugar level. This can familiarize you with their management of diabetes and help if they become hypo- or hyperglycemic.

When we're sick, we're under stress and use hormones to fight the infection. Some of these hormones both raise blood sugar and interfere with insulin. The result is that it's more challenging for people with diabetes to regulate blood sugar when they are sick. A person with diabetes should have a "sick-day" plan, and the trip leader needs to know what that is. The components of a sick-day plan include insulin adjustment, food and fluid intake, and decision points for evacuation, such as urine ketone level, hyperglycemia, and vomiting. Thresholds for evacuation may be: several days of illness without relief; vomiting or diarrhea for more than 6 hours; moderate-to-large amounts of ketones in urine; blood glucose readings consistently greater than normal despite taking extra insulin; early signs of hyperglycemia; loss of a sense of control of blood-sugar levels.

It is important for people with diabetes to eat and medicate at regular intervals. If there is a possibility that insulin could be lost or destroyed—for example, by a boat flipping on the river—make sure that someone else in the group is carrying an extra supply. With control and care, people with diabetes can participate in any activity without problems.

FINAL THOUGHTS

A new physical and social environment, heavy packs, long paddles, altitude, sun, and battling dehydration in the wilderness may be challenges, but we know from experience they do not prevent people with diabetes from enjoying outdoor and wilderness activities. It is important to inform the rest of the group—especially the person's tent mates—about the condition and how to deal with it in an emergency. Supporting a companion living with a chronic medical condition in the wilderness includes understanding the illness, how it is managed, and what your companion would like you to do in the event they become ill and unable to help themself. It's good first aid, and as we'll discuss in Chapter 27, it's good expedition behavior.

Evacuation Guidelines
Diabetes:
- Evacuation thresholds for people with diabetes includes several days of illness without relief
- Vomiting or diarrhea for more than 6 hours
- Moderate-to-large amounts of ketones in urine
- Blood-glucose readings consistently greater than normal despite taking extra insulin
- Early signs of hyperglycemia
- Loss of a sense of control of blood-sugar levels

CHAPTER 20 | SEIZURES, STROKE, AND ALTERED MENTAL STATUS

The nervous system is considered one of the "big three" physiological systems, along with the cardiovascular and respiratory systems. The importance of the "big three" is founded on their roles in basic life support: our brain function, our heart function, our ability to breathe. In Chapter 4 we discussed injuries to the brain and the spine. In this chapter we will discuss illness to the nervous system, including seizures, stroke, syncope (fainting), and response to any event with altered mental status.

SEIZURES

A seizure is a disruption of the brain's normal activity by a massive paroxysmal electrical discharge from brain cells. The seizure begins at a focus of brain cells, then spreads through the brain and to the rest of the body through peripheral nerves. This electrical disturbance may cause violent muscle contractions throughout the body (a grand mal seizure), or result in localized motor movement and possible loss of responsiveness.

The causes of seizures include high fever, head injury, low blood sugar, stroke, poisoning, and epilepsy. Low blood sugar can be a cause of seizures in people with diabetes. Brain cells are sensitive to low oxygen and sugar levels, and if these fall below acceptable levels, a seizure may be triggered.

Causes of Seizures

- Epilepsy
- High fever and heatstroke
- Brain injury
- Alcohol or drug withdrawal or overdose
- Diabetic hypoglycemia

The most common cause of seizures is epilepsy, a disease that manifests as recurring seizures. The onset of epilepsy is not well understood. Often it begins in childhood or adolescence, but it can also be a consequence of a brain injury. Most persons with epilepsy control their seizures with medication. Interruption of the medication or inadequate dosage can be a cause of seizures.

At one time, seizures were attributed to mental illness. The source of these misperceptions may have been the dramatic visual impact of a writhing, moaning person having a seizure. Educating bystanders and group members about epilepsy and seizures can help alleviate such misunderstandings.

Signs and Symptoms of Seizures. The typical generalized seizure begins with a short period, usually less than a minute, of muscle rigidity, followed by several minutes of muscle contractions. The patient may feel the seizure approaching and warn bystanders, or cry out at the onset of the episode. The patient suddenly falls to the ground, twitching and jerking.

As muscular activity subsides, the patient remains unresponsive but relaxed. They may drool, appear cyanotic, and become incontinent. Pulse and respiratory rate may be rapid.

Signs and Symptoms of Seizures

- The patient experiences a feeling of an imminent seizure.
- Unexpected and unexplained collapse.
- Localized or full-body convulsion or temporary disconnection from the present.
- Postictal recovery phase.

The patient may initially be unresponsive or difficult to arouse, but in time—usually within 10 to 15 minutes—the patient becomes awake and oriented.

Treatment of Seizures. When the seizure has subsided, open the airway, assess for injuries, and take vital signs. Place the patient on their side during the recovery phase to help maintain an open airway.

Treatment for a seizure is supportive and protective care. You cannot stop the seizure, but you can protect the patient from injury. The violent muscle contractions of a seizure may cause injury to the patient and to well-meaning bystanders who attempt to restrain the patient. Move objects that the patient may hit. Pad or cradle the head if it is bouncing on the ground. A patient in seizure will not swallow the tongue; however, the airway may become obstructed by saliva or secretions, and the patient may bite their tongue.

An accurate description of the seizure tells the physician much about the onset and extent of the problem. In most cases, a seizure runs its course in a few minutes. Repeated seizures, especially those in which the patient does not regain responsiveness in between, and seizures associated with another medical problem such as diabetes or head injury, are serious medical conditions that require rapid evacuation.

Treatment Principles for Seizures

- Protect from harm, but do not restrain.
- Do not place a bite stick or any other object in a patient's mouth.
- Place patient on side to maintain open airway during the postictal recovery phase.
- Perform a patient assessment to check for injuries.
- Protect the patient's dignity.

A patient with epilepsy who has an isolated seizure requires evaluation by a physician but does not require a rapid evacuation. These occasional seizures are often due to changes in the patient's need for medication or failure to take the medication as prescribed. After recovering from the seizure, the patient should be well fed and hydrated, and assessed for any injury that may have occurred during the seizure.

A STROKE

A stroke results from the same disease process that causes angina and heart attacks, only it is manifested in the brain. A stroke or cerebrovascular accident is the consequence of interruption of the blood supply to the brain by a blood clot or a ruptured blood vessel. The disruption in blood flow deprives the brain of oxygen and can cause injury or death of brain cells.

Signs and Symptoms of Stroke

The signs and symptoms vary with the part of the brain that is injured. They can be permanent, or if the disruption in blood supply to the brain is intermittent, transient, known as the transient ischemic attack or TIA. Assess for altered mental status, a headache (which may be sudden and severe) slurred speech or an inability to talk, one-sided weakness or paralysis evidenced in altered CSMs, loss of bowel or bladder control (incontinence), or changes in vision.

> **Signs and Symptoms of Stroke**
> - Altered mental status
> - Headache (may be sudden and severe)
> - Inability to speak or slurred speech
> - One-sided weakness or paralysis
> - Facial paralysis
> - Incontinence
> - Vision changes

You can perform a focused stroke assessment. Look at the patient's face, ask them to smile and check for facial symmetry. Asymmetry is a sign of possible stroke. Ask them to close their eyes and hold their arms out in front. Arms that drift in relation to each other suggest a stroke. Ask the patient to repeat a simple phrase such as "you can't teach an old dog a new trick." Difficulty with speech suggests a stroke. Documenting these signs and their time of onset, and communicating this to healthcare providers is important; hospital treatment of stroke depends on time, signs, and symptoms.

Treatment of Stroke

Treatment of a possible stroke is founded on early recognition from our patient assessment, supportive care and evacuation. Stroke can be alarming and stressful; emotional reassurance and psychological first aid may be helpful. Transport the patient in a position in which they are comfortable. Paralyzed limbs should be protected. If the patient is unresponsive, place them in the recovery position with the affected side down.

> **Treatment Principles for Stroke**
> - Provide emotional reassurance.
> - Place in a position of comfort.
> - If unresponsive, protect the airway.
> - Document the time of onset of signs and symptoms.
> - Rapidly evacuate.

SYNCOPE

Syncope (fainting) is a brief loss of postural tone followed by a spontaneous and complete recovery. It is often caused by a decreased blood flow to the brain, usually from low blood pressure. It may be due to severe pain, strong emotion, urination, defecation, vomiting, dehydration, or carotid sinus stimulation. Syncope may also be a sign of underlying disease, especially if symptoms associated with the fainting episode do not resolve.

Signs and Symptoms of Syncope
The patient may report dizziness, vision changes, warmth or lightheadedness preceding the fainting episode. They may be momentarily dazed and confused, and then may collapse with a rapid heart rate; pale, cool, clammy skin; and pale mucous membranes. Occasionally they may twitch or have seizure-like activity.

Treatment of Syncope
Lay the patient flat, elevate their legs, and make them comfortable: in the shade, out of the cold, etc. Perform a patient assessment, looking especially for residual signs and symptoms.

If, after recovering, the patient describes symptoms preceding the fainting episode such as dizziness, pallor, diaphoresis, vision changes, warmth, or light-headedness, and these symptoms resolve after the fainting episode, then this is likely low risk syncope and the patient does not need to be evacuated.

If symptoms remain after the fainting episode, the patient should be evacuated. The episode may be due to a heart condition.

ALTERED MENTAL STATUS

Responsive patients can react to the environment and protect themselves from sources of pain and injury. An unresponsive patient or any patient with altered mental status is in danger. They may be mute and defenseless, perhaps unable to rely on their gag reflex to protect the airway. Many conditions cause unresponsiveness or altered mental status: head injury, stroke, epilepsy, diabetes, alcohol intoxication, drug overdose, and fever.

A patient who is unresponsive or has altered mental status for unexplained reasons poses a difficult diagnostic problem. The medical history may provide clues; use ToStop (see sidebar) as a memory aid for common causes of unresponsiveness. Investigate each possibility and look for clues that either rule out or confirm its presence. Obtaining a history of an unresponsive patient may be challenging; carefully question bystanders for any background information they may be able to provide.

ToStop
To: Toxins
S: Sugar/Seizure
T: Temperature
O: Oxygen
P: Pressure

Consider medications, alcohol or drugs, and toxins such as carbon monoxide. Look for medication containers, bottles, and sources of exposure to noxious gas. Look for medical alert bracelets. Try sugar to check if this may be hypoglycemia, remembering that a response to sugar may take a while, and assess for signs of seizure such as loss of bladder or bowel control, excess saliva, a bitten tongue, or a patient who gradually awakens. Are they warmer or cooler than expected? Can you measure their temperature? Might they be hypothermic? Altered mental status may be due to a lack of oxygen, so examine their skin and mucous membranes; dusky or bluish colors suggest hypoxia. Might this be due to increased intracranial pressure—swelling in the brain—from injury or stroke?

Treatment Principles for the Patient with Altered Mental Status
- Protect the spine.
- Manage the airway; consider positioning the patient on the side.
- Search for clues.
- Consider administering sugar.

Regardless of whether you can identify the cause, support and transport patients with altered mental status to a physician for further evaluation. Care for an unresponsive patient includes airway maintenance and spine protection, unless trauma can be ruled out. If you are unsure why a patient is unresponsive, place some sugar between the patient's cheek and gum. This will help a hypoglycemic patient and, as long as you diligently protect the airway, won't hurt a patient who is unresponsive for any other reason.

FINAL THOUGHTS

An episode of altered mental status can be very worrisome for the companion and the responder. You lose the ability to dialogue with the patient and to work together with informed consent with the patient; you also lose having the patient as an active participant in their own healthcare. Trust that a sound patient assessment and use of ToStop to guide your assessment and treatment will reduce the uncertainty and guide your treatment plan, helping you provide excellent care in the wilderness.

Evacuation Guidelines
- Evacuate all patients with syncope that occurs during exertion or without the presence of prodromal symptoms such as dizziness, lightheadedness, pallor, diaphoresis, vision changes, or patients with syncope followed by residual signs and symptoms.
- Rapidly evacuate any patient with signs or symptoms of stroke or with persistent altered mental status
- Rapidly evacuate all events of syncope that are accompanied by chest pain, headache, shortness of breath, abdominal pain, known pregnancy, or signs and symptoms of shock.

CHAPTER 21 | URINARY AND REPRODUCTIVE MEDICAL CONCERNS

INTRODUCTION

If you're leading or participating in wilderness trips, you will encounter people with medical problems involving their urinary and reproductive systems. These can include urinary tract infection, epididymitis and testicular torsion, menstrual pain, vaginal infections, and ectopic pregnancy. The wilderness leader should be knowledgeable about the prevention, assessment, and field treatment of these conditions, and know when they merit evacuation.

ASSESSMENT TIPS

An individual experiencing scrotal pain for the first time may be embarrassed and hesitant to inform the leader. Likewise, a person with a urinary tract infection may not know the significance of burning or frequent urination or that the trip leader has the means to treat it in the field. You have an opportunity to set a tone of openness to talk about urinary and reproductive system medical problems when you discuss, at the start of a trip, how you will manage personal hygiene (more on this later in this chapter).

When you are assessing a person with a urinary or reproductive system complaint, provide a private place to talk. Be straightforward, respectful and nonjudgmental. Use proper medical terminology or terms that you both understand—no jokes or slang. Refer to anatomical organs, not gender. Ideally, a person of the same sex or gender-identity as the patient, or a friend chosen by the patient, should be present during any physical exam. And the patient can help by performing a self-exam.

Avoid assumptions when assessing patients. There are many reasons why we should not make assumptions about the patient's anatomy, gender identity, or biological sex. Traumatic injury, gender-confirming surgery, congenital anatomical differences, surgical removal of gonads due to cancer/pre-cancerous condition, hysterectomies, appendectomies, and other factors can all affect the appearance or function of the reproductive and urinary systems. If it is relevant, we privately and professionally ask about anatomy, medical history, and current treatments.

For patients with ovaries and a uterus, gather information about the patient's menstrual and reproductive history. When was their last menstrual period? How long is their cycle? What is normal for them? Do they use contraception? Have they had sexual activity that could result in pregnancy since their last menstrual cycle? Have they experienced this problem in the past, and if so, how was it treated?

The anatomy, physiology, and medical treatments of transgender and gender non-conforming patients can create medical conditions that may be poorly understood by healthcare providers. Ask the patient about their anatomy, medications, and any ongoing health concerns. Ask what you can do to help. In the reporting context use the patient's words, e.g., "the patient states, 'I'm in the process of transitioning from male to female.'" Use discretion and protect confidentiality.

Urinary Tract Infection (UTI)

A urinary tract infection is an infection in any part of the urinary system—the kidneys, ureters, bladder, and urethra. The kidneys filter waste from the blood and produce about 1 to 2 quarts of urine per day. The urine passes to the bladder via thin tubes of muscle called ureters. The bladder is a hollow, muscular, balloon-shaped organ that serves as a reservoir for urine.

Although you do not control how your kidneys function, you can control when to empty your bladder. The urethra, a tube located at the bottom of the bladder, allows urine to exit the body during urination.

Most infections involve the lower urinary tract—the bladder and the urethra. Urinary tract infections are more common in people with a vagina due to the proximity of the urethra to the vagina and rectum, and the shorter length of the urethra.

Signs and Symptoms of UTI. Urinary tract infections cause increased frequency or urgency of urination, a burning sensation during urination, and sometimes decreased urine volume. The patient complains of pain above the pubic bone and possibly a heavy urine odor with the morning urination. Blood or pus may be present in the urine. Urinary tract infections can progress to kidney infections. If the kidneys are infected, the patient complains of tenderness or pain in the small of the back, and may have a fever and fatigue.

Some people, especially those who are older and have comorbid conditions such as diabetes, may experience more non-specific symptoms, such as fatigue, rather than painful urination. Older people can experience confusion as a dominant symptom of a UTI.

Treatment For UTI. Drinking lots of water every day and emptying the bladder often constitute the best treatment, and aid in prevention as well. You can tell if you are drinking enough by the color of your urine. Unless you are taking vitamins, the urine should be clear, not yellow. Persons taking vitamins may have yellow urine.

Signs and Symptoms of Urinary Tract Infection
- Increase in frequency of urination
- Urgency and a burning sensation during urination

Treatment of Urinary Tract Infection
- Increase fluid intake.
- Avoid foods that irritate the bladder.
- Consider antibiotics and the urinary analgesic pyridium.

The perineal area (between the vagina and anus) should be cleaned with water and mild soap (if available) daily. Taking 500 milligrams of vitamin C daily and eating whole grains, nuts, and fruits may help. Curry, cayenne pepper, chili powder, black pepper, caffeine, and alcohol should be avoided, because these may irritate the bladder.

A urinary tract analgesic (e.g., pyridium) may be helpful for the pain. On extended expeditions, consider carrying antibiotics to treat urinary tract infections. If an infection persists for more than 48 hours despite the use of antibiotics, the patient should be evacuated. Also evacuate patients with symptoms of a kidney infection (painful , burning urination, flank pain, fever) for further evaluation.

TESTICULAR PAIN

Male external genitalia consist of the penis and scrotum. The penis provides a route for urine to be expelled from the bladder and sperm from the testes. The scrotum is a pouch-like structure located beneath the penis. The testes lie within the scrotum and are the site of sperm and testosterone production.

Sperm travels out of the testes via the epididymis, a comma-shaped organ that lies behind the testes. The epididymis consists of approximately 20 feet of ducts. From the epididymis, sperm travel through the ductus deferens, a tube approximately 18 inches long that loops into the pelvic cavity.

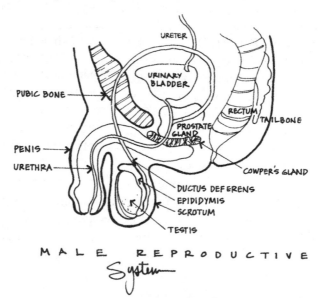

MALE REPRODUCTIVE System

Epididymitis

Epididymitis is an inflammation of the epididymis and can be caused by infections from gonorrhea, syphilis, tuberculosis, mumps, prostatitis (inflammation of the prostate), or urethritis (inflammation of the urethra).

Signs and Symptoms of Epididymitis. The patient suffers from pain in the scrotum, possibly accompanied by fever. The scrotum may be red and swollen. Epididymitis tends to come on slowly, unlike torsion of the testis, which tends to occur rapidly.

Treatment of Epididymitis. The treatment is bed rest, support or elevation of the testes, and antibiotics. Diagnosis can be tricky. The pain and swelling often prevent any activity; thus, evacuation is recommended. Acetaminophen, aspirin, or ibuprofen may decrease the fever and pain.

Torsion of the Testis

Torsion of the testis is a twisting of the testicle within the scrotum. The twisting constricts the ductus deferens and its accompanying blood vessels, decreasing the blood supply to the testis. If the blood supply is totally cut off, the testis becomes ischemic and eventually necrotic, meaning the tissue can die. After 24 hours without blood supply, the prognosis for saving the testis is poor.

Signs and Symptoms of Torsion. The scrotum is red, swollen, and painful, and the testis may appear slightly elevated on the affected side. The patient must be evacuated for treatment.

Signs and Symptoms of Epididymitis and Testicular Torsion

EPIDIDYMITIS
- Usually more gradual onset
- Scrotum is swollen, painful, and red

TESTICULAR TORSION
- Usually acute onset
- Scrotum is swollen, painful, and red
- Testis may be elevated

Treatment of Torsion. If you suspect torsion in the wilderness, there is little to be lost in having the patient attempt to untwist the affected testicle, rotating from the inside to the outside. Increased pain while untwisting is probably a good indicator that you're going in the wrong direction.

MENSTRUAL CONCERNS, VAGINAL INFECTION, AND ECTOPIC PREGNANCY

For most people assigned female at birth, the reproductive organs lie within the pelvic cavity and include the vagina, cervix, uterus, fallopian tubes, and ovaries. The vagina, or birth canal, is approximately 3 to 4 inches long. The vagina is continuously moistened by secretions that keep it clean and slightly acidic. At the top of the vagina is the cervix, which opens into the uterus. The cervix thins and opens during labor to allow the fetus to pass through.

The uterus is about the size of a fist and is located between the bladder and the rectum. Pregnancy begins when a fertilized egg implants in the tissue of the uterus. The uterus is an elastic organ that expands with the growing fetus.

On either side of the uterus, the ovaries lie approximately 4 or 5 inches below the waist. They produce and release eggs and the hormones estrogen and progesterone. Each month, an egg (ovum) is released from one of the ovaries and travels down the fallopian tube to the uterus. The fallopian tubes, approximately 4 inches long, wrap around the ovaries but are not directly connected to them. When the egg is released from the ovary, the fimbriae (fingerlike structures at the end of the fallopian tube) make sweeping motions across the ovary, sucking the egg into the fallopian tube.

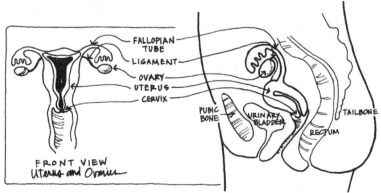

FEMALE REPRODUCTIVE System

The Menstrual Cycle

On average, the menstrual cycle—the monthly release of ova—can begin at about 12 years of age. Hormones regulate the cycle, which continues until menopause, cessation of the menstrual cycle, at approximately 52 years of age.

The endometrial tissue that lines the uterus undergoes hormone-regulated changes each month during menstruation. The average menstrual cycle is 28 days long. From days 1 through 5, the endometrial tissue sloughs off from the uterus and is expelled through the vagina. The usual total discharge is 4 to 6 tablespoons of blood, tissue, and mucus. This is called the "period." During days 6 through 16, the endometrial tissue regrows in preparation for implantation of an ovum, becoming thick and full of small blood vessels.

Ovulation usually occurs around day 14; the egg reaches the uterus around day 20. On about days 16 through 28, the endometrium secretes substances to nourish the embryo. If conception does not occur, the hormones progesterone and estrogen decrease, causing the uterine blood supply to decrease and the lining of the uterus to be shed.

Mittelschmerz. Some individuals experience cramping in the lower abdomen on the right or left side or in the back when the ovary releases an egg. The pain is sometimes accompanied by bloody vaginal discharge. This is called mittelschmerz (*mittel* = middle; s*chmerz* = pain).

Signs and Symptoms. The pain may be severe enough to be confused with appendicitis or ectopic pregnancy, but a careful assessment should allow the first responder to distinguish between the two. Ask the patient where they are in their menstrual cycle. Have they ever had this pain before? Typically, the cramping will be similar to past cycles. Any light bleeding or pain should cease within 36 hours. The abdomen is soft. Individuals using hormonal contraception do not ovulate, so are unlikely to have mittelschmerz. Collecting a careful history about medication adherence can help to determine if someone has missed pills, which could result in ovulation.

Dysmenorrhea. Dysmenorrhea is painful menstruation (cramps). Possible causes include prostaglandins, which cause the uterus to cramp; endometriosis (inflammation of the endo-metrium); pelvic inflammatory disease; or anatomic anomalies such as a displaced uterus.

Treatment. Anti-prostaglandins such as ibuprofen reduce the pain as well as the volume of flow and the length of the period. Relaxation exercises, such as yoga and massaging the lower back or abdomen, can help reduce pain, as will applying heat to the abdomen or lower back.

A change in diet may also help. Decreasing the amount of salt, caffeine, and alcohol in the diet while increasing the B vitamins—especially B6 (found in brewer's yeast, peanuts, rice, sunflower seeds, and whole grains) can offer some relief during cramping. Because exercise causes endorphins (natural opiates) to be released by the brain, cramps may diminish during stren-uous exercise.

Secondary Amenorrhea. Secondary amenorrhea is the absence of menstrual periods after an individual has had at least one period in their life. Causes of secondary amenorrhea include pregnancy, hormonal medications, ovarian tumors, intense athletic training, excessive weight loss or gain, altitude, and physical or emotional stress. Changes in the menstrual cycle are common in the backcountry and may be normal adjustments to unfamiliar stresses. The trip leader can help reduce stress around this by discussing these changes early in the expedition.

Vaginal Infections

The vagina normally contains a plethora of microorganisms. Most of the time these organisms are in balance and create a slightly acidic pH. Vaginal infections can occur when the normal balance of microorganisms and the pH are upset. Antibiotics, hormonal medications, and physical or emotional stress may cause an infection to develop. Uncontrolled diabetes is a risk factor as well. Cuts and abrasions from intercourse or tampons, not cleaning the perineal area, or not wearing clean, dry under-wear can also lead to an infection.

The two most common causes of vaginal infections are can-didiasis (yeast) and bacterial vaginosis.

Signs and Symptoms of Vaginitis. Symptoms of a yeast infection generally include curdy white discharge and itching. The vulva may be swollen and excoriated from scratching. Symptoms of bacterial vaginosis include a grayish, milky, thin discharge. The discharge may be malodorous, and the patient may complain of vaginal pain but not itching. For the purposes of field diagnosis, the symptoms are similar, and initial treatment is the same.

Treatment of Vaginitis. Vaginal yeast infections can be treated with an over-the-counter antifungal cream or suppository, such as miconazole (Monistat 1), clotrimazole, butoconazole or tioconazole (Vagistat-1), or with fluconazole (Diflucan). If these treatments don't provide relief within 48 hours, the patient should be evacuated.

Prevention. The best prevention for vaginal infections is education. To help prevent vaginal infections, wipe front to back after urinating or defecating, clean the perineal area daily with plain water or a mild soap, and promote ventilation by wearing loose-fitting synthetic or cotton underwear or running shorts.

Signs and Symptoms of a Vaginal Infection
- Curdy white discharge or grayish milky discharge
- Malodorous discharge
- Redness, soreness, itching of vaginal area

Treatment of Vaginal Infections
- Apply antifungal cream or suppository.
- Evacuate if symptoms persist for 48 hours despite treatment.

Prevention of Vaginal Infection
- Stay hydrated.
- Decrease sugar, caffeine, and alcohol intake.
- Wear loose-fitting underwear or running shorts for ventilation.
- Wash perineal area daily.
- Change tampons regularly.
- Decrease stress.

Ectopic Pregnancy

Ectopic pregnancies are pregnancies that occur outside the uterus, most commonly in the fallopian tubes. Due to congenital anomalies or scarring caused by infection, the egg implants and begins to grow in the tube, rather than completing its passage to the uterus. In such cases, sperm usually fertilizes the egg in the upper two-thirds of the tube.

Signs and Symptoms of Ectopic Pregnancy

- Rapid onset of unilateral lower abdominal pain
- Vaginal bleeding
- Absence of menstruation
- Signs and symptoms of peritonitis and shock (late developing sign)

Signs and Symptoms of Ectopic Pregnancy. The classic triad of an ectopic pregnancy is absence of menstruation, abdominal pain, and bleeding. The onset of pain is rapid and located on one side of the abdomen. In 4 to 6 weeks, the embryo becomes too large for the fallopian tube, which ruptures. The pain then becomes agonizing, and signs and symptoms of peritonitis develop. The patient may hemorrhage and die from shock, although slow bleeding is more common.

Treatment for Ectopic Pregnancy. Treat for shock and evacuate rapidly.

TIPS FOR HYGIENE IN THE WILDERNESS

If you're a trip leader, or simply traveling with companions, consider a pre-trip conversation about personal hygiene, especially around urination, defecation, and menstrual cycles. Set a tone for a respectful, open, adult, professional discussion of these challenges, which we all face when we are away from showers, faucets, hot water, or toilets. The conversation should encompass how you will handle fecal waste, urine, food waste, toilet paper, and bathing, but in this chapter we will focus on hygiene in the context of our urinary and reproductive systems.

Hand washing is important. Nothing beats soap and water to clean your hands. Alcohol-based hand sanitizers are helpful when water or time is scarce. To help prevent vaginal infections and fungal infections in the groin, wear loose-fitting shorts that allow for adequate ventilation. Baggy running shorts work well. In the winter, long underwear breathes well if you take off your wind protection clothes before going to bed.

Use comfortable, synthetic fabric–based underwear, which is easy to wash and quick to dry. If you are allergic to synthetic fabrics, consider silk or merino wool underwear. When urinating or defecating, wipe from the front to the back to limit introduction of bacteria into the vaginal area. Wash the vaginal area with water (and mild soap, if available) daily.

If you have a vagina and are not planning to use toilet paper to wipe with after urination, consider using a cotton bandanna to wipe. Allow the bandanna to dry in the sunlight between uses and wash frequently.

Changing tampons frequently in spite of the inconvenience in backcountry contexts is important to prevent infection. Used tampons and pads are bagged and carried out of the backcountry. Having a designated system makes proper disposal of tampons, pads, and toilet paper easier. A small stuff sack with a couple of extra plastic bags allows personal organization and privacy. Some people prefer wide-mouthed water bottles or plastic containers for this. Include a small wad of toilet paper in this kit. An aspirin or two placed in the bag or container will help dissipate odor.

How many extra tampons or pads to bring? Bring a little extra for heavier than normal flow, in case your cycle changes and you experience your period twice in a month, or if pads or tampons get wet. If a few people in a group each bring a bit extra, the group can cover almost any emergency without adding a lot of bulk. Remember to wash your hands prior to inserting a tampon. You could also consider using a reusable menstrual cup, in lieu of tampons or pads.

Evacuation Guidelines
- It is recommended that any person with a uterus and lower abdominal pain who is at risk for pregnancy should be evaluated for the possibility of pregnancy. If the patient presents with lower abdominal pain and vaginal bleeding (not associated with their regular menstrual cycle) they should be evacuated rapidly.
- Any person in a remote setting who suspects they may be pregnant should consider evacuation for evaluation by a healthcare provider and routine prenatal care.
- Evacuate any patient with signs and symptoms of a UTI or vaginitis that does not respond to treatment or is accompanied by a fever.

- Evacuate any patient with persistent testicular pain.
- Expedite evacuation for any patient with suspected testicular torsion.

22 MENTAL HEALTH CONCERNS ON WILDERNESS EXPEDITIONS

Written with the assistance of Cynthia B. Stevens, M.D.

INTRODUCTION

When we venture into wilderness, we bring with us our medical and our mental health history. Illness, injury, and mental health concerns that can present in our urban lives may also present in the wilderness. Outdoor leaders and expedition physicians will tell you that they see mental health issues ranging from heightened stress to episodes of anxiety, depression, mania, psychosis, or drug reactions on Denali, at Everest base camp, on treks, river trips, in outdoor programs, and during personal trips. As societal awareness of mental health as a medical issue increases, this topic is finding its way into wilderness medicine curriculum.

Anxiety, mild depression, some post-traumatic stress responses, and mild drug reactions may be managed without having to end the camping experience. More serious episodes will need to be treated by a skilled mental health professional in a more controlled setting. We don't expect first responders to be mental health professionals, but awareness of some of the more common mental health conditions; application of our patient assessment system; and thoughtful, compassionate care can help support these patients.

STRESS RESPONSES

Stress occurs whenever the mind or body has to adjust to a change in the individual's external or internal world. Substantial increases in stress typically result in heightened physiological and emotional states. This can exacerbate preexisting physical conditions (e.g., a change in blood pressure creates greater risk of a cardiac event), and generate symptoms related to anxiety and depression. Stress can also exacerbate chronic mental conditions such as psychotic disorders. Chapter 29 addresses stress injury and psychological first aid.

ANXIETY RESPONSES

Anxiety responses can include an acute anxiety event (also known as panic attacks), phobias, obsessive-compulsive thoughts and behaviors, and post-traumatic stress responses. Anxiety often accompanies physical injury and can interfere with an accurate assessment. Symptoms may include feelings of fear, apprehension, loss of control, and loss of sanity. Signs, which can mimic a heart attack, include heart palpitations; rapid, irregular heartbeat; rapid breathing; pale skin; and sweating.

First aid for stress and anxiety responses includes calming the patient and completing a patient assessment to try to identify physical causes. Patients whose responses abate might be able to stay in the field. An anxiety or stress response that is unpredictable or persistent may be a hazard to the patient and others, and may necessitate an evacuation.

DEPRESSION

Depression typically manifests in withdrawal, isolation, crying, diminished interest in most activities, fatigue or loss of energy, difficulty making decisions, feelings of helplessness and hopelessness, or a change in eating or sleeping patterns. These are not occasional blue moods. This is a deeper persistent affective disorder. Depression can also present with agitation, increased motor activity, ruminating thought processes, and compulsive behaviors. If the depression affects other group members, or limits the ability of the person to participate in the trip or focus on essential risk management tasks, the individual may need to be evacuated.

MANIA/PSYCHOSIS

Individuals experiencing mania or psychosis are out of touch with reality in some way (e.g., hallucinations, delusions, heightened energy levels), which means that the person suffering from psychotic symptoms cannot distinguish internal from external reality. Thus, mania and psychosis are more difficult to manage and can be dangerous if they occur in terrain where falls are a risk, or during an activity requiring focus and precise actions, such as paddling a rapid. Psychotic symptoms can be brought on by heightened stress, change in environment, use of drugs, and/or stopping administration of prescribed medications. Mania and psychoses are generally more serious than anxiety or depression and more likely to require field consultation with a mental health specialist, if available, and evacuation.

SUICIDAL BEHAVIOR

Suicide is the third-leading cause of death among individuals 15 to 24 years of age in the United States. If someone talks about suicide, pay attention.

If suicidal thoughts are suspected because the patient seems very depressed, feels hopeless or helpless, or actually talks about harming themself, talk to the patient specifically and directly about suicide. Opening this conversation may be challenging, but talking about suicide does not cause people to commit suicide. Ask the following five questions:

- Are you thinking of harming or killing yourself?
- Do you have a plan for how you would do this?
- Do you have the means with you now to carry out this plan?
- When are you thinking of doing this?
- Do you have a history of past suicide attempts?

Signs/Symptoms of Mental Health Concerns

ANXIETY RESPONSES
- Respiratory rate and heart rate increase
- Skin: clammy
- Trouble focusing
- Dizziness, trembling
- Stomach distress
- Chest pains
- Tingling sensations
- Excessive fear reactions
- Possible fight/flight/freeze response
- Panic episodes with catastrophic thoughts of dying, losing control, or going crazy
- Compulsive rituals/thoughts

DEPRESSION
- Persistent feelings of helplessness, hopelessness, despair. Agitation and anxiety may also be present
- Withdrawal, isolation, crying, diminished interest in most activities, fatigue or loss of energy, difficulty making decisions, irritability, and/or change in eating and sleeping patterns
- Vital signs that are normal for patient

MANIA/PSYCHOSIS
- Mania: incessant talking, flight of ideas, high energy, decreased need for sleep, altered sense of reality or inability to distinguish internal from external reality
- Psychosis: hallucinations, delusions, and an altered sense of reality

---

The more the person answers affirmatively, the higher the risk to that person.

The policy of an outdoor program may dictate what is to be done if an individual demonstrates any suicidal thoughts or behaviors, but in most cases these individuals ought to be evacuated.

TREATMENT PRINCIPLES

Complete a thorough patient assessment. Psychological problems can have physical causes such as brain tumors and infections, brain injury, substance abuse, hypoxia, hypoglycemia, hypothermia, or hyperthermia, to name a few.

Is the patient on any medications that might be influencing the problem? Does the patient have any history of this problem? If so, what has made it worse or better?

Listen carefully. Use a calm voice, slow breathing, eye contact, and patience. Keep questions simple, honest, direct, and respectful. You may need to repeat questions if a patient has trouble tracking. Ask if the person knows what led to these feelings and reactions.

Remain calm and reassure the patient. Focus on the patient's strengths. Discuss what has helped correct these feelings, thoughts, and reactions in the past, and see if some of these things can be done now.

Evaluate the risk to yourself, the patient, and others. Inform the patient of your treatment plan; don't surprise them. Decide if you can manage this patient in the field.

FINAL THOUGHTS

Evacuation Guidelines
We don't need to fully understand the problem. We can make an evacuation decision based on simple principles.
- Is the mental health condition beyond our ability to manage in the field?
- Does potential harm to other group members outweigh the benefit to the patient? Does the patient require a level of attention or monitoring that is already adversely affecting the cohesion, function, or safety of the group?
- Is the patient a danger to self or others?
- Does the patient feel unsafe or unable to continue?

- If any of these questions are answered in the affirmative, evacuate the patient to the care of a mental health professional.

EXPEDITION MEDICINE

"Judgment in my estimation is the greatest safety factor you can have."
—Paul Petzoldt, NOLS Founder

The first aid we can perform in the field is often limited. The experience and outcome for the patient are strongly influenced by the quality of leadership and expedition behavior, and the decisions we make. Three chapters at the end of this section prepare you for the challenges of leadership, teamwork, communication, decision-making, and the stress of rescue. This section completes the suite of skills we need to effectively lead wilderness medicine problems and blends the medicine with outdoor leadership. The NOLS incident data shows that flu-like illness and gastrointestinal symptoms are by far the most common medical complaints. The chapter on hygiene and water disinfection speaks to this from the perspective of prevention, our most effective treatment. This theme continues as we address hydration, which helps us tolerate heat, cold, altitude, and the exercise that comes with outdoor pursuits.

CHAPTER 23 | HYDRATION

INTRODUCTION

NOLS instructors constantly harp on hydration, urging their students to drink water. They issue large water bottles, mugs, and hydration bladders to encourage drinking. They carry water in the desert and melt snow with a passion in winter environments.

Dehydration is rarely the primary cause of an evacuation at NOLS, but underlying dehydration complicates many of our evacuations. Preventing dehydration on the trail, on the river, and on the ocean is a part of life for wilderness travelers.

It is a myth that hydration, by itself, prevents heat exhaustion, heatstroke, or altitude illness. Proper hydration helps us tolerate heat, altitude, and cold, but the only illness that hydration prevents is dehydration. Dehydration worsens fatigue, decreases the ability to exercise efficiently, and reduces mental alertness. Often fatigue, irritability, poor thinking, body aches, and headache at the end of a day are the first signs and symptoms of dehydration. In extreme cases, dehydration can be a life-threatening medical problem.

PHYSIOLOGY OF WATER BALANCE

Humans are bags of water. Our fluid-filled inner ears enable us to hear, the brain is cushioned by fluid, and the joints are lubricated by fluid. Blood is 90 percent water, and every bio-chemical reaction takes place in a medium of water.

For many, spending extended time outdoors requires adjust-ing to new rhythms and responding to environmental stressors more directly than in our everyday lives. Outdoors, we exer-cise daily and thus lose water through sweating, breathing, and increased metabolic demands. Outdoors, we adjust directly to the environment, whether hot or cold. In the desert we sweat to lose heat, and in the cold we lose water to moisten the cold air we breathe. Outdoors, hydration is not as simple as turning on the tap. It's harder to obtain and store water; we lose more of it responding to the environment, and we need more of it to main-tain health. In the desert we carry, ration, and spend a lot of time searching for water. We may alter our activity patterns to reduce water loss; we rest during the hot midday and work in the cool dawn and evening. In the winter, we must melt the water we drink—a time-consuming process. There is always the difficulty of disinfecting potentially contaminated water sources.

Assessment of Hydration

At L in the SAMPLE history, we explore fluid intake and output, not just today, but over the past several days; dehydration can be cumulative. The signs and symptoms mimic altitude illness, hypothermia, fatigue, heat exhaustion, and shock. Dehydration must be suspected in every patient treated in the outdoors.

General symptoms of a negative water balance are fatigue, heat oppression, thirst, irritability, dizziness, dark smelly urine, and headache. A seriously dehydrated patient may have a rapid pulse; pale, cool, clammy skin; pale mucous membranes; weak-ness; and nausea. Mental deterioration can occur and present as loss of balance and changes in mental awareness. Tenting—in which the skin retains a tent shape when pinched—is a sign of serious dehydration; normal skin is sufficiently hydrated to return to its normal shape.

With a 2-percent fluid deficit, we experience mental deteri-oration, decreased group cooperation, vague discomfort, lack of energy and appetite, flushed skin, impatience, sleepiness, nau-sea, and an increased pulse rate.

A 12-percent fluid deficit results in an inability to swallow, a swollen tongue, sunken eyes, and decreased neurological function. Dizziness, tingling in the limbs, absence of salivation, and slurred speech may also be present. A fluid deficit greater than 15 percent is potentially lethal. Signs include delirium, vision disturbances, and shriveled skin.

Treatment of Dehydration
A mildly dehydrated patient—and all wilderness travelers—should drink clear water to replace fluids. It is the best fluid for hydration.

Electrolyte replacement drinks can help, although some people find they are too sweet. Sugar increases the time it takes for fluid to be absorbed from the stomach. Coffee and tea contain caffeine, a diuretic that stimulates the kidneys to excrete fluid. Some experts consider this effect overrated; nonetheless, coffee, tea, and alcohol (which also increases urine production and fluid loss) should be avoided when rehydrating. Cool water is absorbed faster than warm water, but the difference probably interests only a physiologist. The message is moderation: not too hot, not too cold—whatever is palatable.

A severely dehydrated patient may have electrolyte imbalances as well as a fluid deficit. Such a patient cannot be rehydrated in the field and must be evacuated to a hospital for intravenous fluid therapy.

Hyponatremia
Just as it's possible to become dehydrated, we can get into trouble by drinking too much water. A typical scenario is a hot-weather hiker drinking much more water than needed and developing a situation where hydration status is good, yet blood sodium is relatively low. This is hyponatremia, also known as water intoxication.

Signs and symptoms vary among individuals and depend on the patient's hydration and sodium levels. The patient may appear to have heat exhaustion: headache, weakness, fatigue, lightheadedness, muscle cramps, nausea with or without vomiting, sweaty skin, normal core temperature, and normal or slightly elevated pulse and breathing rates.

Recognizing hyponatremia, versus heat exhaustion or dehydration, depends on an accurate history. Be suspicious if the patient has a high fluid intake—several liters in the last few hours.

Patients with suspected hyponatremia and an altered mental status should be evacuated. Patients with mild-to-moderate symptoms and a normal mental status can be treated in the field. Have the patient rest in the shade with little or no fluid intake and a gradual intake of salty foods, while the kidneys reestablish a sodium balance. Brisk urine production usually indicates things are progressing in the right direction. Oral electrolyte replacement drinks are low in sodium and high in water, and may not help much.

FINAL THOUGHTS

There are several cornerstones to good health in the outdoors: staying warm and dry, eating well, resting, camping comfortably, washing hands, climbing slowly at altitude, and, most important, staying properly hydrated.

How much water should you drink to stay healthy in the wilderness? Current wisdom tempers the water-pounding rhetoric we have seen in recent decades. Hydration needs vary from person to person, climate to climate, activity to activity. We exercise and sweat at different rates in heat and cold, in dry and humid air, at sea level and at altitude. Drink if you are thirsty. Thirst is a fine-tuned mechanism, a sensitive indicator of the need to drink. Beware of the advice to drink to "stay ahead of thirst." This can promote hyponatremia.

Follow the ancient saw "know thyself," and use experience and self-awareness to know when to drink. NOLS's guideline of 3 to 4 liters of fluid a day during summer hiking has served our students well for decades and is a good reference point.

Competitive athletes face the question of whether to drink plain water or sports drinks with sugar. Research supports the recommendation that participants in athletic events for longer than one hour should drink solutions containing 4 to 8 percent carbohydrates. However, on wilderness expeditions, daily nutrient intake should be based on well-balanced meals and on-trail snacks, not sports drinks or energy gels.

CHAPTER 24 | HYGIENE AND WATER DISINFECTION

INTRODUCTION

We commonly see signs at wilderness trailheads warning of disease-causing bacteria, viruses, and protozoa in the water. It's become an accepted belief that wilderness water must be disinfected. Yet, the available science does not support the assumption that all wilderness water, especially from pristine sources, harbors diarrhea-causing pathogens. It is true that diarrhea and related flu-like symptoms are the most common illnesses on wilderness trips, but we can't categorically blame the water. Poor hygiene—particularly poor hand-washing habits—are believed to be a prominent cause of these preventable illnesses.

Water contamination continues to be a major health problem in many parts of the world, and diarrheal illness is a leading cause of death. Unfortunately, it is not always easy to know when a wilderness water source has a low risk of intestinal pathogens and when it has a high risk. Maintaining strict hygiene practices in pristine wilderness can be difficult, and water disinfection may seem unnecessary, but diarrhea is unpleasant and can be dangerous to our health. It may be better to be safe than sorry.

WATERBORNE ILLNESS

Worldwide, waterborne microorganisms account for many cases of infectious diarrhea. The microorganisms causing diarrhea include bacteria, protozoa, viruses, and parasitic worms. Diseases that are spread through contaminated water include typhoid, cholera, campylobacteriosis, giardiasis, and hepatitis A.

Although the protozoan *Giardia* frequently causes diagnosed diarrhea in the United States, other bacteria and viruses are being identified as well. Recently the protozoan *Cryptosporidium* has received attention as a cause of municipal waterborne disease outbreaks, but it is unclear how much risk it poses in wilderness water sources.

Giardia

Giardia is a microscopic protozoan. It has a two-stage life cycle as cyst and trophozoite. The cyst, excreted in mammalian feces, is hardy and can survive 2 to 3 months in near-freezing water. If swallowed, the warmer internal environment causes the cyst to change into its active stage, the trophozoite. The trophozoite attaches itself to the wall of the small intestine and is the cause of the diarrhea associated with *Giardia* infections.

Humans are carriers of *Giardia*. It has also been identified in both domestic and wild animals, specifically in beavers, cats, dogs, sheep, cattle, deer, and elk, as well as in reptiles, amphibians, and fish. Cases of *Giardia* have risen in recent years, but it is not clear if this truly represents a higher infection rate, or simply a higher rate of confirmed diagnoses.

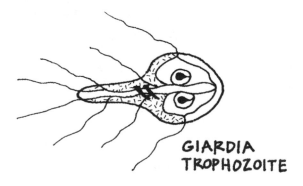

GIARDIA
TROPHOZOITE

Giardia is difficult to diagnose due to the wide variation in symptoms. For a reliable diagnosis, three stool samples should be examined. Most infections are without symptoms, and the unwitting carrier inadvertently spreads the illness. The incubation period from ingestion to the onset of infection is 1 to 3 weeks. Symptoms include recurrent and persistent malodorous stools and flatus, abdominal cramping, bloating, "sulfur burps," and indigestion. Serious infections produce explosive watery diarrhea with cramps, foul flatus, fever, and malaise.

Although drug therapy is available, prevention through hygienic habits and water disinfection makes much more sense. *Giardia* is sensitive to heat and easily filtered, and it can be killed with chemical disinfection.

Cryptosporidium

The microscopic protozoan *Cryptosporidium* is spread by drinking contaminated water, eating contaminated raw or undercooked food, or transferring from hand to mouth cysts picked up from fecal matter.

Some people may not have symptoms. Most have an illness that starts 2 to 10 days after infection, lasts 1 to 2 weeks, and includes watery diarrhea, headache, abdominal cramps, nausea, vomiting, and low-grade fever. In people with compromised immune systems, the infection may continue and become life-threatening.

Cryptosporidium cysts are sensitive to heat and can be filtered but are not reliably killed by iodine or chlorine. People with suppressed immune systems should consider boiling water or using a filtration system to protect themselves from infection.

WATER DISINFECTION

Purifying water eliminates offensive odors, tastes, and colors, but it does not kill microorganisms. Sterilization kills all life forms. Disinfection removes or destroys disease-causing microorganisms. What we commonly refer to as water purification is really disinfection. There are four main methods of water

Methods OF WATER DISINFECTION:

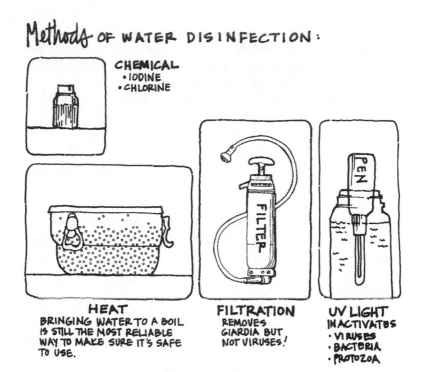

CHEMICAL
• IODINE
• CHLORINE

HEAT
BRINGING WATER TO A BOIL IS STILL THE MOST RELIABLE WAY TO MAKE SURE IT'S SAFE TO USE.

FILTRATION
REMOVES GIARDIA BUT NOT VIRUSES!

UV LIGHT
INACTIVATES
• VIRUSES
• BACTERIA
• PROTOZOA

disinfection: heat, chemical treatment, filtration, and ultraviolet (UV) light.

Heat

Incorrect information persists regarding how long to boil water before it is disinfected. The common diarrhea-causing microorganisms are sensitive to heat and killed immediately by boiling water. The protozoans *Giardia* and *Entamoeba* (the amoeba which causes amebiasis) die after 2 to 3 minutes at 140°F (60°C). Viruses, diarrhea-producing bacteria, and *Cryptosporidium* cysts die within minutes at 150°F (65°C). By the time water boils, it is safe to drink.

The boiling point decreases with increasing elevation, but this does not affect disinfection. The boiling point at 19,000 feet (5,700 meters) is 178°F (81°C), sufficient for disinfecting water.

The advantage of boiling is its effectiveness. However, it is inconvenient on the trail, takes time, and consumes fuel.

Chemical Treatment

Chemical treatment is the addition to water of halogens (either iodine or chlorine) or chlorine dioxide. If used correctly, halogens and chlorine dioxide can reliably deactivate viruses and kill diarrhea-causing bacteria and most protozoa cysts, with the exception of *Cryptosporidium*. The concentration of chemical and its contact time in water determine the degree of disinfection.

Factors that can affect chemical treatment include pH, water temperature, and the chemical binding with debris in the water. All chemical reactions—including those used in water treatment—are affected by pH, but the pH levels of most natural water sources don't have significant impacts. Cold water, on the other hand, can dramatically slow the reaction of either halogens or chlorine dioxide. Compensate for a slower reaction in cold water by increasing contact time. To be on the safe side, allow 30 minutes in warm water (86°F [30°C]), 60 minutes in cold water (59°F [15°C]).

All chemical disinfection methods work most effectively in clear water. When the chemical disinfectant binds with organic and inorganic particles in water, less is available to destroy diarrhea-causing microorganisms and viruses. Reduce debris before adding the chemical: filter murky water with a manufactured filter, or use an improvised strainer such as a coffee filter or a clean bandanna. You can also let water sit until the floating particles settle to the bottom or use alum to clear the water.

Iodine. Iodine, a commonly used halogen, is available as a tablet containing tetraglycine hydroperiodide, sold commercially as Potable Aqua iodine tablets. Iodine crystals in Polar-Pure, 2-percent iodine (tincture), and 10 percent povidone-iodine solutions are also effective.

Iodine is affected less than chlorine by pH, and it has less effect on the taste of the water. Wilderness medicine experts believe that at the levels used to occasionally disinfect water, iodine is safe for most people. Those who spend a lot of time in the wilderness may want to consider other means to disinfect water. Iodine is not recommended for persons with thyroid disease or a known iodine allergy, or during pregnancy.

The aftertaste of iodine and chlorine in water can be improved by adding flavoring. The sugar in drink mixes, however, also binds the halogen. Add flavoring after disinfection. An ascorbic acid (vitamin C) tablet, added after disinfection, improves flavor by chemically reducing the iodine and chlorine to iodide and chloride, which have no taste.

Chlorine. Chlorine has been used as a disinfectant for over 200 years. Chlorine bleach (4 to 6 percent) is commonly used to disinfect water. Halazone and Puritabs are chlorine tablets.

Chlorine Dioxide. Chlorine dioxide products such as Aqua Mira, Micropur, Potable Aqua chlorine dioxide, and the MIOX Purifier are newer products that are effective over a broad temperature range and leave less of an aftertaste in the water. They claim to disinfect *Cryptosporidium*, although contact time needs to be 4 hours, an inconvenience on the trail.

Ultraviolet Light. There are several products on the market that disinfect water using ultraviolet (UV) light, a well-established disinfectant. With the correct light intensity and exposure time, UV inactivates viruses, bacteria, and protozoa, does not require chemicals, and does not alter taste. The UV radiation must bathe the pathogens, so the water should be clear. There is no overdose danger, but there is also no residual disinfection power. Sunlight on transparent plastic bottles, ideally on a dark surface, exposed to UV for a minimum of 4 hours can disinfect water and may be a viable option in an emergency.

Filtration

Filtration physically removes solid materials and microorganisms by forcing water through a filter element. Filter elements can be ceramic cartridges, fiberglass, or structured or labyrinthine mediums of dense, honeycombed material. Several types of filters are available with pore sizes small enough to filter *Giardia* and *Cryptosporidium* cysts, as well as bacteria. A 0.2-micron filter (the number refers to the pore size in the filter medium) is a common standard. Most bacteria are removed by 0.2-micron filters, protozoa by 1.0-micron filters. These are believed to be the most common waterborne pathogens in the North American backcountry.

Viruses are too small to be reliably eliminated by field water filtration. Some filters, labeled purifiers, have an additional process that deactivates viruses by passing water through an iodine- or chlorine-impregnated resin, or by trapping them in a filter medium that carries an electrostatic charge. If you're traveling outside North America, or in areas with a lot of people and poor sanitation, viruses are a greater risk and a purifier may be a better choice than a standard filtration system.

Filters are more convenient on the trail than boiling water, and filtration may reduce the amount of iodine or chlorine necessary to chemically disinfect water. On the downside, filters can be expensive and may clog or develop undetectable leaking cracks.

FOOD-BORNE ILLNESS

Microbes and viruses can be found everywhere. They're in the soil, in water, on our hands, in our noses and mouths. Many are harmless to us. Some cause illness either through the toxins they produce, or as a side effect of colonizing the digestive tract. We can expose ourselves to these pathogens by drinking contaminated water, or through poor hygiene practices in the kitchen. Bacteria such as *Staphylococcus*, *Shigella*, and *Salmonella*, and viruses such as norovirus are common sources of food-borne illness. If we give these pathogens a place to linger, such as a dirty cook pot, they can multiply, produce toxins, and/or be available to enter new hosts along with the next meal.

Those of us with access to modern sanitation don't have to give much thought to hygiene. We're protected by flush toilets, effective waste disposal and sewer systems, reliably disinfected tap water, readily available hot water, and proximity to advanced medical care. The wilderness is a different story; proper human-waste disposal, hand and utensil washing, safe food preparation, and water disinfection need to become habits. For instance, a river guide with poor kitchen hygiene was the source of food poisoning for many of the people on his trip. There are other documented accounts of illness being passed from person to person on wilderness trips. We suspect that poor kitchen and personal sanitation—rather than contaminated water sources—cause most episodes of flu-like and diarrheal illness on NOLS courses.

Hygiene in the Wilderness Kitchen

NOLS has found several practices helpful in reducing the incidence of food-borne illness on our expeditions.

Cook Food Thoroughly. Food that is dry or has a high salt or sugar content inhibits bacterial growth. Moist food that is low in salt and sugar is a good medium for growth, especially if it is warm. Protect yourself by cooking food completely. Boil your pasta, beans, and rice, and cook your meat until it is no longer red (ideally 170°F or 77°C).

Eat Cooked Food Promptly. Heat destroys most bacteria. Cold keeps bacteria from multiplying. Keep cooked food hot or cold, and don't keep it long. The optimal temperature zone for bacterial growth is between 45° and 140°F (7° and 60°C). In only a short period—within an hour in ideal warm and moist conditions—bacteria can multiply to become the source of diarrhea.

Avoid Leftovers. Storing cooked food without refrigeration invites disaster. Plan meals so that all food is consumed when served. Besides promoting bacterial growth, keeping leftovers creates a waste-disposal problem and attracts animals such as bears.

Cold-weather trips have the advantage of natural refrigeration. If leftovers are quickly cooled in air temperatures that stay below 38°F (3.5°C) and the meal is reheated completely, your risk of food-borne illness is less, though not zero. It's always safer to avoid leftovers. Heat-resistant toxins and microbes may colonize stored cooked food. If you do eat leftover food, make sure that the food is hot throughout the dish, not just on the surface. A crispy exterior does not mean that the interior has been well heated.

Clean Pots, Pans, and Utensils. Dirty pots, pans, and utensils are ideal surfaces for microbial life. Cleaning away grease and food in the wilderness can be a challenge, especially if water is scarce. Plan ahead to minimize leftovers. Use sand or snow to scour pots, then rinse with hot water. Hard work to remove food residue can minimize the water needed for a final rinse. Dish soap helps clean, but it must be rinsed well to avoid diarrhea and disposed of properly to leave no trace. Use a strainer to filter out large food particles that should be packed out. Scatter the remaining wastewater widely, away from camp and water sources.

Boil cooking utensils daily. Immersing clean utensils in your water pot as you boil the morning hot drink water will help continue the sanitizing process. Bacteria and protozoa will be killed and viruses deactivated, as the heat disinfects the water.

Large groups frequently use group-cooking setups with chlorine rinses as an important step in keeping utensils clean. The three-bucket method begins with a hot soapy-water scrub, then a warm-water rinse, and finally a 1-minute immersion in a chlorine-rinse bucket. Prepare this 100 to 150 ppm solution by adding 1 tablespoon of 4- to 6-percent chlorine bleach per gallon of water, or one-quarter tablet of Effersan, a commercially available chlorine tablet. Air-dry the cooking gear, rather than wiping with potentially dirty dish rags.

Keep Kitchen Surfaces and Utensils Clean. Keep the food-preparation surface and your utensils clean. Between the grocery store and dinner, your food can be contaminated many different ways. Dirty hands can reach inside, touch, and contaminate the food. Avoid this by pouring food from a bag or box. The spoon used to taste the soup may also be the spoon used to stir or serve. The cook may sneeze or cough and spread germs over dinner. The spatula may be placed on the ground or in a grubby food sack, then used to stir your pasta. An organized and clean kitchen reduces the chance of this cross-contamination.

Fresh Fruit and Vegetables. The surfaces of fruit and vegetables can be contaminated. A rule of thumb for fruit and vegetables is to peel it, boil it, cook it, or avoid it.

Protect Food from Insects and other Animals. Insects and other animals are vectors of disease. Keeping flies and rodents from your food both protects you from disease and keeps the animal from becoming habituated to humans as a source of food.

Don't Share. Sharing your resources, energy, wisdom, and companionship is good expedition behavior. Sharing your microbes with your tent mate is not. Keep your handkerchief, water bottle, cup, bowl, spoon, and lip balm to yourself. Instead of reaching into a plastic bag for a handful of raisins and contaminating the entire bag, pour the raisins into your hand. Serve food with the serving utensil, not your personal spoon. An ill person or one with open cuts on their hands should not prepare food. It takes only one person to be the source of a group-wide illness.

Wash Your Hands. Lastly, but most importantly, wash your hands! Keep nails trimmed and clean. Microbes live on the skin, and hands are an excellent and common medium for transporting these creatures from person to person. Regular hand washing does not sterilize your hands, but it does reduce the chance of infection. Ideally after using the latrine, you should use hot water, lots of soap, and a thorough rinse. Practically speaking, in the wilderness, you'll wash with cold water. At a minimum, you should do this before preparing, serving, or eating food. Large expeditions or base camps often set up a hand-washing station near a latrine or outhouse, or in a central camp location. Waterless soaps are an option when water is not available, or as an extra precaution after hands have been rinsed of grease and dirt.

Using natural toilet paper—leaves, sticks, rocks, or snow—reduces the paper you use and, when done properly, is as sanitary as regular toilet paper. But you need to be proficient to avoid contaminating your hands with fecal material. And of course, always wash your hands afterward.

FINAL THOUGHTS

Some people think that contaminated water accounts for most infectious diarrhea in the U.S. wilderness. Person-to-person exchange from poor kitchen and personal hygiene practices is also thought to be a leading cause. Outside the wilderness, the most common route for infection is believed to be from person to person via hand-to-mouth contact or contaminated utensils.

Infection rates increase with close contact and poor hygiene. Habits of cleanliness and hygiene are essential to health and safety in the wilderness.

Your choice among boiling, filtering, adding chemicals, or using UV radiation to disinfect your water will depend on how contaminated the water might be, personal preference, fuel availability, group size, cost, and reliability. None of the water disinfection methods is foolproof. Each has its limitations, and each must be done correctly. They reduce, but do not eliminate, the risk of getting sick from drinking water.

CHAPTER 25 DENTAL EMERGENCIES

INTRODUCTION

Dental issues are among the most common medical problems encountered on wilderness trips. Enduring a dental problem in the wilderness, several days away from care, can be an uncomfortable experience. Simple field treatments for broken teeth or fillings, knocked-out teeth, impacted wisdom teeth, toothaches, and gum irritations can make life more comfortable during an evacuation.

DENTAL CAVITIES, BROKEN TEETH, OR LOST FILLINGS

Dental cavities, lost fillings and broken teeth can cause discomfort or pain, particularly if hot or cold liquids or spicy foods touch the exposed tooth tissue. Exposure of a nerve, pulp, artery, or vein due to a cavity, lost filling, or a broken tooth causes pain. Various temporary filling materials are available for stopgap treatment of dental cavities, broken teeth or fillings. Cavit is a premixed combination of zinc oxide powder (not the ointment) and a topical anesthetic available as a nonprescription temporary filling in many dental emergency kits. In a pinch, NOLS staff have even had success using sugarless gum and ski wax to cover loose fillings and broken teeth.

Broken Tooth/Lost Fillings

SIGNS AND SYMPTOMS
- Pain when exposed to air
- Obviously cracked or broken tooth
- Bleeding and possible exposed pulp

TREATMENT PRINCIPLES
- Seal painful exposed nerves from air and temperature changes with Cavit, wax, or sugarless gum.
- If biting down fully causes pain, placing rolled-up gauze between back molars can help.
- Consider pain medications.
- Consider evacuation.

Rinse the broken tooth or filling thoroughly before covering with a temporary filling. Roll the temporary material into a small ball and gently press it into the hole in the tooth, sealing the exposed tissue. If biting down fully causes pain, placing pieces of rolled up gauze between the back molars can maintain separation and reduce pain.

AVULSED TOOTH

An avulsed (knocked-out) tooth should be gently rinsed, then slowly and gently placed back into the hole. Irrigate the tooth, but don't scrub it—you may remove tissue that can help the tooth survive. If you can't replace it yourself, save the tooth for replacement. Hank's Balanced Salt Solution (available as Save-A-Tooth) is the medium of choice. Milk, regardless of fat content, is acceptable (as is powdered milk). Next in line, but still decent choices, are physiological saline, the patient's own saliva, and water. You can also wrap the tooth in gauze and have the patient carry it between the cheek and gum or in a cool place. For a good prognosis, a tooth must be replaced within 30 minutes and receive the care of a dentist within a week.

If the socket is bleeding, it can be packed to place pressure on the tissue. A slightly moist tea bag makes an acceptable

---

Avulsed (Knocked-Out) Tooth

TREATMENT PRINCIPLES
- Irrigate but do not scrub the tooth.
- Attempt to replace the avulsed tooth in the socket.
- If the tooth cannot be replaced, it should be kept in an appropriate storage medium.
- Provide pain medications as needed.
- Consider evacuation.

---

packing material. In fact, the tannic acid in non-herbal tea promotes clotting.

IMPACTED WISDOM TOOTH

When molars emerge into the back of the mouth, the gum tissue may remain intact over part of the tooth, causing irritation. Plaque and food debris get stuck under the flap of tissue, and infection and pain set in. In addition, the patient may experience swelling and redness around the partially erupted tooth and gum, as well as swelling and tenderness in the jaw.

The definitive solution is to pull the tooth, which is a job for a dentist. Our first aid in the field is based on keeping the area clean. Assess the inside of the mouth with a light. If you have an irrigation syringe, try to irrigate under the flap of skin, firmly and gently. Brush and floss the area, especially between second and third molars. It may bleed, and the patient can use mouthwash, salt water, or water to rinse and spit. Pain will

---

Impacted Wisdom Tooth

SIGNS AND SYMPTOMS
- Pain
- Swelling and redness around the partially erupted tooth and gum
- Possible swelling and tenderness in jaw

TREATMENT PRINCIPLES
- Irrigate under the flap of skin, firmly and gently.
- Brush and floss the area.
- Use mouthwash, salt water, or water to rinse and spit.
- If biting down fully causes pain, consider placing rolled-up gauze between back molars.
- Consider pain medications.
- Consider evacuation.

---

increase because of the irritation from this treatment but should diminish within 3 to 4 hours. If biting down fully causes pain, consider placing rolled-up gauze between the top and bottom molars. If the pain does not improve, consider evacuation.

ORAL IRRITATIONS AND INFECTIONS

General mouth irritation is usually due to poor hygiene and can be treated with vigorous brushing and rinses with water.

An infection between the gum line and a tooth, commonly the result of trapped food, may become a periodontal abscess. Local swelling and abscesses on the gums indicate infection. Evacuation to a dentist is the best treatment. On remote expeditions, treatment with antibiotics and drainage of the infection may be considered.

Oral Irritations

SIGNS AND SYMPTOMS
- Difficulty eating or drinking due to pain
- Sensitivity to air, temperature, or sweets

TREATMENT PRINCIPLES
- Dental hygiene: Brush teeth and flush mouth with disinfected water.
- Cover/fill holes with Cavit, wax, or sugarless gum, or use Cavit to "glue" crown or filling in place.
- Consider pain management.
- Evacuate if pain is persistent or debilitating.

FINAL THOUGHTS

Preparation for a wilderness expedition includes a visit to your dentist to identify and treat any potential problems. In the field, brush and floss regularly. Anyone who has experienced the woes of a toothache, loose filling, or dental infection in the wilderness knows that the need for dental hygiene does not cease when we venture into the woods.

CHAPTER 26 | COMMON NONURGENT MEDICAL PROBLEMS

INTRODUCTION

These topics are often mislabeled as "common and simple" medical problems. They are indeed common. The data that NOLS has been keeping for over 30 years on field medical incidents tells us that flu-like illness (colds, upper-respiratory infections, sore throat, fever, headaches) and gastrointestinal problems (nausea, vomiting, diarrhea, constipation) comprise 40 percent of reported illness and dwarf all other reported illness categories.

Respiratory symptoms (cough, congestion, runny nose, sore throat) are usually viral upper-respiratory infections, a "cold" or "flu" and can also cause a headache, malaise, fatigue, low-grade fever, muscle aches, and body aches. Gastrointestinal symptoms (nausea, vomiting, and diarrhea) are usually caused by a "stomach bug" or "stomach flu."

However, these problems are not necessarily simple. The symptoms are common to many different medical presentations and can occasionally be the initial symptoms of more serious clinical conditions including Covid, Dengue, Zika, and others.

The wilderness leader's challenge is knowing how to manage these symptoms effectively and deciding when someone is sick enough to warrant an evacuation.

FLU-LIKE ILLNESS

Often these illnesses, known variously as colds, upper-respiratory infections, sore throats, fevers, and headaches, are viral infections of the nasal passages and throat that cause a runny nose, sore throat, cough, sneezing, headache, mild fever, muscle aches, and malaise. "Colds" are self-limiting, but these infections can linger for several weeks, despite all our remedies.

Signs and Symptoms of Flu-like Illness

- Fever
- Headache
- Muscle aches and malaise
- Nasal congestion and coughing
- Increased mucus production
- Cough, sometimes productive
- Sore throat
- Fever
- Malaise

They are transmitted by contaminated hands, and in some cases as respiratory droplets or aerosols. Wash your hands! Cover your cough!

Upper-Respiratory Infection (URI)

URIs are viral or bacterial infections that affect the sinuses, pharynx, larynx, or bronchi. They are uncomfortable for the patient but usually self-limiting.

Sore Throat

The most common causes of a sore throat are simple dryness due to altitude and dehydration, and viral infections such as the common cold. Strep throat, roughly 10 percent of sore throats, is caused by bacteria *(Streptococcus)* and requires a culture to confirm. We can suspect strep if the throat is beefy red with white pus spots, accompanied by fever, headache, vomiting, and—less likely—respiratory signs and symptoms.

Fever

Fever is the body's resetting of our internal thermostat, triggered by the immune system's response to an infection. Other signs and symptoms of illness usually accompany fever.

Headache
Dehydration is thought to be the most common cause of headaches in the backcountry. Other causes include muscular tension, altitude, vascular disorders, trauma, brain tumors, and carbon monoxide (CO) poisoning.

Treatment Principles for Flu-like Illness
The management of flu-like illness is based on treating symptoms to help the patient feel better while these illnesses run their course. We also need to recognize when the illness is more serious or complex, and the patient requires evacuation for evaluation by a physician. Hydration is important, as is hygiene—especially hand washing. These illnesses are communicable, and we want to avoid spreading them through the group.

Rest and patience are cornerstones of treatment. Most of these illnesses are self-limiting—but they can take a week or more to resolve. People don't like to be sick, and impatience will drive decisions to try treatments or to leave the wilderness. Pain medications (acetaminophen, aspirin, or nonsteroidal antiinflammatory drugs) for headache and muscle aches are fine. Decongestants (e.g., pseudoephedrine) and cough suppressants can treat upper-respiratory symptoms.

Evacuation Guidelines
When are these common problems not simple? Evacuation is recommended for flu-like illness if:

- Fever persists for more than 48 hours or is high (>104°F/40°C).
- The patient develops a stiff neck, severe headache, breathing difficulty, or wheezing.
- Signs or symptoms of pneumonia develop (fever, productive cough, noisy lungs).
- Increasing shortness of breath, decreasing exercise tolerance, or worsening malaise.
- The patient is unable to tolerate any oral fluids for more than 48 hours, especially if there is fever, vomiting, or significant fluid losses from diarrhea.

- The sore throat occurs in conjunction with an inability to swallow water and/or maintain adequate hydration.
- The sore throat is associated with a fever and a beefy red throat with white patches.
- The headache does not respond to treatment, is sudden and severe, or is associated with altered mental status.

GASTROINTESTINAL PROBLEMS

Gastroenteritis is an inflammation of the gastrointestinal system. Diarrhea is persistent loose, watery stools. These are common backcountry medical conditions. A study on Denali showed that a third of the climbers had diarrhea, and that their hygiene practices could have used improvement. We may want to blame it on the water, but fecal-oral contamination is probably a more common cause. Wash your hands!

The signs and symptoms of the "mung," as NOLS instructors often call nausea, vomiting, and diarrhea, are familiar.

Treatment of Gastroenteritis. Hydration is a focus of our treatment, as persistent diarrhea and vomiting can cause dehydration and electrolyte problems. If vomiting has been severe, consider electrolyte replacement solutions. Antinausea medications such as ondansetron (Zofran) or bismuth subsalicylate can be helpful. Antidiarrheal medication such as loperamide (Immodium) can be helpful for persistent diarrhea. Try a bland diet.

Signs and Symptoms of Mild Gastroenteritis

- Gradually increasing, diffuse abdominal pain, often worse in the lower quadrants
- Intermittent cramping, with frequent loose stools
- Hyperactive bowel sounds
- Nausea and vomiting, occasionally with low-grade fever
- Usually resolves within 1-3 days

Signs and Symptoms of Severe Gastroenteritis

- Persistent or worsening pain over 24 hours, especially if the pain becomes localized and constant
- Inability to tolerate fluids
- Stools with blood and mucus
- Signs and symptoms of shock
- Fever >102°F (38°C)

Evacuation Guidelines

When are these gastrointestinal problems not simple? Evacuation is recommended if:

- There is bloody or coffee-ground vomit, the vomiting persists despite treatment, or the patient is unable to hydrate.
- The diarrhea becomes bloody or persists despite treatment, or the patient is unable to hydrate.
- Abdominal pain persists or worsens over 24 hours.
- Fever abruptly increases.
- The patient is unable to tolerate oral fluids for more than 48 hours, especially if accompanied by diarrhea or vomiting.

EYE INJURIES

Foreign Body in the Eye

Usually eyelashes, tears, and blinking defend the surface of the eye from foreign particles, but if a speck of dust, dirt, or leaf lands on the eye or inside the eyelid, it can be painful and irritating. Foreign objects in the eye may also scratch the cornea, adding to the irritation.

If a patient complains of a painful eye, examine the eye carefully. Don't rub it. Pull the lower lid down and have the patient look up. This allows you to see the lower part of the eye and inside the lower eyelid. Flip the upper lid over a small stick or cotton applicator and have the patient look down. This allows you to see the upper part of the eye and inside the upper eyelid.

Remove foreign material by irrigating with clean water, or, if it's on the eyelid and not the eye itself, with gentle use of a piece of gauze. If the object is stuck, leave it in place. Never try to remove something from the eye with force. Close the eye and bandage it shut with a folded gauze pad or sterile eye shield, and evacuate the patient. Patients with irritated eyes but no obvious foreign object embedded should be evacuated if pain is great, or if the irritation persists for 24 hours.

THE EYE

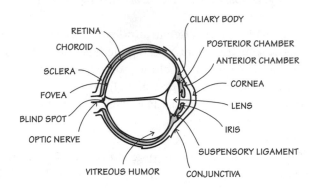

If the foreign object is impaled in the eye, do not remove it. The eye contains precious fluids that may leak out, and extracting the object can cause additional damage. Stabilize the object in place with gauze; cover and protect it against being banged. In contrast to traditional first aid advice, bandage only the injured eye. While our eyes do track together, they also react to sound and other stimuli. Leaving one eye open results in less overall eye movement, in part because when eye movement causes pain we instinctively turn our heads like an owl and limit eye muscle movement. Evacuate the patient.

Subconjunctival Hemorrhage

A subconjunctival hemorrhage is bleeding under the conjunctiva, the outer covering of the eye, and over the sclera, the white part of the eye. A subconjunctival hemorrhage may happen after hard coughing, increasing blood pressure, or a direct blow to the eye. Most cases cause no pain to the patient and are noticed by someone else. Usually the hemorrhage is on only one eye. By itself, it rarely indicates a significant problem and is not a reason for evacuation. If it is the result of a blow to the eye, examination by a physician is advised.

Hyphema is bleeding into the anterior chamber of the eye, often after a blow to the eye. Blood may be seen in the iris (the colored ring around the pupil). A patient with hyphema should always be evacuated.

Evacuation Guidelines
- Hyphema (blood in the anterior chamber of the eye)
- Any loss of vision, blurred vision, or double vision
- An object impaled in the eye
- Acute, severe eye pain
- A foreign body in the eye that you can't remove
- Eye irritation that persists more than 24 hours

SKIN PROBLEMS (DERMATITIS)

Dermatitis is a general term referring to skin inflammation. It can have a variety of causes, including cosmetics, plant juices, household chemicals, sun, and medication allergy. Dermatitis occurs in many forms, usually involving an itchy rash on swollen, reddened skin. Dermatitis is a common condition that usually isn't life-threatening or contagious, although it can make the patient miserable.

Signs and Symptoms. Dermatitis presents with red, swollen, itchy skin that may blister, ooze clear-to-yellow fluid, develop a crust, or flake off.

Treatment Principles. Field treatment is symptom management. Consider corticosteroid creams, antihistamines, wet compresses, covering the skin, and avoiding irritants.

Fungal Infections of the Skin

One form of dermatitis is fungal skin infections that commonly occur in the groin and on the feet. Fungus grows well in hot, sweaty, poorly ventilated conditions. The signs and symptoms are red, itchy skin that scales and may blister and crack. Treatment principles include washing the area thoroughly with soap and water, then keeping the area dry. A thin layer of over-the-counter antifungal cream may help. Preventing these irritating problems is easier than treating them. If you have a tendency to get these infections, consider wearing cotton or well-ventilated underwear. Wash the groin and feet daily, and air-dry regularly.

Sun Bumps

The itching, red, blistered rash we know colloquially as "sun bumps" has a real medical name—polymorphous light eruption (PMLE). PMLEs are unusual reactions to light that, as far as can be determined, are not associated with other diseases or drugs.

Sunlight in general, UVA specifically, is thought to be the causative factor in PMLE, although the overall natural history of the eruption is probably intertwined with skin type, diet, sun exposure, altitude, sensitizing cosmetics, sunscreen use, and other factors. It's more common in people from high latitudes and reported three to four times more in women than in men.

Medical experts say that 30 minutes to several hours of exposure are required to trigger the eruption, which will subside over 1 to 7 days without scarring.

Signs and Symptoms. In the field, it is difficult to distinguish these lesions from the many rashes that look similar: chilblains, pernio, salt rashes, and other forms of dermatitis. As the name implies, these eruptions come in different forms, but commonly present as a red or pink raised rash and small blisters that can coalesce into plaques. They can itch miserably and sometimes cause stinging sensations and pain.

Treatment. Short-term management treats symptoms, primarily itching. Antihistamines and topical steroid creams are recommended by some experts but really don't work well. Unfortunately the reaction seems to run its course despite our efforts to shorten the discomfort. Prevention includes wearing protective clothing, using sunscreen, and ensuring gradual exposure to the sun. We know from experience that this does not work for everyone, and the medical literature agrees. There are a variety of drugs used for people with recurrent reactions, none of which seems to be particularly effective.

A related condition to PMLE is phytophotodermatitis (PPD), a reaction from exposure to certain plants along with subsequent exposure to sunlight. PPD can occur through ingestion of the plant or, more commonly, through topical contact. Common plants implicated include celery, giant hogweed, parsnip, fennel, parsley, lime, lemon, rue, fig, mustard, scurf pea, and chrysanthemums. Plant oils in perfumes are also implicated in these reactions.

Phytophotodermatitis can look like PMLE, with initial burning pain and a raised, red, itchy rash followed by blistering. Treat mild reactions with cool, wet dressings, topical steroid creams, and nonsteroidal anti-inflammatory drugs. Severe reactions, where the patient is intolerably uncomfortable from itching, may require evacuation for prescription steroid medications.

SKIN PROBLEMS: POISON IVY, OAK, AND SUMAC

Poison ivy, oak, and sumac grow in all of the Lower 48 states. Poison oak is more common west of the Rockies, poison ivy east of the Rockies, and poison sumac in the Southeast. Individuals vary in their sensitivity to urushiol, the oil present on the surface of the plants—some react to very casual contact, others seem immune as they walk through thick patches. Urushiol can be transferred to the skin regardless of whether the plants have their leaves, as the oil is found on the stems, as well. Inhaled smoke from burning plants can also cause a significant reaction.

Signs and Symptoms of Urushiol Reaction. This contact allergic reaction causes the skin to become red and itchy with a blistered rash and scaly, crusting wounds. Contrary to myth, the blister fluid is harmless. The rash spreads over time, due not to the fluid but to the varying time it takes different parts of our skin to react to the urushiol.

Treatment for Urushiol Reaction. We can't stop this rash. Our best efforts can prevent additional contact and treat symptoms. Try to wash the area immediately after exposure with soap and cool water. There are commercial soaps that claim to more effectively remove urushiol than plain soap does. You may be able to remove some of the oil before you react.

Wash all clothes and equipment that may have been exposed. Urushiol persists on clothing, ropes, and plants for years.

Apply a thin layer of one-percent hydrocortisone cream or calamine lotion, and try oral antihistamines to reduce itching.

In severe cases, your physician may prescribe a steroid to help reduce the itching and swelling.

Prevention. Learn to recognize poison ivy, oak, and sumac. Nothing works as well as avoiding contact. Barrier creams for hypersensitive individuals may be considered.

CHAPTER 27
LEADERSHIP, TEAMWORK, AND COMMUNICATION

INTRODUCTION

A NOLS Wilderness Medicine EMT course was in its second week. In addition to the technical skills and knowledge of an EMT, this course had spent the first week building a learning team—a course community with shared expectations for teamwork and competence. Without warning, a student collapsed in the classroom.

In less than a minute, the student was on the floor, receiving CPR and supplemental oxygen and being analyzed for a shock by an AED—they were in cardiac arrest. Fifteen minutes after that, an ambulance was on the scene, and the patient, once again breathing on his own, was being packaged for transport to a helicopter and advanced cardiac care.

The incident is a case study on leadership, teamwork, and communication. The instructors—all experienced EMTs—instantly flipped from welcoming students back after a break to managing the airway, performing relentless chest compressions, hooking up an AED, and managing the scene. Students in the class found the AED, called 911, got oxygen, shoveled snow off the walkway, moved furniture, assisted with chest compressions and airway management, met the ambulance, and took notes. When the ambulance arrived, the instructors and rescue team worked together on advanced life support and also made a phone call to NOLS headquarters to inform them of the situation and ask for support.

About two weeks later, the student came by the course for some hellos and lessons learned.

An EMT course is a resource-rich environment for this type of crisis, but just as much as gear, what saved this student's life was the teamwork and leadership exhibited by the course.

Skilled medical and rescue teams, aircrews, and wilderness leaders have found themselves in similarly challenging situations in which communication, teamwork, and leadership are not optimal and things don't work out well. Aircraft have crashed because flight crews failed to perform a routine task, or a team member didn't speak up to report a problem. Ineffective communication of snowpack and terrain observation has contributed to avalanche incidents. Maps and headlamps left behind have embarrassed wilderness travelers caught in approaching darkness. Medication errors that were not resolved have led to adverse patient outcomes. Experts have unclipped from their climbing anchors, avoiding a dangerous situation only when their observant partners noticed the error.

Wilderness and mountain rescuers know that human error contributes significantly to many backcountry and mountain incidents. When the airline industry realized that well-trained and technically proficient crews could crash airworthy aircraft because of inadequate crew communication or interaction, it developed a series of programs—known as crew resource management (CRM)—to focus on leadership, teamwork, and communication. This training has since expanded into medicine, the military, law enforcement, search and rescue, and other disciplines. In organizational cultures that are traditionally hierarchical, CRM shifts leadership away from autocratic and individualistic styles toward an approach that is based on mutual interdependence and shared responsibility. This is an environment where people can share observations and ask questions, where the depth of talent on the team is acknowledged and utilized, where task loads are shared and it is ok to say you are tired, where communication is effective and the team functions with a shared vision.

Error trapping is the identification and isolation of problems and errors. A core goal of CRM is to create a superb, self-correcting team, so when an individual makes a mistake—something we all do—or an unplanned challenge arises, the team works together to "trap the error," keep it from becoming worse, and accomplish the mission.

SKILLS, BEHAVIORS, AND HABITS OF EFFECTIVE TEAMS

There are two equally important roles on our medical and rescue teams: leading and following. In this context, leading means providing vision—a shared mental model of the mision—and a nexus of accountability, responsibility, communication, and direction. Effective following, on the other hand, means staying active and engaged, constructively questioning team direction, and supporting other team members. Both roles share a set of skills, behaviors, and habits that the scholarship of CRM and the experience of those who participate on skilled teams have identified. In this chapter we highlight a set of these characteristics we consider pertinent to effective teams: expedition behavior, service to the mission, competence, self-awareness, tolerance for adversity and uncertainty, communication, and vision and action.

Expedition Behavior
In the medical and search and rescue world it is common to hear the word teamwork used to refer to the combined actions of a group of people, or the actions of an individual in service to the group. Teamwork has a tangible side: actions taken to support our teammates. However, teamwork also has an intangible side: a spirit, a culture that binds the team together. At NOLS, that sense of spirit and culture is embodied in the concept of expedition behavior.

Expedition behavior—teamwork—is a virtue we strive for at NOLS because decades of experience have proven the value of working together, serving the mission, and treating each other with dignity and respect. Expedition behavior is inclusive of every person who may be part of the team and recognizes that diversity in perspective brings depth to a team. Demonstrating good expedition behavior is not about leading. It's an intentional choice to be a good teammate, a good follower, and a good citizen. And for a leader, demonstrating good expedition behavior gives the team a model of how everyone should act. Our culture tends to value leading more than following, but expedition behavior has a rightful place on the podium alongside leadership.

Good expedition behavior is demonstrated by practical tangible tasks done to support the team. It is team members taking care of one another, watching for fatigue and hazards, lending a helping hand without being asked, and asking for help when needed. People demonstrating good expedition behavior treat others with respect and politeness. Their actions are sincere— done without desire for reward or accolade. Expedition behavior is picking up after yourself and your teammates, getting out of bed on a stormy night to check everyone's tents, carrying extra weight when your companion is ill, and allowing your weight to be carried when you are ill. It is cleaning gear after a rescue, responding when it is inconvenient, learning and using your teammates' names and pronouns, saying thank you, and please. It is acting without being asked, without complaining, and with the good of the group in mind.

Service to the Mission
One of the attributes of effective teams identified in the CRM work is a sense of a shared mission. People engage in search and rescue for many reasons. We want to help people. We enjoy the wilderness. We're proud of using our skills. We want the challenge. Yet, sometimes we're assigned boring tasks or we disagree with the plan. The trap is to freelance, to do what we think is best, or what is of interest to us, not what follows the plan. Freelancers are rescuers who drop a task when they are drawn to something more exciting, or searchers who leave their assigned pattern to look in areas they deem more likely for a find. Freelancers are poison to a team.

It's our job to work with the team and within the plan. The mission is the patient.

Competence

A characteristic of effective teams is competence, their proficiency in technical (in our context outdoor, rescue, and first aid) and group-management skills. Ideally, our skills are sharp, and we train to keep them fresh. Effective teams are composed of lifelong learners, and they share knowledge and experience within the team.

Lifelong learners are honest about their current proficiency as individuals, and as a team. The competence diagram below is a conceptual model showing stages of competence from the novice, new at a skill and possibly not able to understand where their competence lies; to the beginner, still new but more aware and able to understand their limitations; to the proficient practitioner who can perform a skill thoughtfully, deliberately and with competence; to the expert, who can perform a skill automatically, with little deliberate thought. One mindset flowing from this position of expertise is toward complacency, to a potentially false assumption that a skill or set of knowledge is durable and will be retained without practice and study. Avoiding this complacency trap leads the expert down the path of the reflective, or mindful, practitioner, who continually seeks to understand where their competency lies and values deliberate practice and honest evaluation and feedback. (Read more on this in Chapter 28, "Judgment and Decision Making.") These are the teams and the individuals who train on a regular basis, challenge each other to improve, and never assume they are truly competent.

> The phrase "expedition behavior" is unique to NOLS, and may be our catchiest phrase, but the concept of being nice to each other and serving our community, our country, our team, our mission, our family, or expedition is not unique to NOLS; it is found wherever people work together for a greater good.

Share Knowledge and Experience. A leader who acts directively, a common style in a crisis, should not act in isolation. Ideally, the leader utilizes the team's skill and experience to make the best decisions, and to efficiently and effectively perform the needed tasks. If the team leader is wise they capitalize on the

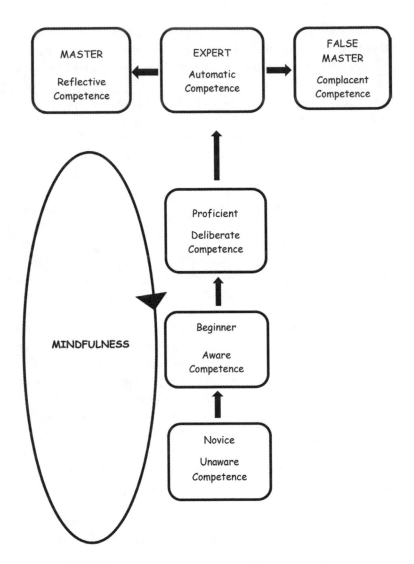

abilities of the team; they do not need to be a master of every group-management or technical skill. For example, in a large rescue operation, a leader may not be the most experienced medical person or the technical rescue system expert. They delegate these tasks to those on the team who are competent in the skill while they attend to the overall vision and flow of the event.

The effective leader both leads and teaches. They take the initiative and time to share pertinent details of the medical or evacuation plan with team members. They answer questions and listen to input. They explain and practice techniques before using them on the patient. Likewise, team members with excellent expedition behavior serve in an environment where they can share their knowledge and experience up the ladder, thereby contributing to the overall efficacy of the team. Shared knowledge and effective communication strengthen the team. Everyone feels respected and engaged. Higher-quality decisions are more likely to be made.

Self-Awareness
Self-aware leaders and team members learn from their experiences by acknowledging their abilities and successes, facing their limitations, admitting their mistakes, and seeking feedback from others. They know themselves well enough to understand their habits and their tendencies, some of which are good, others bad. Perhaps when under stress they slip into the procrastination syndrome, the hurry-up syndrome, the do-it-all syndrome, or the perfectionist syndrome. Perhaps they are insightful and see the moment when a teammate needs an encouraging word, a compliment, or simply a drink of water. Self-awareness is hard and ongoing work. The following are some behaviors that the self-aware use to support their team.

Recognize and Resolve Fatigue. In the excitement of an emergency, you may ignore the effect of fatigue on your performance. Actively plan and schedule for operational phase transitions, rest periods, the night shift—not just for team members, but for yourself, as well. Will you need to rest, feed people, or find fresh folks to help carry the litter? Outdoor leaders and rescue personnel often work in an organizational culture where fitness and competence are valued. They may have unrealistic conceptions of their vulnerability to stress and fatigue. I learned a valuable lesson when I was assigned to the night shift on a multi-day search. Not wanting to rest when others were working hard, I found something to do. The incident commander noticed this, confirmed that I was on the night shift, and told me in no uncertain terms, "It's your job to sleep. I need you at 100 percent tonight." Said another way, good leadership means creating a culture where self-care and rest are acceptable, and good expedition behavior means acknowledging when you need to rest.

Recognize and Report Work Overloads. Avoid trying to fix everything yourself and taking on too many tasks. The culture of emergency services and outdoor leadership can drive a strong work ethic and a sense that it is inappropriate for the helper to ask for help. Leaders need to be able to step back and keep their eyes on the big picture, and everyone needs to avoid the distraction of becoming mired in tasks best done by others. It's a measure of wisdom and maturity—good expedition behavior—no matter what your role on the team, to be able to say, "I'm overloaded. Can you help?" The instructors in the story that opens this chapter did not hesitate to call for help, and their expedition mates at the school's headquarters did not hesitate to respond.

Reflect and Learn from Your Experiences. Identify not only the technical details of an action, such as snowpack analysis, map reading, the thoroughness of a patient assessment, the gear that worked, and the gear that failed, but also the quality of communication and teamwork, the decisions, and the distractions. What went well, what could have gone better, and when were you more lucky than competent? Effective teams of mindful practitioners reflect on and learn from these experiences.

Tolerance for Adversity and Uncertainty

In addition to managing patients where we may not be sure of the underlying condition, or the urgency of evacuation, wilderness medicine can be a world of lengthy transport times, arduous conditions, inclement weather, and lack of resources—a test of any responder's tolerance for adversity and uncertainty. Wilderness medical responders must be able to live with uncertainty, endure hard work and challenge, and make do or improvise what they lack. Even in this era where communication out of the wilderness tends to be reliable and helicopter transport is an assumed option, NOLS courses (or just people or expeditions) have carried patients for days in awful weather over difficult terrain. They have struggled due to lack of people to move patients short distances up steep slopes of loose rock. They have hunkered down and waited days for the weather to improve, caring for both the patient and their teammates.

Prepare for Contingencies. Weather will turn bad. Helicopters will be delayed. Radios will break. Stable patients will take turns for the worse. Spring snow that's firm and supports weight in the morning can become soggy pudding in the afternoon. High-performing teams anticipate, consider more options, plan for glitches, and plan early. Stay ahead of the curve by analyzing your plan over and over, and asking, "What if?" What if one of us sprains an ankle? It's sunny and warm now, but can I keep the patient dry if it rains?

Get Ready for the Long Haul. It's easy to be focused during the initial stages of a crisis. In wilderness medicine, the rubber often meets the road when you move into the long hours of work in difficult conditions as you carry a litter or wait through a storm for the helicopter. This is where a rescue becomes an expedition, and expedition behavior becomes crucial. Leaders and engaged team members understand this phase change. They stay connected to the group, keeping everyone, including the patient, informed and focused on the task. They, and the team members, make sure everyone is eating, drinking, and staying warm and dry. They keep the process moving, energy and enthusiasm high, and focus on the mission of the patient.

Learn to Be Comfortable with Uncertainty. Medicine is a world of uncertainty, and wilderness medicine doubly so. There are times we don't know exactly what injury or illness a patient may have. We may be unsure how best to treat this illness or injury. We often work without the information we need in unpredictable and changing weather or in a fluid and evolving event. Learn to be comfortable in this arena; it's wilderness medicine.

Communication
Effective leaders and team members master communication skills. They state what they think, feel, and want, and they listen with openness to different viewpoints. Leaders keep their

groups informed and give clear, usable, and timely feedback. All members of a team contribute to creating a safe forum where every group member can discuss ideas and contribute to the decision-making process.

Clearly State and Acknowledge Decisions. When decisions are made, whether by leaders or team members, they are clearly stated, then repeated back to "close the loop." Effective teams clarify instructions and ask questions to check for understanding: "We're going to rig an anchor here and use it to belay the patient to the ground. Let's go around the group and have everyone say what they will do."

Brief Effectively. Brief to keep your team informed, share information and state decisions and plans. Briefings help develop a "shared mental model." They prepare the team for the planned course of action by focusing individual plans and intentions on the "big picture." They create a space for inquiry, concerns, and suggestions.

Effective briefings are clear, complete, and interesting. In addition to technical details, they address team coordination and communication as well as planning for potential problems. The team puts aside social conversation or low-priority tasks, pays attention, and asks pertinent clarifying questions. They identify roles and responsibilities, cite names, and use simple, clear, common language. Expectations are set for handling unusual conditions or possible deviations from normal operations. For example: "We sent four people—Charlie, Juliet, Mike and Oscar, with Juliet in charge—walking to the road head to ask for help carrying Victor. They should arrive tonight. If we don't hear from them by tomorrow noon, we'll send a second team."

A briefing should be brief. Concise briefings help people remember details. Several 5-minute briefings may be more effective than one 20-minute briefing. Keep it simple. Strive for the three-sentence briefing. Brief at phase changes: at the start, when the assessment is done, when you reach an obvious rest stop or obstacle in a litter carry. Address both who will do specific tasks, and how they will do them. Team members should clearly understand their roles and tasks: "Thanks for staying alert for hazards. I'll stay at the head of the patient, monitor the airway and protect the spine. Jack, finish the head-to-toe assessment and measure the vital signs. Jill, find a foam pad and sleeping bag for the patient."

Include as many team members as possible in the communication flow; brief and update them as needed on weather, delays, plans, and schedules. Students in outdoor-education groups, clients in guided trips, helpful bystanders, your patient, and local rescue personnel all may be part of your team.

Build a Team Environment. One of the concepts in CRM is that the answer is often in the cockpit; someone on the team has a critical observation, piece of information, or insight that solves a problem. As a member of any team, make it your goal to build an inclusive environment that acknowledges and respects the skills and experiences of every team member and invites their contributions to the mission. Listen with patience, do not interrupt or "talk over," and do not rush through a discussion. Avoid focusing only on the loud voices in the group. Seek the quiet voices and include them in the conversation; there may be a moment when they are thus empowered to share critical information, insights, observations, and suggestions; there may be a moment when they save the day.

Effective Inquiry: Ask and Listen. Foster an environment where questions can be asked regarding information, actions and decisions. Teams struggle constantly to prevent unconfirmed or false pieces of information from entering a narrative and driving decisions. If people do not understand, they should be encouraged to speak up and ask for clarification of unclear instructions or confusing or uncertain situations. Develop a team habit of healthy skepticism and verification of facts. If speculative information finds its way into a conversation,

---

A Simple Briefing Format

LEADER TO TEAM

- Here's what I think we face.
- Here's what I think we should do.
- Here's why.
- Here's what we should keep our eye on.
- Now, talk to me.

AFTER-ACTION REVIEW/ HOT DEBRIEF

- What was planned?
- What actually happened?
- Why did it happen?
- What can we do next time?

quickly and clearly identify and control it; trap and control this error. For example:

> Why are we putting a tourniquet on this snakebite wound? I thought tourniquets weren't indicated for snakebite.

> You said you can't hear breath sounds; do you mean it's too noisy to listen, or the patient is not breathing?

> The subject may or may not have a red jacket; this is unconfirmed. We need to stop talking about a red jacket.

> The point last seen is Wolf Ridge, not Coyote Gulch.

Give and Accept Appropriate Feedback. Give performance feedback at appropriate times. Make it a positive learning experience for the whole crew. Feedback must be specific to the issue at hand, objective, based on observable behavior, and given with respect and politeness. Likewise, accept feedback objectively and without defensiveness. Unreceptive responses to feedback within a team have inhibited communication, preventing people with vital insights from speaking, and played a causal role in accidents.

Use Appropriate Advocacy and Assertion. Foster an environment in which your team can speak up and state their information until there is resolution and decision, where questioning is not seen as insubordination or sabotage. As a team member, seek clarity when uncertain about a task, speak up when seeing an unacknowledged danger, and recognize that minor differences in approach to a problem are acceptable. There are sad tales of a team member or leader making a mistake, while another team member had the correct information but did not speak up or assert their perspective. For example: "I'm uncomfortable with your delay in starting an evacuation. John has a persistent high fever. I think we should take him to a doctor." And there are times where you listen to a plan and think you might do it differently, but the proposed plan is sound, and in the spirit of expedition behavior, you support it.

As a leader, model advocacy by checking in with your team and listening to their responses. "Are you getting enough direction from me about what you need to be doing? If anyone disagrees, please speak up."

Address Conflict. Disagreements occur. Personalities clash. Conflicts can impede communication and cooperation, and contribute to accidents. In a moment of crisis a leader may need to step in, identify the issue, and ask the team to put aside interpersonal differences until the emergency is over, addressing only immediate issues that are impeding progress or affecting safety. Later, when the crisis has passed, it's important to debrief about these issues and emotions, work to manage the conflict, increase the team's ability to deal with its differences, and use the experience to inform the team's response for similar issues in the future. A conflict during a crisis may mean that expectations, roles, and responsibilities are unclear. People don't know what is expected of them or others, are missing information, or don't have a sense of the big picture. Clarify structure and expectations. The bottom line—the patient should be the winner of every conflict.

Vision and Action
Leaders assure that the group stays focused on the mission. They understand the importance of the planning phase of any expedition or rescue. They keep team members informed about the plan. They convey mission goals and priorities. They are decisive when the situation requires decisiveness and patient when it is appropriate to wait or gather more information. They are forward-looking and flexible, revising the plan as necessary.

Set a Tone Appropriate to the Situation. Effective leaders set a tone appropriate to the level of urgency. Listen for insidious threats to the team's culture, often heard in the use of profanity, obscenity, sexual, ethnic, and racial comments. Even if not directed at an individual, they erode dignity and respect, and they undermine the team.

If the situation isn't dire, you may need to slow down your team. "Let's take it easy. We've finished the assessment, and the scene is safe. Next we have to splint the patient's fractured leg, then log roll the patient onto a sleeping bag and treat for shock. Let's take it one step at a time." Conversely, you may have to remind your team to keep conversation and attention on the situation at hand. "Let's worry about dinner later. Right now, let's prepare this landing zone." Leaders, and followers practicing good teamwork, ensure that nonoperational factors such as social interaction or conversation do not interfere with necessary tasks (e.g., small talk does not interfere with climbing signals). In aviation this is known as keeping a "sterile cockpit," that is, when there is a task at hand, the team is disciplined and focused.

Scene Awareness. Many people call this situational awareness. Researchers observing NASA shuttle crews call it vigilance or watchfulness. It is the responsibility of everyone on the team. Pause after scene size-up and initial assessment. Lift up your head and look over the scene. Take a deep breath. Organize yourself and your gear. Seek hazards. Formulate a plan for the next few minutes, but be careful of the trap of creating too much organization. Many scenarios are fluid. Stay alert and flexible.

There are phases to operations: some need immediate action; others allow time for care and thoughtfulness. Effective teams identify what needs to be done now, and what they have to prepare to do later. In a search, this may be the situational awareness to quickly deploy teams into the field, followed by planning for the next operational phase. In a rescue, this may be stabilizing the patient, while at the same time preparing for the evacuation by securing a landing zone, organizing a litter team, or positioning support personnel.

Workload Management: State Clear Expectations of Roles and Responsibilities. Clarify roles, responsibilities, and the big picture:

> "I'll keep myself visible and in the open in case the rest of the group comes by. Jose and Laura scout for the best trail through these boulders back to camp. Check back with me before a half hour is up. Javier, you're in charge of patient care. Stay with the patient and monitor vitals. Blow your whistle three times if you need me."

A team works well when people know what they have to do and have a sense of where they fit in the big picture. Clear expectations prevent people from doing unnecessary tasks or getting in one another's way. Let others know what you expect of them and what they can expect from you. "Folks, let's splint this arm first, then move the patient to the litter."

Provide Adequate Time for Completion of Tasks. Hurried tasks, such as complex land coordinate conversions, have sent rescue teams to the wrong location. Litter straps have been left loose when a team stopped one task to start another, only to be tripped on when the litter carry began. Identify your key tasks, tell people what needs to be done, allow enough time, and complete each task one by one. Complex tasks can be checked with a checklist, or double checked by a teammate.

Stay Vigilant During Both High and Low Workloads. Look around, check details, and check in with people both when you're busy and when workload is low. It's easy to focus your attention when you're on duty and in the middle of the event. It's harder when the initial excitement ebbs, and the work of a long and apparently routine situation sets in. Accidents can happen when you overlook the obvious, missing the moment when you could have intervened or prevented a problem. How many of us have walked away from a rest break without looking around or noticing the water bottle and map left on the rock? How many of us have thanked a teammate for noticing that forgotten water bottle and map?

FINAL THOUGHTS

In the incident that opened this chapter, the team lived the concepts of CRM. Over 15 desperate yet controlled minutes we focused on the mission—the patient. Communication was excellent: closed loop with simple language. Procedural questions were resolved promptly and professionally. People accomplished their roles and tasks without hesitation; some because we effectively delegated, and others because team members had scene awareness and took initiative. Recognizing fatigue, switching the person doing chest compressions was frequent and fluid; compressions were uninterrupted except for AED use. The tone was tense, yet calm. We moved efficiently through the incident because we worked thoughtfully. The patient survived, both due to the team's competence in basic life support, and to their teamwork.

CRM has identified, through observations in simulators and in the real world, lessons to learn from effective teams. Three, which focus on communication and error trapping—preventing mistakes from becoming problems—are relevant for people working together in wilderness medicine and rescue contexts.

First, good technical skills cannot protect against the effects of poor communication; you may be able to navigate to a precise location, but if your support team has a different set of coordinates, your skill is for naught. Second, team performance is more closely associated with the quality of communication than with technical proficiency; you may never have prepared epinephrine for delivery to a patient with anaphylaxis, but if your teammate confirms your work, the task can be completed correctly. Third, it is the ability of crews to communicate effectively that prevents their errors from becoming adverse outcomes; if your team can hear and respond to questions, you're much less likely to allow an error to cascade.

In my years of wilderness expeditioning, emergency medicine, and rescue, I have found that the medicine we can practice in the wilderness is often limited; sick and injured people need doctors and hospitals. The quality of care we provide the patient often hinges not on our first aid skill but on the quality of our leadership, teamwork, and communication—the effectiveness at which we work together, make sound decisions, and get things done. Quality care is built on a foundation of skills competence that flourishes on a team with excellent leadership and expedition behavior.

CHAPTER 28 | JUDGMENT AND DECISION-MAKING

INTRODUCTION

Patient care is a series of decisions. Some are common and simple, like whether to treat a blister. Others, such as whether to evacuate someone with a bellyache, are unusual and complex. These decisions affect the patient's health, the safety of your expedition members, and the safety of those who may come to assist in your evacuation or rescue.

In many cases, our choices weigh risks of harm and loss against potential benefits. For example, when we choose to take a medication, even a common non-prescription pain medication such as ibuprofen, there are risks of stomach irritation and GI bleeds alongside benefits from the anti-inflammatory and pain relief properties of the medication. When we choose to close a cut—even a small one—with a bandage, there are benefits for healing and risks for infection, despite our diligence with wound cleaning. Thawing frostbite in the field may quickly restore circulation, but there may be a risk of refreezing causing a more serious injury. If we choose to try to cross a mountain pass in building weather, we balance the risk of being caught in a storm against the benefit of being on the other side.

Decision-making is a process of forming an assessment; analyzing and comparing the information, risks, benefits, and options; and then laying down an opinion. Many decisions are simple and routine; we have the information and experience we need, and thoughtful people to consult. Yet there are other times when we must make decisions challenged by missing data, conflicting information, and urgency. We're at the edge of our experience and training, making decisions without being able to consult a higher authority. Where a medical decision might feel easy in an urban context, we may have less experience making this decision in a wilderness context where logistical and weather considerations can play a prominent role in the decision. This is where judgment—the ability to come to a sensible conclusion when a decision is novel or unclear—is invaluable.

Humans have developed fascinating and complex ways to reach decisions, and we often do so without giving the process much thought. We may use a rule of thumb, follow a protocol or algorithm, or make a guess. We may act quickly based on experience, or gather information and make a reasoned decision. Whether we are experts or novices, we want to support good judgment by being thoughtful and skilled decision-makers. Wilderness medicine is practiced in a resource-limited environment. The only resource we will have with us 100 percent of the time is our judgment. It's our best tool, so it pays to learn to use it as well as we would a map and compass. This chapter takes a brief tour of common ways we make decisions, their pros and cons, and some traps we want to avoid.

GUESSING

The self-aware decision-maker knows that, faced with a choice about what to do, everyone guesses from time to time. Guessing, or (more formally) using intuition uninformed by data and possibly misinformed by experience, isn't always bad. If consequences are of small significance, guessing saves time and provides the solace of action. However, when a person's health is at stake, we don't want to guess. Take a wilderness medicine course, learn to make a patient assessment, and bring with you into the wilderness a reference or set of protocols to give you guidance.

RULES OF THUMB

Heuristics, simple "rules of thumb," are common problem-solving aids, mental shortcuts based on collective and personal experience. We use heuristics in everyday decisions, often without thinking. We "measure twice, cut once" to avoid error. We benefit from the cold weather camping experience of our elders by adhering to the saw to "go to bed warm to sleep warm." We evaluate weather by considering the mariner's rhyme, "Red in the morning, sailor take warning; red at night, sailor's delight." We avoid the irritation of poison ivy by remembering, "Leaves of three, let them be."

Using mental shortcuts can be expeditious. We think, then act. They are valuable tools, as long as they are accurate and relevant to the decision we need to make. We trust heuristics because we assume they are proven over time and supported by statistics or science. In fact, they may not be accurate in every context. "Red and yellow, kill a fellow. Red and black, venom lack" is used to identify the coral snake found in the U.S. Unfortunately, if you cross the border into Mexico and head south, this heuristic may actually be dangerous. Much of the Americas are home to deadly coral snakes with red and black adjacent bands. Consider the heuristics you use and whether they are both accurate and relevant to the situation at hand.

PROTOCOLS, TREATMENT, AND EVACUATION GUIDELINES

Medical professionals use protocols, standing orders, and algorithms—predetermined decision points—that are helpful in guiding the novice and reminding the expert. Outdoor professionals use local operating plans, bear camping practices, and evacuation guidelines in the same manner. These tools may be checklists to remind us of things to do, steps to follow, information to gather, and protocols to consider.

It can be very helpful to have decisions made before you encounter a given situation, especially if those decisions are the work of thoughtful, careful, and experienced professionals.

Thank goodness we don't need to choose the compression rate every time we do CPR. We can use the protocol of a minimum of 100 compressions per minute, the heuristic "push hard, push fast," or the memory of practicing to the beat of "Staying Alive."

The focused spine assessment is a decision protocol. We use it to evaluate a patient for a possible spine injury. It is based on sound medical science as well as field experience and expert opinion. It is reliable if the protocol is executed properly and invaluable in guiding us through a high risk decision. Here, when we may not have professional expertise, we can rely on the expertise of professionals to guide our decision.

A word of caution: in the medical world, algorithms and decision protocols are often designed around classic signs and symptoms. Over-reliance can discourage independent and creative thinking when the picture is vague. There may be a patient who does not formally meet criteria for a protocol—for example, your program's abdominal pain guidelines—but still warrants evacuation for logistical reasons. You may be leading a peak climb, knowing you plan to turn around at a certain time, yet decide to descend earlier due to building weather. Protocols are not a substitute for judgment. Cookbooks are best used by thinking cooks who recognize when recipes need to be changed.

EXPERIENCE

We make decisions based on our experience. We recognize specific patterns, find clues within those patterns, and compare this to what's happened before. Experts intuitively recognize a situation and evaluate, accept, or reject choices. This is called the expert decision model, expert intuition, natural decision-making, or a pattern-recognition model. It's fast: see the pattern, make the decision.

An experienced medical provider can look at a patient's appearance, see subtle clues, recognize a pattern, and come up with a hunch as to what is wrong: "This guy is having a heart attack." An experienced rescuer can look at a map and quickly know whether a litter carry will be over shortly or take all night.

The Logbook

Pilots keep flight logs, and avalanche professionals keep slope assessment logs. Medical professionals keep logs of patient contacts to review their experience. A logbook or journal can help remind you of what you have actually seen and the decisions you have made, grounding your memory in your actual experience.

The important word is experience. Most of us are outdoor professionals first, and medical providers second. We need to be honest about our medical experience—or lack of it. We need to be candid about what we have learned from our experience—learning that often comes from the hard work of acknowledging errors. We need to be careful about reaching conclusions from one or two experiences. We can confuse correlation with cause, or fall into the trap of thinking the patient had one problem when in fact it was another.

INFORMATION-GATHERING MODEL—THE PATIENT ASSESSMENT SYSTEM (PAS)

The Patient Assessment System (Chapter 1) is decision-making based on the old-fashioned virtue of careful, deliberate, and systematic thinking. We gather information, weigh alternatives, and then decide.

Gather Information

The initial assessment identifies threats to life and the chief complaint, which will likely be the focal point of your patient care. The SAMPLE history and head-to-toe exam complete the gathering of subjective and objective information.

Identify Options, Choices, and Alternatives

The assessment catalogs our findings. The plan lists the alternatives, and our treatment and evacuation decisions. There are many important decision points in wilderness medicine (e.g., deciding if abdominal pain warrants an evacuation), and less acute questions (e.g., determining the usability of an injured ankle), but the ultimate goal is identifying who is sick and who is not—hence, the importance of good data-gathering in the PAS.

Are there clear boundaries for our decisions on treatment and evacuation, such as limits to your resources or route options? For example, there are no helicopters available, or you cannot cross the river on the evacuation route. Do you have treatment or evacuation protocols, or orders from your medical director or organization to guide or dictate your decision?

Decide, Implement, and Evaluate

In wilderness medicine, we have extended patient contact time, which allows us to repeat our assessment to check unclear findings, to look for changes in our patient's status, and to evaluate the efficacy of our actions. Our decision-making continues throughout our patient care.

An organized analytical approach can be thoughtful, careful, and thorough. It also can be slow. There are certainly situations in which we don't have the time for this approach; but consider that in wilderness medicine, we usually don't have the option for rapid transport. We can use time to help us make good decisions.

THE HUMAN HAZARD

There isn't a perfect way to make a decision; every method has its pros and cons. If you're self-aware as a leader, you're doing the hard work to understand your tendencies and biases. Here are just a few of these decision-making hazards, and some thoughts on how to avoid them.

Cognitive Biases. Cognitive biases are thinking habits, both conscious and subconscious, built up over time and experience. We may think we are being thoughtful, but our biases impact what information we pay attention to, and how we evaluate that information in making decisions. We may anchor our decision on a convenient diagnosis without considering options. We may fill in a blind spot in a pattern with information we desire, but which is not really there.

Wishful Thinking. Wishful thinking is the familiar trap of making the terrain fit the map. In medicine this can cause us to attach a label to the patient despite discrepancies in the evidence, or to ignore a finding that does not fit our desired narrative.

Pattern Recognition. Identifying only a few features of an illness, or missing the clue—not seeing the rock in the river, the building thunderstorm, the swollen ankle—can cause a pattern recognition error. We close our minds to new information and alternative explanations and solutions.

Common Diagnosis. When we hear headache in the wilderness, we think dehydration, the common diagnosis. Common things are common; yet we must be cognizant of the most potentially serious alternative diagnosis, though it may be uncommon. Treat the patient for the statistically probable problems on your list and, in case you are wrong, identify the worst case scenario and keep it in mind.

Emotional Hooks. Decision-making is not an objective rational process free from emotion. Emotional hooks from recent or vivid experience affect cognition and judgment. Be wary about "going with your gut" when the gut is a strong emotion, positive or negative, about a patient.

"WHAT WERE YOU THINKING?"

Students of decision-making develop the habit of mindful or reflective practice: the ability to think about their thinking. Reflective practice is an intentional attentiveness to thoughts, sensations, emotions, interpretations, judgments, and heuristics. It's honest self-evaluation, pertinent feedback, attentive observation, an ability to take different perspectives, and presence of mind. As we discussed in Chapter 27 in our model of building competence, reflective practice is what defines true mastery of a skill.

Honest Feedback. Reflective practitioners seek honest feedback. They need to know, as best they can, what really happened. Only by debriefing and reflecting can we truly learn whether the decision was appropriate, whether it was the actual cause of the outcome, and whether we should make the same decision in a similar future situation. If we are not open to conflicting information and not willing to admit error, we may base future decisions on an inconsequential intervention or a flawed observation.

Tolerance for Uncertainty. Reflective practitioners see each situation as unique and avoid prematurely slapping a label on a problem and closing the mind. They are aware when they are making the rapid expertise-based decision and are able to pause and reflect on the information and observations they are choosing to value. They clarify unclear information and language. They verify alleged facts. If uncertain about the patient history or physical exam, they do it again.

Reflective practitioners are able to see a situation from multiple and opposing perspectives, intentionally considering other explanations and challenging their first impressions. They ask what is most likely, what is the worst case, and what can be ruled out. At the same time, they tolerate uncertainty. They may not be able to answer all questions or gather all the data. They make the best decision with the information at hand.

Presence of Mind. Cultivate the presence of mind to be watchful, observant, open, curious, flexible, and present when faced with anxiety, uncertainty, and chaos. Rituals as simple as pausing and taking a breath can remind you to be mindful. Repetitive training can give you the confidence to perform tasks with competence and give you the mental reserve to think.

Self-Awareness. Be self-aware. "Did I ignore any data?" "What emotions are operative in me, in this situation?" "What about this situation is different?" "What assumptions am I making?" Everyone stumbles into decision-making traps. Self-awareness and watchfulness give you a better chance to catch yourself before you fall.

Effective Communication. Often the first step into the error trap is miscommunication. The medical-error literature has many examples of vital signs, medical history, or drug doses incorrectly reported and leading to poor decisions from the cascade of flawed information. Listen actively. Restate key points. Use concise, distinctive speech, without mumbles or fillers, with recognized vocabulary, controlled tone of voice, and minimal jargon.

Use Your Team. Effective teams create a culture where the team members can pool their wisdom by asking questions, clarifying information, and understanding when to advocate for alternate perspectives.

FINAL THOUGHTS

The best wilderness medicine practitioners are lifelong learners. They willingly work on the rough edges of their competency to help them navigate the real world. Knowing that real-world decision-making is not as simple as choosing the correct heuristic or protocol, they thrive on practicing both their skills and their judgment.

CHAPTER 29 | STRESS AND THE RESPONDER

INTRODUCTION

First aid training has traditionally concentrated on the nuts and bolts of treatment and transport—things such as assessment, splinting, and airway maintenance. Yet the emotional aspects of emergency medical care are equally important.

Although there are limited data on wilderness rescuers or outdoor leaders specifically, there is a growing body of literature on the effects of stress—a state of physical or psychological tension—on emergency workers. Research shows that high attrition rates, burnout, and stress-related illness and injury are common among emergency personnel who shoulder the burden of caring for the ill or injured and for the safety of their teammates.

STRESS ON THE JOB

The demands on emergency personnel create an environment in which turnover and stress-related illness are common. Beyond the immediate stress of patient care, emergency situations may subject wilderness responders to pervading noise such as wind, rushing water, screams, and sirens; the confusion of the emergency scene; the fatigue that comes with making decisions amidst prolonged extreme weather; bystanders who may never be satisfied with the rescuer's performance; equipment failures and inadequate equipment; and long hours of hard physical work. Lengthy rescues, situations in which the patient dies, multiple-casualty incidents, and incidents in which emergency workers or friends are injured are particularly stressful.

Certainly, emergency stress affects an outdoor leader or anyone thrown into the role of rescuer. Experience may help a person cope with these stresses, but it does not confer immunity.

The leader of an expedition experiences significant extra stress when weather, group dynamics, faulty equipment, or complex logistics build on each other. In addition to caring for the ill or injured under these difficult conditions, the leader continues to be responsible for the safety and welfare of the group.

EFFECTS OF STRESS

Stress—a perceived threat, challenge, or change in the environment—can be a positive factor in creativity, growth, and productivity. For example, healthy exercise that increases your physical capability is good stress. Yet continuous hard exercise without rest or adequate nutrition can become unhealthy stress—a destructive force with negative effects on your health, your family, and your life.

Noises, confined spaces, extremes in weather, and other aspects of the environment may stress you. In the social environment, conflicts within a group, or with the boss or family members, are all stressors. You're also stressed by inactivity and boredom. Sources of stress can be obvious—the approaching storm, the difficult patient—and they can be insidious, building over time, without our awareness.

Stress produces intricate biochemical changes in the body. The brain becomes more active; hormones such as cortisol, secreted by the endocrine system, cause uscles to tighten, pupils to dilate, and heart rate, breathing rate, and blood pressure to increase. Biochemicals in the blood such as protein, glucose, and markers of inflammation, rise.

These physiological changes prepare you to meet a challenge by making you more alert and ready for physical activity. In the short term, they can be helpful. In the long term, the effects of stress can adversely affect your physical and psychological health by wearing you down and making you susceptible to a variety of physical, cognitive, and emotional problems. Many nontraumatic causes of death such as coronary artery disease, high blood pressure, ulcers, and cancer are caused or aggravated by stress.

Stress injury, either from an isolated event or from the cumulative effects of years of tension, is a reality of a responder's experience. We have known about stress injuries for millennia, yet these injuries are often unrecognized or ignored as something that "comes with the territory." Stress injuries cannot be treated if they are not recognized. Increasing the awareness of this injury type will support treatment.

ASSESSMENT: RECOGNIZING STRESS REACTIONS

Stress in the short term may produce fatigue, nausea, anxiety, fear, irritability, lightheadedness, headache, memory lapses, sleep disturbances, changes in appetite, loss of attention span, and indecision. These are normal reactions by normal people to abnormal events.

Symptoms lasting less than a month are an acute stress disorder. If symptoms persist, posttraumatic stress might be developing. Long-term effects of stress include difficulty concentrating, intrusive images (recurring dreams or sensations of the traumatic event), sleep disturbance, fatigue, and diseases such as ulcers, diabetes, and coronary artery disease. Emotional signs include depression, feelings of grief and anger, and a sense of isolation. Emergency workers suffering from cumulative stress may respond by avoiding emergency situations, taking excessive sick leave, or being easily aroused or startled. It is beyond the scope of this book to discuss intervention for cumulative stress reactions.

TREATMENT: MANAGING STRESS IN THE FIELD

Preparation for the challenges ahead—before rescuers deploy—includes an honest appraisal of the anticipated difficulties of rescue and of your personal and your team's ability to cope. Rescue work, especially wilderness rescue, can be long and tedious. Good outcomes are not guaranteed. There may be value—both for a leader and their team—for a leader to define success more narrowly: by reaching a patient, providing comfort, assuring that the patient is not alone and suffering, and completing the rescue without any further injuries.

Among emergency personnel on the scene of a serious rescue, most will experience at least some symptoms of stress. Short-term stress symptoms can be managed by attending to the physical need for rest, food, and hydration; by briefing the group on the sights, sounds, and emotions they may experience

Acute Stress Reactions

PHYSICAL	EMOTIONAL	COGNITIVE
• Fatigue	• Anxiety	• Memory loss
• Muscle tremors	• Fear	• Indecision
• Nausea	• Grief	• Difficulty problem solving
• Glassy eyes	• Depression	• Confusion with trivial issues
• Chills	• Hopelessness	• Loss of attention span
• Dizziness	• Irritability	• Feeling overwhelmed
• Profuse sweating	• Anger	

Delayed Stress Reactions

- Macabre humor
- Excessive use of sick leave
- Reluctance to enter stressful situations
- Intrusive images
- Obsession with the stressful incident
- Withdrawal from others
- Suicidal thoughts
- Feelings of inadequacy

during a long evacuation; and by debriefing the group after the incident.

Stress reactions on a scene can be managed by separating a struggling person from the source of their stress. Give simple, clear directions to the person and assign productive tasks that can help shift their focus away from the immediate incident. Such tasks might include providing food and drink, building a litter, and setting up tents.

If an emergency caregiver is distressed, detached from reality, or disruptive, they become a patient. Someone may need to stay with them to lend a sympathetic ear. You can help such persons cope by talking with them and offering assurances that their feelings are valid, real, and perfectly appropriate. Provide emotional support with honesty and direct, factual answers to their questions.

Psychological First Aid

Multiple mental-health, disaster, and medical-response organizations support the use of psychological (or stress) first aid (PFA) for victims, survivors, and responders who exhibit acute stress responses following disasters, mass violence, and other traumatic emergency situations.

PFA is basic, nonintrusive, and pragmatic psychological support intended to be applied by a layperson. It is not a therapeutic intervention provided by a mental-health professional, nor is it the discredited and largely abandoned Critical Incident Stress Debriefing (CISD). It does not necessarily involve a discussion of the event that caused the distress.

PFA is designed to enhance three components of resiliency: re-creating a sense of safety, encouraging social

SENSE OF SAFETY
- Help people meet basic needs for food, shelter, and first aid.

PROMOTION OF CALM
- Offer accurate information about the disaster and the relief or rescue efforts.

SELF-EFFICACY
- Give practical suggestions that steer people toward helping themselves.

CONNECTION
- Help people contact friends and loved ones.

HOPE
- Direct people to support services.

support, and reestablishing a sense of self-efficacy. Psychological first aid entails listening, empathy, and assessing needs. It creates a sense of safety, ensuring that basic physical needs are met and protecting the patient from additional harm. It promotes calm with friendship and compassion, and the use of accurate information about the disaster or trauma and the relief efforts underway. It supports self-efficacy, steering people toward helping themselves. It helps people connect with family, clergy, or friends for support. It creates a sense of hope.

These simple tools can be used with any patient and ideally are part of our patient assessment system. They can also be used to provide support among teams of responders. Psychological first aid is increasingly becoming accepted as a necessary and natural culture within search and rescue, ski patrol, emergency services as well as outdoor programs. The responder should help the patient understand that the scene is safe, meet basic physical needs, bring calm to confusion and order to chaos, give the patient agency, and connect them with support groups and powerful tools to manage stress.

The Field Debriefing

Following a rescue, first attend to the physical needs of the rescuers by providing food, water, clean clothing, and shelter. Light exercise may help relieve tension built up over the course of the rescue.

Provide emotional support to rescuers, staff, and course participants who experience unusual stress. In wilderness education, many participants are young and may be experiencing their first real-life stress. Emotional reactions are normal and should be expected, but people who don't know this may compound their own anxieties, making the stress even worse for themselves. The majority are short-term reactions with no lasting consequences.

A simple, voluntary debriefing or a conversation around the fire with a trusted mentor or friend can help people manage the emotions of an event, connect people with their support groups, and identify a person who needs additional help. These conversations can give people a map to work through the emotional and cognitive wilderness after a serious incident.

FINAL THOUGHTS

Rescuers should understand that their reactions—while uncomfortable—are natural, normal reactions to abnormal events, and that healing may take time and assistance. For both patients and rescuers, psychological first aid may be as important to their ultimate recovery as our physical care.

30 MEDICAL LEGAL CONCEPTS IN WILDERNESS MEDICINE

INTRODUCTION

There are several medical legal concepts—in this chapter based on law in the United States—that are pertinent to the wilderness responder. At first glance these legal concepts can be framed as possible trigger points for a lawsuit. They can also be framed as reminders of the style in which we should provide care: we should do what we have been trained to do, do it well, and treat our patients with respect and politeness.

WILDERNESS PROTOCOLS

Doing your job well, consistent with the standards and practices on which you have trained, is excellent protection against lawsuits. Medicine uses the phrase "scope of practice" to describe what care a provider can provide, and "standard of care" to describe the yardstick by which that care is measured. The standard of care by which you will be judged is determined in part by your level of training and the protocols under which you practice.

Most of the care wilderness first responders provide is straightforward and widely accepted first aid. If someone is bleeding, it's expected that we will apply direct pressure and elevation. If we assess a fracture, it is accepted practice that the prehospital treatment is to immobilize the limb.

Administering medication, relocating dislocations and making evacuation decisions are examples of practices outside the normal scope of practice of prehospital medicine, yet very appropriate and consistent with the standard of care in wilderness medicine. To clarify the standards of care you should provide, we encourage all our wilderness medicine students who may find themselves in a leadership position to affiliate with a medical director who can develop a set of protocols, review your training and experience, and provide support for the context in which you will practice medicine. They can develop treatment and evacuation protocols that guide your training, and your program's needs, and help reduce decision-making stress and fatigue on the part of responders, which in turn means better patient care.

Documentation. In the chapter on patient assessment, we discussed written patient notes—the SOAP report. These serve as a form of communication between medical care providers, and they serve as documentation of what you did, when you did it, and how you did it.

Written documentation can be invaluable if your level of care is challenged in a legal process and you must try to reconstruct an event in the past. An axiom of medicine is "If you didn't write it down, you didn't do it." This serves as a reminder of the limits of our memory and the importance of documenting our assessment, our treatment, and any changes in the patient's condition while they are under our care.

Duty to Act and the Good Samaritan? It can be argued that, as a trip leader, whether paid or volunteer, you have a duty to provide assistance in the event of a medical problem. Your patient is not a stranger; you have a prior relationship with the patient as a participant in an activity you lead. You would also have a duty to provide assistance if you respond as part of a rescue or ambulance team.

You will be a Good Samaritan both legally and in the eyes of your society if you provide care voluntarily when you don't have a duty to the patient—for instance, if you stop to help an injured hiker by the side of the trail. To encourage us to provide care in this circumstance, many states have some form of Good Samaritan legislation that provides legal protection for our care as long as we are not grossly negligent. Good Samaritan laws vary from state to state, but common conditions for protection are that we don't have a preexisting duty to the patient, and that the care has to be voluntary—often on an unplanned and unforeseen emergency basis.

Consent
It's simple politeness to ask a person for permission to treat. We do this as part of our initial assessment when we introduce ourselves and ask if we can help. It's also a legal principle that people have control of themselves, and we can't practice medicine on them without their permission.

Informed consent is the process, ongoing throughout our care, where a reliable patient—sober, not distracted, able to focus on the situation, and A+Ox3 or 4—agrees to treatment after being informed about the risks and benefits. The dialogue we have while we assess and treat our patient keeps them informed and, again, is simply polite and respectful.

The law assumes that an unreliable patient, one with an altered mental status who is not fully alert and oriented to person, place, and time, would want help during an emergency situation. This is the concept of implied consent.

Implied consent also applies to minors whose parents or legal guardians are not available to give consent. The laws regarding minors are complex and can vary from state to state. If you're working with minors—in most cases anyone under the age of 18 years—it's wise to seek legal advice that is pertinent to your program and your state.

Confidentiality
As you assess and treat a patient, you will learn aspects of personal and medical history that, out of politeness and respect, should be considered confidential. The findings from your assessment and care can and should be communicated verbally, and in writing, to another medical provider who needs to know

those facts to continue care for the patient. Outdoor leaders who learn a student's or client's medical history from a routine pre-trip screening process have an obligation to only share this information appropriately and must be cautious when discussing medical history with colleagues. Inappropriate disclosure of medical information would breach your "patient to provider" confidentiality. In addition to being disrespectful, you also may be committing slander (defaming a person's character verbally) or libel (defaming in writing).

Be careful about what you say on the radio or to other members of your program or expedition. On the radio, state your facts, avoid identifying the patient unless it is necessary, and avoid speculation. For example, you may note the patient's breath odor and odd behavior as facts, but to state they are intoxicated without a blood test can be slander, as well as being incorrect.

Abandonment

Abandonment happens when you stop care too soon or transfer the patient to someone who is not able to provide the care the patient needs. This can arise when a trained medical provider begins care and gives the impression that they will help the patient, then leaves the patient or turns them over to someone with less training. A scenario for this in outdoor education could be a trip leader turning the patient over to a co-leader or a program support person. The trip leader needs to consider the level of care the patient needs and whether the co-leader or program support person can provide that care.

FINAL THOUGHTS

Fear of being sued can restrain people from taking training or responding to an emergency. This is unfortunate when it prevents people from helping one another. We can talk about the legal climate in our society and the details of law, but there is no arguing that if we can help and fail to do so, we violate the expectations of medicine and our society. Reb Gregg, a long-time legal advisor to NOLS and to the entire outdoor recreation and education community, has given sage advice that is summarized in the two key points in this chapter: Do what you are trained to do, and treat people with respect and politeness. These simple rules will help you provide the best of care—the key to staying out of court.

| # FIRST AID KIT

These are the contents of a standard first aid kit designed for a group of twelve on a monthlong trip. (This is the inventory of a NOLS Field Instructor's Kit.) Requirements will vary with group size, medical qualifications, trip length, location, and remoteness.

General Supplies	No.
Biohazard bag	1ea
Nitrile gloves	1 pair
Latex gloves	4 pairs
Micro shield	1ea
Thermometer (digital)	1ea
Signal mirror	1ea
Whistle	1ea

Foot Repair	No.
Scissors	1ea
Ace bandage	1ea
1" Athletic tape	1ea
Moleskin (2" x 3")	2ea
Molefoam (2" x 3")	2ea
Adhesive knit (2" x 3")	2ea
Second Skin (2" x 3")	2ea
K-tape (2" x 3")	2ea

Wound Care	No.
2" x 2" gauze pad	4ea
3" x 4" nonstick gauze pads	2ea
Opsite Transparent dressing	2ea
4" x 4" gauze pad	2ea
Band-Aids	12ea
Steri-strips	6ea
3" gauze roll	1ea
Tweezers	1ea
Cravats	1ea
Oval eye pads	2ea
Safety pins	2ea
12cc syringe	1ea
Bactracin $1\frac{1}{32}$ oz	2ea
Cortisone $1\frac{1}{32}$ oz	2ea
Benzoin 1 oz	2ea
Betadine 1 oz	1ea

GLOSSARY OF
FIRST AID TERMS

Anaphylaxis. A hypersensitive reaction of the body to a foreign protein or drug.

Anorexia. A lack of appetite.

Appendicular. Refers to the limbs, the legs and arms.

Ataxia. Incoordination of muscles. Usually seen when voluntary movement is attempted; e.g., walking.

Avulsion. A forcible tearing away of a body part. It can be a piece of skin, a finger, toe, or entire limb.

Axial. Referring to the midline through the skeleton, the skull, vertebrae, and pelvis.

Axillary. Referring to the armpit.

Bacteria. Unicellular organisms lacking chlorophyll.

Basal metabolic rate. The metabolic rate of a person at rest. Usually expressed in kilocalories per square meter of body surface per hour.

Basal metabolism. The amount of energy needed to maintain life when the body is at rest.

Brachial. Refers to the arm, usually the brachial artery or nerve.

Brain stem. The portion of the brain located below the cerebrum, which controls automatic functions such as breathing and body temperature.

Campylobacter. A genus of bacteria implicated in diarrheal illness.

Capillary. The smallest of the blood vessels; the site of oxygen, nutrient, and waste product exchange between the blood and the cells.

Cerebellum. The portion of brain behind and below the cerebrum, which controls balance, muscle tone, and coordination of skilled movements.

Cerebrum. The largest and upper region of the brain. Responsible for higher mental functions such as reasoning, memory, and cognition.

Comminuted. A fracture in which several small cracks radiate from the point of impact.

Congenital. A condition present at birth.

Conjunctiva. The mucous membrane that lines the eyelid and the front of the eyeball.

Convection. Heat transferred by currents in liquids or gases.

Cornea. The clear transparent covering of the eye.

Crepitus. A grating sound produced by bone ends rubbing together.

CRT. Capillary refill time. For example, "Capillary refill time is 3 seconds."

Cyanosis. Bluish discoloration of the skin, mucous membranes, and nail beds indicating inadequate oxygen levels in the blood.

Diabetes. A disease resulting from inadequate production or utilization of insulin.

Distal. Farther from the heart.

Electrolyte. A substance that, in solution, conducts electricity: Common electrolytes in our body are sodium, potassium, chloride, calcium, phosphorus, and magnesium.

Embolism. An undissolved mass in a blood vessel; may be solid, liquid, or gas.

Epilepsy. Recurrent attacks of disturbed brain function; classic signs are altered level of consciousness, loss of consciousness, and/or seizures.

Eversion. A turning outward (as with an ankle).

Giardia. A genus of protozoan, a simple unicellular organism that causes an illness that is often characterized by diarrhea.

Globule. Any small rounded body.

Hematoma. A pool of blood confined to an organ or tissue.

Hyperglycemia. High blood sugar.

Hypoglycemia. Low blood sugar.

Intercostal. The area between the ribs.

Irrigate. To flush with a liquid.

Kilocalorie. A unit of heat; the amount of heat needed to change the temperature of 1 gram of water 1 degree centigrade.

LOC. Level of consciousness.

Meninges. The three membranes that enclose and help protect the brain.

MOI. Mechanism of injury for an accident.

Morbidity. The state of being diseased.

Occlusive dressing. A dressing impermeable by moisture.

Palpate. To examine by touching.

Paraplegia. Paralysis affecting the lower portion of the body and both legs.

Paroxysmal. A sudden, periodic attack, spasm, or recurrence of symptoms.

PFD. Personal flotation device (life jacket).

Plasma. The liquid part of blood.

Prodromal. The initial stage of a disease.

Quadriplegia. Paralysis affecting all four limbs.

Rales. Crackly breath sounds due to fluid in the lungs or airways.

RR. Respiratory rate.

SCTM. Skin, color, temperature, and moisture.

Seizure. A sudden attack of a disease as in epilepsy.

Signs. An indication of illness or injury that the examiner observes.

Sprain. Trauma to a joint causing injury to the ligaments.

Strain. A stretched or torn muscle.

Symptoms. Pain, discomfort, or other abnormality that the patient feels.

Tendinitis. Inflammation of a tendon that connects muscle to bone.

Varicose veins. Distended, swollen, knotted veins.

Vasoconstriction. Narrowing of blood vessels.

Ventricular. Referring to the two lower pumping chambers of the heart, the ventricles.

Vertigo. The sensation of objects moving about the person or the person moving around in space.

Virus. A microscopic and parasitic organism dependent on the nutrients inside cells for its reproductive and metabolic needs.

Wheezes. Whistling or sighing breath sounds resulting from narrowed airways.

BIBLIOGRAPHY

Scope of Practice Documents and Evidence Reviews

Johnson D, Schimelpfenig T, Hubbell F, et al. Minimum Guidelines and Scope of Practice for Wilderness First Aid. *Wilderness Environ Med.* 2013: 24;456–462.

Johnson D, Schimelpfenig T, Hubbell F, et al. Minimum Guidelines and Scope of Practice for Wilderness Advanced First Aid. https://www.wildmededucationcollaborative.org/

Johnson D, Schimelpfenig T, Hubbell F, et al. Minimum Guidelines and Scope of Practice for Wilderness First Responder. https://www.wildmededucationcollaborative.org/

Millin M, Johnson D, David E, Schimelpfenig T, Conover K, Sholl M, Busko J, Alter R, Smith W, Symonds J, Taillac P, Hawkins S. Medical Oversight, Educational Core Content, and Proposed Scopes of Practice of Wilderness EMS Providers: A Joint Project Developed by Wilderness EMS Educators, Medical Directors, and Regulators Using a Delphi Approach. *PreHospital Emergency Care.* Published online: 28 Jun 2017. http://dx.doi.org/10.1080/10903127.2017.1335815

Schumann SA, Schimelpfenig T, Sibthorp J, Collins RH. An examination of wilderness first aid knowledge, self-efficacy, and skill retention. *Wilderness Environ Med.* 2012; 23:281–287.

Schimelpfenig T, Johnson D, Lipman G, McEvoy D, Bennett B. Evidence-Based Review of Wilderness First Aid Practices. *Journal of Outdoor Recreation, Education, and Leadership* 2017, Vol. 9, No. 2, pp. 216–238 https://doi.org/10.18666/JOREL-2017-V9-I2-8226

Wilderness Medicine Textbooks

Wilderness Medicine. Paul Auerbach, Tracy Cushing and N. Stuart Harris, ed. 7th ed. Elsevier Press. 2017.

Wilderness EMS. Seth Hawkins, ed. Wolters Kluwer. 2019.

Houston, Charles. *Going Higher: Oxygen, Man, and Mountains.* 4th ed. Seattle: Mountaineers Books, 1998.

Stewart, Charles E. *Environmental Emergencies.* Baltimore: Williams & Wilkins, 1990.

Wilkerson, James A., ed. *Medicine for Mountaineering and Other Wilderness Activities.* 5th ed. Seattle: Mountaineers Books, 2001.

Wilderness Medicine Practice Guidelines

Luks A, McIntosh S, Grissom C, Auerbach P, Rodway G, Schoene R, Zafren K, Hackett P. Wilderness Medical Society Practice Guidelines for the Prevention and Treatment of Acute Altitude Illness: 2014 Update. *Wilderness Environ Med.* 2014; S4-S14.

Gaudio F, Lemery J, Johnson D. Wilderness Medical Society Practice Guidelines for the Use of Epinephrine in Outdoor Education and Wilderness Settings: 2014 Update. *Wilderness Environ Med.* 2014; S15-S18.

Paterson R, Drake B, Tabin G, Butler F, Cushing T. Wilderness Medical Society Practice Guidelines for Treatment of Eye Injuries and Illnesses in the Wilderness: 2014 Update. *Wilderness Environ Med.* 2014; S19-S29.

Bennett B, Hew-Butler T, Hoffman M, Rogers I, Rosner M. Wilderness Medical Society Practice Guidelines for Treatment of Exercise-Associated Hyponatremia: 2014 Update. *Wilderness Environ Med.* 2014; S30-S42.

McIntosh S, Opacic M, Freer L, Grissom C, Auerbach P, Rodway G, Cochran A, Giesbrecht G, McDevitt M, Imray C, Johnson E, Dow J, Hackett P. Wilderness Medical Society Practice Guidelines for the Prevention and Treatment of Frostbite: 2014 Update. *Wilderness Environ Med.* 2014; S43-S54.

Lipman G, Eifling K, Ellis M, Gaudio F, Otten E, Grisson C. Wilderness Medical Society Practice Guidelines for the Prevention and Treatment of Heat-Related Illness: 2014 Update. *Wilderness Environ Med.* 2014; S55-S65.

Zafren K, Giesbrecht G, Danzl D, Brugger H, Sagalyn E, Walpoth B, Weiss E, Auerbach P, McIntosh S, Nemethy M, McDevitt M, Dow J, Schoene R, Rodway G, Hackett P, Bennett B, Grissom C. Wilderness Medical Society Practice Guidelines for the Out-of-Hospital Evaluation and Treatment of Accidental Hypothermia: 2014 Update. *Wilderness Environ Med.* 2014; S66-S85.

Davis C, Engeln A, Johnson E, McIntosh S, Zafren K, Islas A, McStay C, Smith W, Cushing T. Wilderness Medical Society Practice Guidelines for the Prevention and Treatment of Lightning Injuries: 2014 Update. *Wilderness Environ Med.* 2014; S86-S95.

Russell K, Scaife C, Weber D, Windsor J, Wheeler A, Smith W, Wedmore I, McIntosh S, Lieberman J. Wilderness Medical Society Practice Guidelines for the Treatment of Acute Pain in Remote Environments: 2014 Update. *Wilderness Environ Med.* 2014; S96-S104.

Quinn R, Williams J, Bennett B, Stiller G, Islas A, McCord S. Wilderness Medical Society Practice Guidelines for Spine Immobilization in the Austere Environment: 2014 Update. *Wilderness Environ Med.* 2014; S105-S117.

Quinn R, Wedmore I, Johnson E, Islas A, Anglim A, Zafren K, Bitter C, Mazzorana V. Wilderness Medical Society Practice Guidelines for Basic Wound Management in the Austere Environment: 2014 Update. *Wilderness Environ Med.* 2014; S118-S133.

Kanaan NC, Ray J, Stewart M, Russell KW, Fuller M, Bush S, Caravati EM, Cardwell MD, Norris RL, Weinstein SA. Wilderness Medical Society Practice Guidelines for the Treatment of Pitviper Envenomations in the United States and Canada. *Wilderness Environ Med.* 2015 Dec;26(4):472-87.

Schmidt AC, Sempsrott JR, Hawkins SC, Arastu AS, Cushing TA, Auerbach PS. Wilderness Medical Society Practice Guidelines for the Prevention and Treatment of Drowning. *Wilderness Environ Med.* 2016 Jun;27(2):236-51.

Van Tilburg C, Grissom CK, Zafren K, McIntosh S, Radwin MI, Paal P, Haegeli P, Smith WW, Wheeler AR, Weber D, Tremper B, Brugger H. Wilderness Medical Society Practice Guidelines for Prevention and Management of Avalanche and Nonavalanche Snow Burial Accidents. *Wilderness Environ Med.* 2017 Mar;28(1):23-42.

Wilderness Medicine Epidemiology

Gentile DA, Morris JA, Schimelpfenig T, Auerbach PS: Wilderness Injuries and Illness. *Ann Emerg Med* July 1992;21:853–861

Leemon D, Schimelpfenig T: Wilderness Injury, Illness and Evacuation: NOLS Incident Profiles 1999–2002. *Wilderness and Environmental Medicine*, 14, 174 182 (2003)

McIntosh SE, Leemon D, Schimelpfenig T, Visitacion J, Fosnocht, D: Medical Incidents and Evacuations on Wilderness Expeditions. *Wilderness and Environmental Medicine*, 18, 298, 304 (2007).

INDEX

ABOUT THE AUTHOR

TOD SCHIMELPFENIG

As a wilderness educator and a volunteer EMT on ambulance and search and rescue squads for the past forty-four years, Tod Schimelpfenig has extensive experience with wilderness medicine and risk management. He began his NOLS Field Instructor career in 1973, leading numerous courses and course types, culminating in the first father-son instructor team at NOLS. He served as the NOLS Risk Management Director for eight years, the NOLS Rocky Mountain School Director for six years, and for three years on the board of directors of the Wilderness Medical Society (WMS). He has received the Reb Gregg Award for contributions to the field of Wilderness Risk Management, twice received the WMS Warren Bowman Award for contributions to the field of wilderness medicine, and was elected a Fellow of the Academy of Wilderness Medicine. Tod is the founder of the Wilderness Risk Managers Committee, has spoken at numerous conferences on pre-hospital and wilderness medicine, and has taught wilderness medicine around the world. He has written numerous articles on educational program, risk management, and wilderness medicine topics, and he currently reviews articles for the *Journal of Wilderness and Environmental Medicine*. Tod recently retired after serving for 18 years as the Curriculum Director of NOLS Wilderness Medicine.